LEAN OR LAVISH

"Judith Pacht lets us eat our rich cake and have it lean too in this eclectic assortment of dual purpose recipes. *Lean or Lavish* provides a good study in rethinking food in healthy terms."

> —JUDITH OLNEY, author of
> *The Farm Cookbook* and five other cookbooks

"This book's title teases any cook to look through its pages. And, they should, for Judith Pacht has imaginatively presented each of her recipes twice: once lavishly, with butter, cream, sugar, salt, and similar ingredients added without guilt, and once 'leanly,' where these ingredients have been lowered, replaced, or omitted for those who must watch what they eat. How original to offer cooks two choices!"

> —BETTY ROSBOTTOM, author of
> *Betty Rosbottom's Cooking School Cookbook*
> and director of LaBelle Pomme Cooking School

LEAN OR LAVISH:

Two Tempting Versions of Each Dish

JUDITH PACHT

Nutritional Analysis by Tomi Haas, M.S., R.D.
Wine Selections by Hank Rubin

WARNER BOOKS

A Time Warner Company

Lean or Lavish is not intended to offer medical advice. As with any change in your diet, check your plans with your physician.

Warner Books, Inc., 666 Fifth Avenue, New York, NY 10103

W A Time Warner Company

Printed in the United States of America
First printing: May 1991
10 9 8 7 6 5 4 3 2 1

Library of Congress Cataloging-in-Publication Data

Pacht, Judith.
    Lean or lavish : two tempting versions of each dish / Judith Pacht;
nutrition analysis by Tomi Haas; wine selections by Hank Rubin.
        p.   cm.
    Includes bibliographical references and index.
    ISBN 0-446-39221-9
    1. Cookery.   I. Haas, Tomi.   II. Rubin, Hank.   III. Title.
TX714.P333   1991
641.5—dc20   90-49359
                                                                  CIP

Cover design by Anne Twomey
Cover photo by Aaron Rezny
Book design by Giorgetta Bell McRee

For Jerry

CONTENTS

ACKNOWLEDGMENTS

A book such as this can only be written with the help and generosity of others. My work has been eased and enriched by friends and colleagues who have shared their considerable talents with me.

My friend, *Bon Appétit*'s wine critic Hank Rubin, has graciously made his extensive knowledge available to me at my convenience, not always at his. The care and thought he has given to pairing each wine (or beer) with a corresponding dish brings breadth and light to the menus.

From the start dietician Tomi Haas contributed her ideas along with the essential numbers, weights and measures. Her flexibility and humor made it possible for us to meet deadlines with grace. Janice Harper, Tomi's helper, performed miracles at the computer as she transformed food into nutrient values.

My heartfelt thanks to Marilou Vaughan and Kit Snedaker for their unending encouragement and fine editing skills; their ideas and support have helped me to refine the book's form and content and have made writing it a satisfying adventure. My thanks also to Dorothy Kolts, who encouraged me to write, and to Peg Rahn, Judythe Roberts, Denise Vivaldo and Natalie Zeidman, who tasted words, recipes and ideas and improved on all of them.

Selma Morrow turned recipe-testing into a pleasure rather than drudgery. Her patience and sense of invention rose above the pressures of time and demands of the book's structure.

Early on, Barbara Kafka taught me to prune away the ordinary and reach for the extraordinary. She and many others helped to shape my thinking, cooking and writing. My thanks to Giuliano Bugialli, Elizabeth David, M.F.K. Fisher, Joyce Goldstein, Diana Kennedy, Richard Olney, Alice Waters and Paula Wolfert, among others, for the inspiration of their work. Any errors or miscalculations in this book are mine, not theirs.

Thanks are also due to the late Elaine Woodard, Jeannette Egan and Rebecca LaBrum for their availability and thoughtful suggestions.

When, as we put the book together, I couldn't find a place for a section or an idea, it was Warner Books' Harvey-Jane Kowal who came to the rescue. And Iris Linares cheerfully typed the additions and changes on no notice at all.

Finally, my special thanks to Warner Books editor Olivia Blumer. Her intelligence, good humor and sense of balance added a welcome and final dimension to the book as a whole. Olivia's guidance has been more than generous—it's been a pleasure.

From the beginning, my job would have been infinitely more difficult without the help of friends and family. I deeply appreciate Anne Kupper's knowledge, ongoing faith in my work and wise counsel, and the unfailing availability and encouragement offered by Elliot and Charlene Elgart, Peg Leavitt, Susan Loewenberg and Becky Novelli, who wrestled words and ideas with me.

My thanks for sharing their recipes, advice and educated palates to Irma Bravo, Sally Brody, Gladys Castillo, Midge Cowley, Olivia Erschen, Lynn Greenberg and the late and loved Harvey Brenner, Judy Harris, Susan Loewenberg, Patty and Lou Snitzer, Alison Stein, Georgeann Tenner, Jane Ullman, Magda Waingrow, Dorothy Wolpert, Ray and Riva Weinshenker and Edith Zolotow.

My parents, Dorothy and Edgar Roedelheimer, and my children, Jane and Michael Monson, Robert Pacht and Cynthia Gwinn, and Carolyn and Jonathan Siegel, have uncomplainingly swallowed my best and worst efforts. Above all I have depended on my husband, Jerry, for his judgment, kindness and support. Without him this book would not have been possible.

AUTHOR'S NOTE ON SAFE EATING

Keep dishes that are high in protein—meat, poultry and fish, egg dishes, custards and creamy sauces—hot or chilled. Harmful bacteria grow when these foods are left at tepid temperatures for long periods. Although I prefer many dishes at room temperature, I'm careful to serve them just when the chill is off, or just when they've become tepid, after cooking.

The safest dishes to hold at room temperature are those made with fruits, vegetables or marinades, because acid in the marinade slows bacterial growth.

And speaking of safety scrub unpeeled vegetables and fruits before they are prepared to remove pesticides. Be sure your meat, fish and eggs are cooked through; when undercooked they may contain harmful parasites or bacteria.

Since there is now concern about eating dishes that contain these uncooked ingredients, some cooks may not wish to prepare or serve Mayonnaise (page 23), Seafood Tartare (page 40), Cold Beet Borscht (page 64), the lean versions of Chilled Prune Mousse (page 240) and Lemon Meringue Mousse (page 242), or Chocolate Ramekins (page 258).

As for me, I continue to enjoy steak and fish tartare, prune, lemon and chocolate mousse. When I prepare them I buy the freshest, best ingredients I can find and take my chances. But to be safe, don't do what I do, do what I say.

FOREWORD

I love simple food and pure flavors. To me, a perfectly poached fresh egg is a feast. Cooking doesn't need to be complex to be delicious, but it must be honest and done with affection. When you love what you cook, chances are you'll cook it well.

My mother knew how to make ordinary food taste good, because she regarded it with affection and respect. During the Great Depression, when I was growing up in our New York City apartment, Mother's special talent and sense of adventure made affordable ingredients exciting enough for company.

Years later and 3,000 miles away, style may have changed, but not substance: my idea of a perfect supper remains sharing soup and crusty bread with family and friends. A steaming, fragrant bowl of clam chowder or rich, golden chicken soup fortified with backs and wings still completely satisfies me. For me, good food and good talk make the best meals.

LEAN OR LAVISH

THE COOK'S CHOICE: LEAN OR LAVISH

When Ralph Waldo Emerson suggested that consistency is the hobgoblin of little minds, he might have been describing me in my kitchen. I often cook light, natural dishes, but sometimes (with great pleasure) I go astray. While meals in my house frequently end with a dessert such as blueberry ice, I'll occasionally whip up a rich blueberry cream.

In this book, cooks can choose between two versions of the same recipe, using either a lean variant (lower in calories, animal fats, salt and sugar) or a lavish one (when butter, sugar and salt are of no concern). Or you may want to start with either version as a base, then alter the ingredients to suit your own preferences and needs. In Moroccan Eggplant (page 32), for example, you might omit the lamb and salt, but increase the olive oil. Such adjustments will make each dish just right for you, and in the process you will generate ideas for converting your own recipes.

The recipes in this book are drawn from many cultures and take on fresh tastes and colors from today's exciting mix of cooking styles and ingredients. Asian-inspired Fish in Lemon-Ginger Sauce (page 113), fragrant Mediterranean-style Roasted Garlic Heads with Rosemary (page 26), a spicy Chile Pepper Soup with Tortilla Chips with South American overtones (page 82), and America's own Lemon Meringue Mousse (not pie!), page 242, happily blend local and ethnic traditions.

Interesting combinations of texture, temperature, color and flavor make these recipes special. The play of textures—soft with crunchy, smooth with chewy—adds appeal to dishes such as Steak Tartare (page 50) and Seafood Tartare (page 40). In the lean version of Steak Tartare, water chestnuts are included along with sweet red onion for a delicious surprise; both versions of Roasted Winter Fruit (page 230) offer a pungent mix of flavors and textures.

Contrasting temperatures bring drama to a dish or meal. Try hot, melting cheese under crisp chilled salad greens, or spread cool Moroccan Eggplant over creamy Brie in wedges of steaming pita bread.

Aroma is critical to flavor, so try to imagine the taste and smell of the finished dish as you put it together. The spicy scent of freshly grated nutmeg enhances acorn squash; a fragrant herbal marinade or sauce offers a delicate contrast to unseasoned poached chicken. But blending sweet ripe raspberries into a thick plum sauce would mask the delicacy of both fruits.

Beautiful presentation makes a delicious dish taste even better. I like to garnish monochrome food such as poached fish or plain boiled potatoes with fresh herbs and small, colorful blanched vegetables. Minced sautéed red pepper, sprigs of flat-leaf parsley and bright sauces help, too. White-fleshed fish fillets appear almost jewel-like when served on a pool of fresh tomato puree and sprinkled with snipped chives.

Color on the table can come from more than just garnishes. A platter of carefully arranged blanched or sautéed vegetables makes a natural still life and centerpiece; so do shiny eggplants, or a field-fresh, half-open leafy cabbage surrounded by unshelled nuts, a few tiny limes, a persimmon, and perhaps some lemons, green leaves, and an apple or two.

ABOUT COOKING LEAN

As you read this book, you'll find the cooking methods used in lean dishes may differ from those in lavish recipes. Sweating, steaming and blanching often replace sautéing, frying and braising: rather than sauté an onion in butter, for example, you may blanch or sweat it. Cooking techniques have been chosen to produce appetizing dishes that most closely resemble the original recipes.

Lean recipes use natural seasonings such as herbs, juices and stocks to heighten flavor while cutting calories, fats and salt. If ingredients such as butter or cream are important to the texture or flavor of a dish, they are reduced as much as possible, made optional, or replaced with a leaner choice. When lean ingredients are substituted for richer ones, I have tried to select foods which are compatible with the concept of the dish. In lean Roasted Garlic Heads with Rosemary (page 27), for example, an easy-to-make lowfat cheese replaces the chévre (goat cheese) called for in the lavish recipe. And sometimes, I substitute a quite different, but equally tasty ingredient. A velouté sauce made with chicken stock and non-fat milk will never taste the same as one made with butter and cream, but a sauce of shallots softened in a simmer of sherry, cooked chicken juices, nutmeg and lemon juice is a splendid low-calorie replacement, full of rich flavor.

All good food should appeal to the senses, but lean dishes in particular depend on beautiful presentation and a sensitive balance of color, texture, temperature and flavor to make up for their lack of richness. At the end of each recipe, you will find hints for making the finished dish inviting.

As might be expected, not all recipes work equally well in both versions. When a lavish original just doesn't fit a lean mold, I have discarded it (or meant to)—so if a contrived dish has slipped through, I hope the reader will consider it an innocent mistake. Lean or lavish, each recipe should taste and look good.

Fats

When I began to write this book I was already adjusting recipes for my family and cooking classes in a general way, to lower fats, calories, cholesterol and salt.

I learned that some foods contain mostly saturated fats, some predominantly monounsaturated fats and some polyunsaturated fats. Oil, I found out, is a fat. Liquid fats (oils) made from plants are (except for palm and coconut oils) largely made of poly- or mono-unsaturated fats. Most saturated fats come from animal sources.

Many authorities believe saturated fats raise blood (serum) cholesterol and increase dangerous plaque in the arteries while monounsaturated and polysunsaturated fats appear to have no undesirable effects. The recommended daily fat intake, many authorities say, should not exceed 30 percent of our total daily calories.

I looked closely at the fat in my lean recipes to see whether it exceeded the 30 percent recommendation, and to see what kind of fat it was.

The results were interesting. Fewer than a third of the lean recipes and subrecipes are over the recommended 30 percent limit, and most of those only slightly above. In this group the fats used are largely monounsaturates and polyunsaturates.

The best way to stay within the 30 percent fat recommendation is to balance daily intake and menus. If you have a main course dish such as Pork with Red Cabbage & Apples (page 154) for dinner, keep the rest of the day's meals low in fat.

But even within a recipe there's room for adjustment. In the lean version of Warm Beets with Onions & Marjoram (page 191), for example, 1 tablespoon of extra virgin olive oil is used to season the dish. A teaspoon or two of a more aromatic, fruity Greek olive oil (replacing the whole tablespoon) cuts the fat content of the recipe to below the 30 percent recommendation, and still seasons it well.

Use the ingredients and methods suggested here as guidelines; experiment and develop combinations of flavors that taste good to you and are healthful eating. Look carefully at the ingredients, and you'll see how to reduce fats without sacrificing flavor.

Sometimes the loss in flavor just isn't worth the change, but often, as with the Warm Beets, you don't even notice the difference.

NUTRITIONAL DATA

The nutritional analysis for each recipe is calculated on the basis of one serving.

Sodium in salt is not calculated in recipes that call for "salt to taste."

Nutrition values are based on 5-ounce cups of cooked meat or cheese unless otherwise noted.

Differences in meat and chicken weights called for in a (Lean and Lavish) recipe set are based on differences in the *cooked* meat's edible portion. For example, edible portions of chicken white meat are calculated based on two-thirds purchase weight; dark meat and whole chickens are calculated based on one-half purchase weight.

To determine the percentage of fat calories from a recipe's total calories: multiply by 9 to convert that recipe's fat grams (gm) to kilocalories (kcal), then divide that fat kcal number by the kcal (calorie) number. The result (quotient) is the percentage of fat in a given recipe.

ABBREVIATIONS FOR NUTRIENT VALUES

kilocalorie: kcal
carbohydrate (gm): carb
fat (gm): fat
cholesterol (mg): chol

sodium (mg): Na
iron (mg)
calcium (mg): Ca

MENU SUGGESTIONS

Each menu lists a suggested wine or beer to accompany the main course dish.

♦

Garden Soup, page 66
Cold Marinated Sole with Raisins & Pine Nuts, page 120
Grilled Basted Vegetables, page 200
Crusty Hot Bread or Rolls
Custards in Berry Sauce, page 254
Wine: *Sauvignon Blanc or Pinot Grigio (both dry, white)*

♦

Fresh Tomato Soup with Clams, page 98
Cold Steamed Chicken Breasts with Herbal Sauce, page 134
Carrots with Tarragon & Ginger, page 194
Lia's Rice, Leek & Asparagus Custard, page 204
Apple Pudding with Raspberry Vinegar, page 238
Wine: *Chardonnay (fresh, young, white) or Brut Blanc de Blanc Champagne*

♦

Fresh Artichoke Soup, page 74
Lamb in Mustard-Thyme Sauce (served on a bed of spinach), page 156
Roasted Barley & Pine Nuts, page 208
Pears Poached in Two Wines, page 234
Wine: *Zinfandel (dry, red) or Barbaresco (rich, red) or Napa Gamay (dry, red)*

◆

Summer Soup with Pear & Avocado, page 62
Lettuce-Wrapped Rock Cod with Carrot Sauce, page 124
Orange & Tomato Salad with Cilantro, page 216
Warm Potato Salad, page 226
Berries!, page 236
Oatmeal Cookies, page 270
Wine: *Alsatian Sylvaner (dry, white) or Riesling (medium-dry, white)*

◆

Seafood Tartare, page 40
Spicy Chicken with Cumin & Lime, page 146
Black Beans Chiapas, page 210
Grilled Basted Vegetables, page 200
Custards in Berry Sauce, page 254
Wine: *Gewürztraminer (spicy, white—can be sweet or dry) or Mexican beer*

◆

Cold Beet Borscht, page 64
Braised Beef with Green Chiles & Orange, page 168
Roasted Potatoes & Garlic, page 202
Cucumber & Yogurt with Cardamom, page 214
Baked Apples California, page 232
Wine: *Petite Sirah (fruity, rich, red) or malt beer*

◆

Tortilla-Pizza with Smoked Duck, Pear & Garlic, page 58
Homestyle Fish Fillets, page 122
Tender Greens with Garlic, page 192
Steamed New Potatoes
Rice Pudding with Apricot Sauce, page 246
Wine: *Zinfandel (medium-bodied, red) or Gewurztraminer (white)*

◆

Roasted Garlic Heads with Rosemary, page 26
Chile Pepper Soup with Tortilla Chips, page 82
Chicken with Two Cheeses & Fresh Sage, page 138
Sautéed Tomatoes & Spinach, page 196
Roasted Winter Fruit, page 230
Jane Ullman's Dark Chocolate Diamonds, page 272
Wine: *Chardonnay (rich, white) or Chablis (steely, white) or Pinot Blanc (white)*

♦

Cilantro Cheese with Garlic, page 28
Braised Pork with Four Spices, page 148
Polenta with Toasted Buckwheat, page 206
Salad of Mixed Garden Greens
Chilled Prune Mousse, page 240
Wine: *Cabernet Sauvignon or Red Bordeaux (both dry, red)*

♦

Homemade White Cheese, page 30
Cold Beef & Garlic Salad, page 182
Crudités (raw carrots, radishes and Niçoise olives)
Hot Crusty Bread or Rolls
Lemon Meringue Mousse, page 242
Wine: *Sauvignon Blanc (white) or White Bordeaux (dry, white)*

♦

Corn Chowder with Green Chiles, page 78
Grilled Fish & Potato Salad, page 172
Warm Beets with Onions & Marjoram, page 190
Chocolate Ramekins, page 258
Wine: *Chardonnay (white) or White Burgundy (dry, white)*

♦

Ceviche, page 42
Bread Soup, page 86
Salad of Mixed Garden Greens
Blueberry Ice Cream, page 260
Chocolate Cake with Fresh Orange Glaze, page 262
Wine: *Tocai Friulano (fruity, dry, white) or Seyval Blanc (white) or Rioja (soft, dry, red)*

BASICS

When cooks make the most of natural juices and flavors, food tastes better and the calorie count drops. One way to add flavor to many dishes is to prepare them with homemade stock (see page 13), then season them with spices, herbs and complementary vegetables. Spiced Cabbage & Beef Soup (page 106), for example, is especially good made with stock instead of water, and so are most sauces and gravies. Meat, poultry, fish and vegetables often taste better when poached in stock. (Stock recipes in this book do not call for salt, letting the cook decide whether or not to use it.)

Soups and sauces can be enriched through texture as well as flavor. Butter, cream and *crème fraîche* add a silky finish to many dishes; even small quantities of these rich ingredients give lean recipes a smoother texture. (If you want to keep lean dishes entirely lean, omit the enrichment or replace it with non-fat yogurt.)

Butter and flour cooked together (a *roux*), whipping cream and egg yolks are delicious thickeners, but there are alternatives. Remember when flour dissolved in liquid was the all-purpose thickener? It still works—and if the flour is lightly browned, it adds a subtle, nutty flavor to savory dishes. I keep a jar of oven-browned flour on hand and use it for thickening such dishes as Golden Chicken in Port with Prunes & Garlic (page 142). *To brown flour*, simply spread a cup or two on a baking sheet and bake it in a 375F (190C) oven 5 to 6 minutes or until lightly colored.

To thicken desserts, you can use arrowroot, cornstarch or tapioca —out of fashion for a time, but now back in favor. Pureed foods are ideal thickeners for desserts as well as sauces and soups, because they add both flavor and body. Vegetables braised with a roast may be pureed and combined with the pan juices or with stock to make gravy. If the puree and liquid separate, sprinkle in a few tablespoons of flour, then simmer to bring the sauce or gravy back together.

Flavor and texture go hand in hand. That traditional flavor enhancer, salt, is no longer on everyone's table, but citrus zest and juice, spices and snipped fresh herbs make tasty substitutes. Even contrasting slivers of fruits and vegetables add interest.

Lemon juice with a pinch of sugar heightens flavor in savory dishes yet adds few extra calories. If the dish needs no additional liquid, you might try using a few drops of concentrated lemon juice (reduced to a syrup over medium heat) with sugar or dry sugar substitute. This tart-sweet combination approximates the flavor of salt and can be used to season a dish such as Cilantro Cheese with Garlic, page 28, without changing its consistency.

''Light'' soy sauce is a widely used low-sodium alternative to full-strength soy sauce, but I prefer the flavor of a good-quality full-strength soy sauce used only in small quantities or diluted by half with lemon juice or wine. (Full-strength soy sauce contains a sixth less sodium than the equivalent measure of salt.)

Fruit juice concentrates, full-strength juices and juices reduced to syrup make good substitutes for sugar, but keep in mind that such sweeteners are caloric, too.

Walnut oil, hazelnut oil and fruity olive oil are other natural seasoners that can be spooned onto food just before serving. Whether you use just a little (in lean recipes) or a bit more (in lavish ones), you should have at least two kinds of olive oil on hand. For ordinary cooking, I use a mild, pure olive oil. Most pure (virgin) olive oils have an acidity of 3.1 to 4% and can be heated to 400F (205C) without smoking. For enhancing the texture and flavor of uncooked dishes such as salads, precooked ones such as tortilla-pizzas (pages 54, 58) and dishes cooked over very low heat, use a cold-pressed extra-virgin olive oil; most of these have 1% acidity and a smoking point of 300F (150C) or less. They can be used sparingly (a good thing, since they're expensive). I like the aromatic, fruity Greek or Italian extra-virgin olive oils.

Oil (or oil and butter) heated in an iron skillet or a sauté pan will brown food, build flavor and give dishes a head start in cooking; the deglazed crusty bits left in the pan add complexity to gravies and sauces. To cut down on fat and calories, brown foods in a non-stick pan or one lightly coated with a non-stick spray. After browning the meat or vegetable (in little or no fat), deglaze the pan, cover it and braise the food until done. This kind of cooking fully develops natural flavors.

Dishes that don't need to be sautéed or browned for flavor can be steamed, sweated or blanched to bring out their natural goodness and reduce calories as well as fat. I've used these alternative techniques in lean recipes whenever possible.

In cooking, the whole is greater than the sum of its parts. Perfecting a dish takes more than a list of ingredients and a few basic techniques. Be willing to experiment, to try alternative cooking methods and new ingredients—it is your own discoveries that make cooking an adventure with delicious results.

STOCKS

Making stock takes little effort and yields a great reward: stock is an ideal base for soups, sauces, stews, and other dishes. Meaty bones, knuckles, poultry carcasses or fleshy fish scraps simmered with vegetables and seasonings provide rich flavor; gelatin from the bones gives body to the liquid. When you use the stock in cooking, your choice of spices, herbs and complementary vegetables adds yet another dimension to its flavor and to the taste of the dish in which it is used.

My stock recipes don't call for salt, but it can be added if you like. Remember, though, that vegetables such as celery, chard and beet greens are relatively high in sodium; when these are cooked in stock, they will add more sodium (and natural minerals) to the simmered liquid.

Stock can be stored in the refrigerator, but it takes up space, and meat and chicken stocks must be simmered every 3 days to keep from spoiling. For these reasons, it's more convenient to freeze stock in small, easy-to-use quantities, or to boil it, uncovered, over medium-high heat until it's reduced by half before storing it. I find it handy to freeze 1 or 2 tablespoons of regular-strength or double-strength (reduced) stock in each section of an ice-cube tray, then store the frozen cubes in a plastic bag to be thawed as needed. Frozen poultry and meat stocks keep at least 2-½ months, vegetable stock up to 6 months; fish stock is best used the day it's made, but may be frozen up to 2 weeks.

To save space, chicken and meat stocks can also be reduced to a syrup before refrigerating or freezing. Such reduced stocks, known to the French as *glace de viande* ("meat glaze"), are natural taste enhancers that intensify the flavor of sauces, gravies and soups, yet add little liquid and few calories. Heated stock syrup can be sprinkled over lean dishes instead of salt to season and moisten them.

To make stock syrup, boil stock over medium-high heat, watching carefully to prevent scorching as the liquid evaporates. When the stock is thick enough to coat the back of a wooden spoon, it's done. Pour the syrup into containers; let it cool, then cover and refrigerate up to 2 months or freeze up to 6 months. Stock syrup sets into a jelly when chilled (and even at room temperature). To change it back to stock again, simply stir it over low heat with a little water or other liquid until it dissolves; then add as much liquid as desired.

While a robust stock is perfect base for soups and sauces, it can also stand alone as a respectable broth. Sip it plain, or add seasonings and slivered vegetables to make a light, fresh-tasting soup in no time. I like to enhance steaming-hot, clarified stock with julienned green onions, blanched peas and carrots. Cool, sparkling jellied meat stock is delicious with a slice of orange or lemon and a sprinkling of chopped chives, particularly if the stock has been flavored with fresh ginger.

To clarify cloudy meat or chicken stock, first be sure that the stock and all utensils are completely free of grease. If meat, vegetables and seasonings are added to enrich the stock, simmer it 1 hour to extract flavors; then pour through a fine sieve into a container, pressing down on the solids with a wooden spoon to extract all the liquid. If the stock is gelatinous, warm it just enough to liquefy. Mix in 1 beaten egg white for every 2 cups of stock; bring to a boil over high heat, then reduce heat and simmer slowly, undisturbed, 15 minutes. When the egg white is cooked, gently ladle the stock into a cheese-cloth-lined sieve or colander. Do not press to extract liquid. Discard solids and cool stock uncovered; then cover and refrigerate or freeze.

If you're short on time, you can substitute good-quality canned or frozen stock, salted or unsalted, for homemade. To give commercial stock a fresher flavor, simmer it about 20 minutes with chopped carrot, onion, celery and other seasonings.

CHICKEN STOCK

I like chicken stock with garlic and without gizzards, but that's the cook's choice.

4 to 5 pounds chicken bones
(from about 4 chickens)
3 to 4 pounds bony chicken
parts, such as necks, wings
and backs
3 medium-size carrots,
coarsely sliced
Leafy green tops of 2 celery
stalks
3 onions, quartered
Bouquet Garni
6 quarts cold water, or to
cover

BOUQUET GARNI
1 teaspoon dried leaf thyme
or several fresh thyme
sprigs, bruised
1 bay leaf, crumbled
3 parsley sprigs (preferably
flat-leaf)
2 garlic cloves, unpeeled,
halved

Place chicken bones and parts, carrots, celery, onions and Bouquet Garni in a 10-quart soup or stock pot. Add cold water to cover and bring to a boil over high heat. Reduce heat to medium and simmer, uncovered, 10 minutes; remove fat and scum with a skimmer or spoon as it forms on the surface. Reduce heat, partially cover pot and simmer 4 hours, adding water as necessary to keep ingredients covered. Pour through a fine strainer into a container. Cool uncovered. Cover and refrigerate; when stock is well chilled, remove fat from surface. Cover stock tightly and freeze up to 2½ months (see page 14 for freezing suggestions); thaw before using. Or cover stock and refrigerate up to 3 days (refrigerated stock must be simmered every 3 days to prevent spoilage). Makes about 3 quarts.

Bouquet Garni: Tie all ingredients in a piece of washed cheesecloth.

TIP

You may use 2 cups dry white wine in place of 2 cups of the water. Simmer wine and all ingredients except water 15 minutes, uncovered; then add water and proceed as directed.

(1 cup)

kcal	carb(gm)	fat(gm)	chol(mg)	Na(mg)	iron(mg)	Ca(mg)
39	1	1	1	65	.05	9

BEEF STOCK

Equal parts of meat and bones make the most flavorful broth. Veal bones are especially gelatin-rich and add body and texture.

3 pounds veal knuckle bones
5 pounds meaty beef bones,
   such as shanks or cross ribs
4 celery stalks, chopped
6 large carrots, chopped
2 large onions, coarsely
   chopped
Bouquet Garni
1 cup dry white wine
6 quarts cold water

BOUQUET GARNI
2 teaspoons *each* dried leaf
   tarragon and dried leaf
   thyme
12 parsley sprigs (preferably
   flat-leaf)
3 bay leaves, crumbled
2 garlic cloves, unpeeled,
   halved

Preheat oven to 475F (245C). Place veal bones, meaty beef bones, celery, carrots and onions in a shallow roasting pan; roast, uncovered, turning once, 20 minutes or until bones and meat are browned. Then transfer bones, meat and vegetables to a 12-quart soup or stock pot. Add Bouquet Garni and wine; bring to a boil over high heat. Reduce heat to medium and simmer, uncovered, 15 minutes.

Add water; bring to a boil over high heat. Reduce heat, partially cover pot and simmer about 5 hours or until stock is reduced by about two-thirds, removing fat and scum with a skimmer or spoon as it forms on the surface. Pour stock through a fine strainer into a container. Cool uncovered. Cover and refrigerate; when stock is well chilled, remove fat from surface. Cover stock tightly and freeze up to 2½ months (see page 14 for freezing suggestions); thaw before using. Or cover stock and refrigerate up to 3 days (refrigerated stock must be simmered every 3 days to prevent spoilage). Makes about 3 quarts.

Bouquet Garni: Tie all ingredients in a piece of washed cheesecloth.

TIPS

Oven-browning the bones, meat and vegetables gives this stock its hearty flavor. For a more delicate stock, omit the browning step.

As the stock simmers, set the pot partly off the heat source. Scum will form on only one area of the surface, making it easier to remove.

(1 cup)

kcal	carb(gm)	fat(gm)	chol(mg)	Na(mg)	iron(mg)	Ca(mg)
26	7	.5	1	68	.4	16

FISH STOCK

Since fish spoils faster and at lower temperatures than meat and poultry, this very simple fish stock is best used within a day of being made. If necessary, it can be quickly frozen at the lowest freezer setting and stored up to 2 weeks.

4 pounds very fresh fish heads and bones from white-fleshed fish such as halibut, turbot, sole or sea bass
1 large onion, coarsely chopped
1 garlic clove, coarsely chopped

Leafy green tops of 2 celery stalks
10 parsley sprigs (preferably flat-leafed)
2 bay leaves crumbled
Freshly ground pepper to taste
2 cups dry white wine
4½ cups cold water

Place all ingredients in a 10-quart soup or stock pot. Bring to a boil over high heat. Reduce heat, partially cover pot and simmer 1 hour, removing scum with a skimmer or spoon as it forms on the surface, then stirring to bury bones in liquid. Pour through a fine strainer into a container; press down on solids with a wooden spoon to extract liquid. Cool uncovered. Cover and refrigerate; when stock is well chilled, remove fat, if any, from surface. Refrigerate up to 1 day, or cover tightly and freeze up to 2 weeks (see page 14 for freezing suggestions); thaw before using. Makes about 6½ cups.

(1 cup)

kcal	carb(gm)	fat(gm)	chol(mg)	Na(mg)	iron(mg)	Ca(mg)
63	2	2	11	50	.3	35

VEGETABLE STOCK

Vegetables become even more flavorful when simmered in this stock. To save space in the freezer or refrigerator, the stock can be reduced to double strength or to syrup and used as a vegetable essence for seasoning soups and other dishes.

6 medium-size carrots,
   coarsely sliced
Leafy green tops of 2 celery
   stalks
2 large onions, sliced
Bouquet Garni
9 dried or fresh lemon grass
   leaves, if desired
3 cups dry white wine
3 quarts cold water

BOUQUET GARNI
5 fresh thyme sprigs, bruised,
   or 1½ teaspoons dried leaf
   thyme
5 parsley sprigs (preferably
   flat-leaf)
2 bay leaves, crumbled
2 garlic cloves, unpeeled,
   halved, if desired

Place carrots, celery, onions, Bouquet Garni and lemon grass, if desired, in an 8-quart soup or stock pot. Add wine and bring to a boil over high heat. Reduce heat to medium and boil, uncovered, 15 minutes. Add water and return to a boil over high heat. Reduce heat, partially cover pot and simmer 45 minutes. To make double-strength stock, uncover and continue to simmer over medium heat about 20 minutes longer or until liquid is reduced by half. Pour through a fine strainer into a container; press down on solids with a wooden spoon to extract liquid. Cool uncovered, then cover and refrigerate up to 1 week. Or cover tightly and freeze up to 6 months (see page 14 for freezing suggestions); thaw before using. Makes about 3 quarts full-strength stock or 1½ quarts double-strength stock.

Bouquet Garni: Tie all ingredients in a piece of washed cheesecloth.

TIP

For vegetable stock with a more pronounced flavor, add mushroom peelings, asparagus stalks, and greens or vegetable scraps that have complementary but not overpowering flavors. Vegetables in the cabbage family, for example, have a strong, distinctive taste, ideal for hot borscht but decidedly less desirable in delicate sauces.

(1 cup, full strength)

kcal	carb(gm)	fat(gm)	chol(mg)	Na(mg)	iron(mg)	Ca(mg)
25	4	0	0	26	.2	14

PERFECT POACHED CHICKEN

Lavish and Lean

♦

This adaption of the Chinese poaching method produces incredibly succulent, moist meat. It's delicious straight out of the pot, in sandwiches and salads, or dressed up with Guatemalan Marinade, page 180.

The large amount of salt called for doesn't make the cooked chicken unduly salty. Substituting soy sauce for salt gives the chicken an Asian flavor, so keep in mind how you plan to serve the meat when you choose seasonings. If you are cutting out salt entirely, poach the chicken in unsalted stock or water.

5 green onions, sliced
   lengthwise
5 tablespoons chopped fresh
   gingerroot
1 (3½- to 4-lb.) chicken

¼ cup coarse salt or 1½ cups
   soy sauce, if desired
About 5 quarts cold Chicken
   Stock, page 15, or
   commercial, or water

Place a third of the green onions and a third of the gingerroot in chicken cavity. Set chicken in an 8-quart pot; scatter remaining green onions and gingerroot over it. Add salt or soy sauce, if desired; pour in stock or water to cover. Bring to a boil over high heat. Reduce heat, cover and simmer 3 minutes. Remove pot from heat and let stand, covered, 45 minutes. Uncover pot and cool chicken in stock. If prepared ahead, cover and refrigerate up to 2 days. Serve at room temperature; if chicken is reheated, flavor and texture will change. Makes about 5½ cups cooked meat.

VARIATION

Substitute 1 (5½-lb.) bone-in turkey breast for whole chicken. Increase simmering time to 15 minutes over very low heat.

TIP

After cooking chicken or turkey, strain, cool and freeze the broth. It can be reused, with or without the addition of fresh green onions and gingerroot (additional salt is unnecessary). With each use, the broth will become more flavorful from the chicken juices and added seasonings.

(poached in un-salted liquid)	kcal	carb(gm)	fat(gm)	chol(mg)	Na(mg)	iron(mg)	Ca(mg)
lean & lavish:	166	0	8	58.5	54.5	1	9

CREAMY NON-FAT YOGURT

A delicate starter produces mild, calcium-rich yogurt.

1 quart Enriched Non-fat Milk	ENRICHED NON-FAT MILK
1 tablespoon plain non-fat yogurt	1 quart non-fat milk
	1 (3.2-oz.) envelope instant non-fat dry milk powder

Prepare Enriched Non-fat Milk and pour into a 2-quart saucepan. Heat over low heat until small bubbles form around side of pan. Cool until tepid, about 94F (35C). Mix yogurt with about ½ cup milk; add to remaining milk and blend well. Pour into a 1½-quart bowl, cover and let stand undisturbed at warm room temperature (about 78F, 25C) 6 hours or until yogurt jiggles slightly when shaken. Then refrigerate, covered, up to 10 days; flavor will become stronger as yogurt matures. Makes 1 quart.

Enriched Non-fat Milk: Pour milk into a 1-quart container. Stir in one package non-fat milk powder until blended. Refrigerate. Makes 1 quart.

(1 cup)

kcal	carb(gm)	fat(gm)	chol(mg)	Na(mg)	iron(mg)	Ca(mg)
170	24	1	9	252	.2	586

MAYONNAISE

For best results, have all ingredients and cooking equipment at room temperature.

4 egg yolks
2 tablespoons Dijon-style
   mustard
½ teaspoon salt, or to taste
1 tablespoon white wine
   vinegar, or to taste

2 teaspoons fresh lemon juice,
   or to taste
1½ cups light vegetable oil
1½ cups olive oil
¼ to ½ cup half and half or
   whipping cream

In a blender or a food processor fitted with a metal blade, process egg yolks about 1 minute or until thick. Add mustard and salt; process 30 seconds. Add vinegar and lemon juice; process 1 minute. With blender or processor motor running, add oils very slowly in a thin, steady stream until oils are absorbed and mayonnaise is thickened. Then add enough half and half or cream to give mayonnaise the desired consistency. Season with additional salt, vinegar or lemon juice as needed. Makes about 1 quart.

(1 cup)

kcal	carb(gm)	fat(gm)	chol(mg)	Na(mg)	iron(mg)	Ca(mg)
1540	2	172	280	364	1.4	62

APPETIZERS & FIRST COURSES

I love the choices appetizers offer. In fact, I'd as soon sample an array of tempting first-course dishes as sit down to a full dinner.

Start with whatever the season brings. Slender asparagus spears are a sign of spring and are best eaten with fingers if you like them plain, as I do. Spring vegetables need only the simplest cooking to enhance their sweetness and fragrance. Blanched Vegetables with Garlic & Curry Sauces (page 36), for instance, take advantage of early fresh flavors but not of your time. Serve them with the yogurt-based sauce if you are watching fats and calories or the mayonnaise-based if you're not.

Summer brings sweet, mild garlic, fresh from the earth and ideal for roasting or even for mincing raw with parsley to garnish baked new potatoes. If you prefer garlic with no bite at all, prepare Roasted Garlic Heads with Rosemary (page 26), and spread the buttery-soft cloves over toasted French bread for an easy, aromatic appetizer that's fun to eat.

Ceviche, South American-style marinated raw fish, is low-calorie eating any time of year. Air freight flies seafood from the Pacific and Atlantic everywhere, every day; tossed with local tomatoes and green onions, they make an international appetizer.

Many of the appetizers in this chapter rely for their flavor on simple, fresh foods that require little cooking. For this reason, you'll find only small differences between the lean and lavish versions of some recipes. Just be sure you use only the best and tastiest ingredients.

ROASTED GARLIC HEADS WITH ROSEMARY

Lavish

♦

Cooked garlic has a mild, delicate flavor and spreads like butter—pinch the cloves with your fingers and squeeze the tender garlic onto toasted or grilled French bread. In late spring or early summer when garlic is at its mildest and sweetest, look for large heads with plump cloves, ideal for roasting. To really enjoy this dish, you have to dive in, so be sure to have a generous supply of napkins on hand.

8 unpeeled whole garlic heads with firm, plump cloves
½ cup extra-virgin olive oil
Salt and freshly ground pepper to taste
5 fresh rosemary sprigs or 3 tablespoons dried leaf rosemary
1 small baguette (French bread loaf), cut in ½-inch-thick slices

Additional extra-virgin olive oil
8 (about 1-oz.) slices mild fresh goat cheese, such as Montrachet
16 Niçoise olives
1 lemon, cut in 8 wedges, seeded
Additional rosemary sprigs for garnish

Preheat oven to 300F (150C). Cut tips from unpeeled whole garlic heads; set heads, cut sides up, in a large, shallow baking pan. Spoon 1 tablespoon oil over each garlic head.

Season with salt and pepper. Bruise 5 rosemary sprigs to release essence, then remove needles from stems (or rub dried rosemary). Sprinkle rosemary over garlic. Bake, uncovered, 1½ hours or until garlic feels tender when gently pinched. Garlic can be served warm or prepared up to 8 hours ahead and kept loosely covered at room temperature. Just before serving, toast sliced French bread and brush with additional oil.

To serve, arrange garlic, toasted bread, cheese and olives on a medium-size platter. Garnish with lemon wedges and rosemary sprigs. Makes 8 appetizer servings.

Lean

The lowfat cheese in this version has only one-third the calories of goat cheese, but you'll hardly notice the difference when it's spread over the soft garlic cloves and toast.

8 unpeeled whole garlic heads with firm, plump cloves
8 teaspoons extra-virgin olive oil
Freshly ground pepper to taste
5 fresh rosemary sprigs or 3 tablespoons dried leaf rosemary

1 cup lean Homemade White Cheese, page 30, or non-fat or lowfat cottage cheese
1 small baguette (French bread loaf), cut in ½-inch-thick-slices
1 lemon, cut in 8 wedges, seeded
Additional rosemary sprigs for garnish

Preheat oven to 300F (150C). Cut tips from unpeeled whole garlic heads; set heads, cut sides up, in a large, shallow baking pan. Spoon 1 teaspoon oil over each garlic head. Season with pepper. Bruise 5 rosemary sprigs to release essence, then remove needles from stems (or rub dried rosemary). Sprinkle rosemary over garlic. Bake, uncovered, 1½ hours or until garlic feels tender when gently pinched. Garlic can be served warm or prepared up to 8 hours ahead and kept loosely covered at room temperature.

In a blender or a food processor fitted with a metal blade, process cottage cheese 2 minutes or until smooth (no need to process Homemade White Cheese). Spoon into a small serving dish, cover and refrigerate. Just before serving, toast sliced French bread.

To serve, arrange garlic, toasted bread, cheese and lemon wedges on a medium-size platter. Garnish cheese with 1 small rosemary sprig; garnish platter with additional rosemary sprigs. Makes 8 appetizer servings.

	kcal	carb(gm)	fat(gm)	chol(mg)	Na(mg)	iron(mg)	Ca(mg)
lavish:	527	42	39	25	537	2.2	229
lean:	205	30	6.5	1	319	2	125

CILANTRO CHEESE WITH GARLIC

Lavish

♦

Cilantro gives the cheese its garden-green hue; ground cumin adds a delightful flavor.

1 large garlic clove
8 ounces cream cheese, cut in
   3 or 4 pieces
¾ cup fresh cilantro leaves
1½ teaspoons ground cumin

⅓ cup whipping cream
¼ to ½ teaspoon salt
Corn or tortilla chips
Cilantro sprigs and cherry
   tomatoes for garnish

Turn on motor of a blender or a food processor fitted with a metal blade; drop in garlic and mince. Add cheese; process until smooth. Add cilantro leaves and cumin; process until cilantro leaves are finely chopped (they should look like green flecks). Add cream; process until blended. Season with salt. Remove to a small bowl. Cover and refrigerate until cheese thickens and flavors meld, at least 8 hours (or up to 3 days). Remove from refrigerator about 15 minutes before serving.

To serve, spread cheese over half of each corn or tortilla chip, then arrange chips on a medium-size platter. Garnish with cilantro sprigs and cherry tomatoes. Or mound cheese in small bowl and surround with chips. Makes about 1½ cups (about 8 appetizer servings).

VARIATION

Herbed Cheese: Here's an ideal replacement for cheeses such as Boursin, often served with crackers before or after a meal. For ground cumin, substitute ½ teaspoon dried leaf tarragon and ¼ teaspoon *each* dried leaf thyme, dried leaf oregano and dried dill weed. For cilantro, substitute ¼ cup fresh parsley leaves (preferably flat-leaf). Add leaves from 4 marjoram sprigs, if desired.

Note: To add a garden flavor to this variation, use all fresh herbs. Replace dried thyme, tarragon and dill with 3 times the quantity of fresh herb leaves (for example, ¼ teaspoon dried leaf thyme is equivalent to ¾ teaspoon fresh thyme). Replace dried oregano with 4 times the quantity of fresh.

Fresh herb leaves may become bitter upon standing, especially if they have been snipped. To keep them tasting fresh, blanch them in boiling water 30 seconds, then drain and pat them dry. (This step isn't necessary for cilantro.)

Lean

The cheese in this recipe has only one-fourth the calories of cream cheese. If you find it too dry, add a bit of whipping cream with the sour cream.

½ cup fresh lemon juice
1 large garlic clove
8 ounces hoop cheese or 1
   cup non-fat or lowfat
   cottage cheese
¾ cup fresh cilantro leaves
1½ teaspoons ground cumin
⅓ cup Creamy Non-fat
   Yogurt, page 22, or
   commercial (omit if using
   cottage cheese)

1 tablespoon dairy sour
   cream, if desired
Pinch of sugar, if desired
About 6 medium-size carrots,
   peeled, cut in 4-inch sticks
1 jicama or 2 turnips (about 1
   lb. *total*), peeled, cut in ¼-
   inch-thick slices
Cilantro sprigs for garnish

In a small saucepan, reduce lemon juice over medium heat by about half or until syrupy. Set aside. Turn on motor of a blender or a food processor fitted with a metal blade; drop in garlic and mince. Add cheese; process until smooth. Add cilantro leaves and cumin; process until cilantro leaves are finely chopped (they should look like green flecks). Add yogurt, if used; process until blended. Remove to a small bowl. Blend in sour cream, if desired. Season with lemon syrup, adding a few drops at a time; add sugar, if desired. Cover and refrigerate until cheese thickens and flavors meld, at least 8 hours (or up to 3 days). Remove from refrigerator about 15 minutes before serving.

To serve, spread cheese over half of each carrot stick and jicama or turnip slice; arrange vegetables on platter. Garnish platter with a cluster of cilantro sprigs. Makes about 1½ cups (about 8 appetizer servings).

VARIATION

Herbed Cheese: Follow directions for Herbed Cheese, page 28.

TIPS

Carrots can be prepared up to 1 day ahead, sprinkled with water, tightly covered and refrigerated. Jicama or turnips can be prepared up to 1 day ahead, dropped into 1 quart of lemon water (1 tablespoon lemon juice to 1 quart water), covered and refrigerated. Unlike many white vegetables, jicama and turnips don't discolor when cut, but they do dry out; lemon water keeps them moist, crisp and flavorful.

For a more pungent flavor, toast cumin seeds in a 350F (175C) oven 5 minutes or until they begin to pop. Cool, then grind.

	kcal	carb(gm)	fat(gm)	chol(mg)	Na(mg)	iron(mg)	Ca(mg)
lavish:	291	18	22	42	320	1	72
lean:	63	10	.6	1	164	.8	66

HOMEMADE WHITE CHEESE
Fromage Blanc

Lavish

♦

Here's a homemade American version of a creamy, slightly tangy Burgundian cheese with small curds. At Restaurant Mail in Bourg-en-Bresse, France, fromage blanc is served after the main course, as either a sweet (with cinnamon and sugar) or a savory (with minced garlic and parsley). I like it before dinner, sprinkled with snipped chives and spread on French bread, or with fresh fruit for a light lunch.

1 (½-gallon) carton whole
  milk
¼ cup whipping cream
¼ cup minced flat-leaf parsley
  leaves

Salt and freshly ground
  pepper to taste
2 garlic cloves, minced
French bread, sliced

Fold a large piece of washed and dried cheesecloth into 3 or 4 thicknesses to make a piece about 1 foot square. Open milk carton completely. Loosely cover opening of carton with folded cheesecloth. Allow milk to stand undisturbed at room temperature 2 to 5 days or until curds form: milk will look like a solid mass (curds) surrounded by a watery film (whey). Line a sieve, strainer or colander with the folded cheesecloth. Gently pour curds and whey into cheesecloth. Let drain undisturbed at cool room temperature 8 hours or until cheese is creamy and semisolid; the longer it drains, the firmer it becomes. Transfer to a small bowl; stir in cream and refrigerate until ready to serve or up to 2 days.

To serve, spoon cheese into a small serving dish. Garnish with a pinch of parsley. Serve with salt, pepper, bowls of garlic and parsley and French bread. Makes about 2 cups (8 appetizer servings).

TIP

Reserve the whey and use it in place of liquid when making pastry. It's a natural tenderizer for crusts and is rich in calcium.

Lean

Prepare as directed opposite, but substitute 1 (½-gallon) carton nonfat or lowfat milk for whole milk and omit the cream. Makes about 2 cups (8 appetizer servings).

	kcal	carb(gm)	fat(gm)	chol(mg)	Na(mg)	iron(mg)	Ca(mg)
lavish:	227	20	12	41	258	1.2	249
lean:	141	20	2	4	231	1.2	255

MOROCCAN EGGPLANT

Lavish

♦

Fill warm pita bread with ripe Brie cheese and spoonfuls of lemony eggplant spread. Vary the seasonings to suit your taste; the spread should be tangy with a sweet undertone.

2 (1¼- to 1½-lb.) eggplants
1 garlic clove, pressed
About 3 tablespoons extra-
   virgin olive oil
3 tablespoons paprika
2 teaspoons ground cumin
Salt and freshly ground
   pepper to taste

2 to 3 tablespoons fresh
   lemon juice
1 tablespoon sugar
6 ounces ground lamb,
   sautéed, fat drained off,
   meat lightly salted
Pita bread, cut in quarters
8 ounces ripened Brie cheese

In a large pot, bring about 4 quarts of water to a boil. Peel eggplants, cut lengthwise in quarters and drop into boiling water. When water returns to a boil, reduce heat, cover and simmer 10 minutes or just until eggplant is limp. Drain eggplant in a colander; press with a plate to extract as much water as possible. In a large chopping bowl, chop eggplant medium-fine; or coarsely chop in a food processor fitted with a metal blade, using 5 or 6 (1-second) pulses and scraping down sides of work bowl as needed to redistribute pulp. Do not overprocess; texture should be like that of slightly lumpy applesauce.

Transfer chopped pulp to a medium-size bowl. Add garlic and enough oil to coat eggplant lightly. Gently stir in paprika and cumin. Season with salt and pepper. Add lemon juice and sugar. Gently stir in sautéed lamb. If prepared ahead, omit garlic; cover and re-frigerate up to 2 days. Add garlic several hours before serving. Re-move from refrigerator about 15 minutes before serving.

To serve, spoon eggplant mixture into a serving bowl. Wrap pita bread in foil; warm in a low oven. Serve eggplant mixture with warmed pita bread and cheese. Makes 8 to 10 appetizer servings.

Lean

Chopped, seasoned eggplant wrapped in cups of butter lettuce makes an ideal low-calorie appetizer or first-course salad. To serve the dish as a salad, arrange it on a bed of greens and surround with blanched sweet carrots sprinkled with freshly snipped chives.

2 (1¼- to 1½-lb.) eggplants
1 garlic clove, pressed
1½ tablespoons extra-virgin olive oil
3 tablespoons paprika, or to taste
1 teaspoon ground cumin, or to taste

Freshly ground pepper to taste
¼ cup fresh lemon juice, or to taste, see TIP
1 teaspoon sugar
Butter lettuce cups

Cook, drain and chop eggplant as directed for Moroccan Eggplant, opposite.

Transfer chopped pulp to a medium-size bowl. Add garlic and oil. Gently stir in paprika and cumin; season with pepper. Stir in lemon juice and sugar.

If prepared ahead, omit garlic; cover and refrigerate up to 1 day. Add garlic several hours before serving. Remove from refrigerator about 15 minutes before serving.

To serve, spoon eggplant mixture into butter lettuce cups. Arrange on a large platter. Makes 8 to 10 appetizer servings.

TIP

For finished lean Moroccan Eggplant with less liquid, reduce the ¼ cup lemon juice in a small saucepan over medium heat to about 1 tablespoon.

	kcal	carb(gm)	fat(gm)	chol(mg)	Na(mg)	iron(mg)	Ca(mg)
lavish:	302	20	20	49	256	2	80
lean:	84	14	3	0	8	1.4	22

AVOCADOS & ORANGES CUERNAVACA

Lavish

♦

Guests serve themselves from a festive bowl, using tortilla chips instead of forks. Optional chiles make the dish spicy-hot. For an informal starter, serve the salad in butter lettuce cups on individual plates.

1½ cups ¼-inch cubes of Mexican *queso ranchero* or jack cheese (about 8 oz.)

1 cup thinly sliced sweet red onion

⅓ cup ¼-inch cubes of peeled jicama or peeled sweet white turnip

2 medium-size navel oranges, peeled, sectioned, cut in ⅓-inch cubes

3 tablespoons finely chopped red bell pepper

1 teaspoon finely diced jalapeño or serrano chile, if desired

⅓ cup extra-virgin olive oil

2 large ripe avocados

About 3 tablespoons fresh lemon juice

2 tablespoons fresh lime juice, or to taste

Salt to taste

Tortilla chips

⅓ cup fresh cilantro leaves

In a large bowl, combine cheese, onion, jicama, oranges, bell pepper and chile, if desired. Toss with oil. (At this point, you may cover and refrigerate up to 4 hours.)

Half an hour before serving, pit and peel avocados and cut in ⅓-inch cubes; in a small bowl, gently toss avocados with 2 teaspoons lemon juice. Add avocados to cheese-onion mixture and gently toss again. Season with remaining lemon juice, lime juice and salt. Cover and let stand at room temperature 30 minutes before serving.

To serve, heat tortilla chips. Add cilantro to salad and toss gently; spoon into a large serving bowl or individual bowls. Accompany with warm tortilla chips; forks are optional. Makes 8 to 10 appetizer or first-course servings.

Lean

This crunchy, lighter version of the preceding recipe depends on sweet onion and red bell pepper for taste as well as texture.

¾ cup ½-inch cubes of lowfat (skim milk) Mexican *queso ranchero* or jack cheese (about 4 oz.)

1 cup thinly sliced sweet red onion

1 cup ½-inch cubes of peeled jicama

2 medium-size navel oranges, peeled, sectioned, cut in ½-inch cubes

3 tablespoons finely chopped red bell pepper

1 tablespoon minced orange zest

1 teaspoon finely diced jalapeño or serrano chile, if desired

2 tablespoons extra-virgin olive oil

1 small ripe avocado

About 3 tablespoons fresh lemon juice

2 tablespoons fresh lime juice, or to taste

2 tablespoons Japanese rice vinegar

⅓ cup fresh cilantro leaves

In a large bowl, combine cheese, onion, jicama, oranges, bell pepper, orange zest and chile, if desired. Toss with oil. (At this point, you may cover and refrigerate up to 4 hours.)

Half an hour before serving, pit and peel avocado and cut in ½-inch cubes; in a small bowl, gently toss avocado with 1 teaspoon lemon juice. Add avocado to cheese-onion mixture and gently toss again. Season with remaining lemon juice, lime juice and vinegar. Cover and let stand at room temperature 30 minutes before serving.

To serve, add cilantro to salad and toss gently; spoon into individual bowls and serve with forks. Or spoon into a large serving bowl and serve with wooden skewers or picks. Makes 8 to 10 appetizer or first-course servings.

	kcal	carb(gm)	fat(gm)	chol(mg)	Na(mg)	iron(mg)	Ca(mg)
lavish:	341	17	27	106	166	1.4	258
lean:	133	11	9	7	39	.8	91

BLANCHED VEGETABLES WITH GARLIC & CURRY SAUCES

Lavish

♦

Carefully cooked and attractively arranged in a basket or on a platter, simple vegetables make an edible centerpiece—appetizer, vegetable and salad, all in one. The recipe expands to serve a crowd.

GARLIC SAUCE
1 cup Mayonnaise, page 23, or commercial
1 large garlic clove, pressed
¼ cup fresh lemon juice
1 tablespoon Worcestershire sauce

CURRY SAUCE
1 cup Mayonnaise, page 23, or commercial
1 teaspoon curry powder
½ teaspoon *each* ground cumin and chili powder

¼ cup fresh lime juice, or to taste
1 teaspoon sugar, or to taste

BLANCHED VEGETABLES
2½ pounds broccoli, cut in flowerets with 2-inch stalks
1 pound baby or small sweet carrots with tops
1 red bell pepper
1 yellow bell pepper
1 pound asparagus
½ medium-size cauliflower
1 lemon

Prepare Garlic Sauce and Curry Sauce; refrigerate. Prepare Blanched Vegetables.

To serve, arrange vegetables around dipping sauces on a large platter or in a flat, plastic-lined basket. Or compose a salad on individual plates; spoon a ribbon of either sauce over vegetables. Makes 8 to 10 appetizer or first-course servings.

Garlic Sauce: Blend Mayonnaise and garlic. Add lemon juice and Worcestershire sauce; stir until smooth. Pour into a small serving dish. If prepared ahead, omit garlic; cover and refrigerate up to 3 days. Add garlic 1 hour before serving. Makes 1¼ cups.

Curry Sauce: Blend Mayonnaise with curry powder, cumin and chili powder. Add enough lime juice and sugar to give dip desired flavor and consistency. Pour into a small serving dish. If prepared ahead, cover and refrigerate up to 3 days. Makes 1-¼ cups.

Blanched Vegetables: Bring a large pot of salted water to a boil over high heat. Meanwhile, wash vegetables; cut as directed below. Blanch each vegetable for suggested time; for tender-crisp vegetables, begin counting cooking time when water returns to a boil after vegetables have been added. Reduce heat and gently simmer for minimum time, then test; remember, vegetables continue to cook a bit after they have been removed from water. Use a skimmer or tongs to lift vegetables from water. Quickly refresh them in cold water, then blot dry on paper or cloth towels. When cool, cover loosely and keep at room temperature several hours. Or prepare up to 1 day ahead, wrap in plastic wrap and refrigerate. Return to room temperature before serving.

CUTTING DIRECTIONS & SUGGESTED TIMES
FOR BLANCHED VEGETABLES:

Broccoli: Make a ¾-inch "X" in bottom of each floweret's stalk. To blanch, hold stalk end and dip broccoli head into boiling water. Then flip stem portion over into water. Blanch 1 to 2 minutes.

Carrots: Peel or scrape carrots; leave 2 to 3 inches of green tops attached. Blanch baby carrots 3 to 4 minutes. Larger carrots take longer.

Bell Peppers: Cut in half; remove seeds and white pith, then cut in ½-inch-wide strips. Blanch 1 minute.

Asparagus: Break off tough bottom portion of stalks. If asparagus stalks are thicker than ¼ inch, peel them downward from tips. Blanch 2 to 5 minutes, depending on thickness of stalk.

Cauliflower: Core cauliflower and remove any brown spots. Break flowerets into bite-size portions. Cut lemon in half. Squeeze juice from lemon; add juice and juiced rinds to boiling water. Blanch flowerets about 4 minutes.

Lean

GARLIC SAUCE
¾ cup Creamy Non-fat
    Yogurt, page 22, or
    commercial
¼ cup Mayonnaise, page 23,
    or commercial
1 large garlic clove, pressed
1 teaspoon Worcestershire
    sauce

CURRY SAUCE
¾ cup Creamy Non-fat
    Yogurt, page 22, or
    commercial
¼ cup Mayonnaise, page 23,
    or commercial
1 teaspoon curry powder
½ teaspoon *each* ground
    cumin, chili powder and
    sugar
2 tablespoons fresh lime juice,
    or to taste

Prepare Garlic Sauce and Curry Sauce; refrigerate. Prepare Blanched Vegetables as directed for lavish recipe, but omit salt from cooking water.

Makes 8 to 10 appetizer or first-course servings.

Garlic Sauce: Blend yogurt, Mayonnaise and garlic. Stir in Worcestershire sauce until smooth. Pour into a small serving dish. If prepared ahead, omit garlic; cover and refrigerate up to 3 days. Add garlic 1 hour before serving. Makes about 1 cup.

Curry Sauce: Blend yogurt and Mayonnaise. Blend in curry powder, cumin, chili powder and sugar. Season with lime juice. Pour into a small serving dish. If prepared ahead, cover and refrigerate up to 3 days. Makes about 1¼ cups.

(for 3 tablespoons sauce)

	kcal	carb(gm)	fat(gm)	chol(mg)	Na(mg)	iron(mg)	Ca(mg)
lavish garlic:	242	2	26	19	211	.4	9
lean garlic:	50	3	3	5	89	.7	56
lavish curry:	244	3	27	19	190	.5	9
lean curry:	43	4	3	3	82	.1	55
vegetables:	67	15	1	0	40	1.6	71

SEAFOOD TARTARE

Lavish

♦

For the best possible tartare, use fresh fish and a sweet onion. Smelt eggs are sold in Japanese markets and in the imported food sections of many supermarkets; salmon eggs (salmon caviar) are sold in small jars in most grocery stores.

1 pound fresh boneless fillet of yellowtail
2 tablespoons smelt eggs (*masago*) or salmon eggs
⅓ cup minced red onion
1½ teaspoons Japanese rice vinegar
¾ teaspoon prepared wasabi (Japanese horseradish paste) or 1 teaspoon prepared hot mustard
2 tablespoons Mayonnaise, page 23, or commercial

2 tablespoons extra-virgin olive oil
Salt
Few drops of lemon juice
Butter lettuce or other greens such as lamb's lettuce (mâche) and endive
Additional smelt eggs for garnish
1 lemon, for garnish
Rice crackers or melba toast rounds

Remove skin and dark spots from fish fillet; pull out any small bones with tweezers or your fingers. Cut fish into small dice with a sharp knife. Place in a medium-size bowl. Add 2 tablespoons smelt or salmon eggs, onion, vinegar, wasabi or mustard, Mayonnaise and oil. Gently toss ingredients together, then season with salt and lemon juice. Toss again. Serve immediately. Or, if prepared ahead, cover and refrigerate up to 6 hours. Remove from refrigerator 20 minutes before serving.

To serve, mound tartare over lettuce leaves or other greens on a small platter. Indent center of mound; spoon in 1 teaspoon smelt or salmon eggs. Cut lemon in half lengthwise, then cut crosswise into slices. Fan lemon slices over lettuce. Or mound tartare on 8 individual lettuce-lined plates; garnish each serving with a few smelt or salmon eggs and a fan of lemon slices. Serve with rice crackers or melba toast rounds. Makes 8 appetizer or first-course servings.

Lean

Fresh tuna has great flavor but fewer calories and only half the fat of yellowtail. When you are planning to prepare fish tartare or ceviche, check with your market to make sure the seafood is extremely fresh and from deep, cold waters.

1 pound fresh lean top fillet of yellowfin tuna, skinned
1½ teaspoons finely grated fresh gingerroot
½ cup diced sweet red onion
3 tablespoons minced chives
1½ teaspoons Japanese rice vinegar
1 tablespoon fruity extra-virgin olive oil
¾ teaspoon prepared wasabi (Japanese horseradish paste) or 1 teaspoon prepared hot mustard

3 tablespoons fresh lemon juice, or to taste
2 teaspoons soy sauce, if desired
1½ teaspoons toasted sesame seeds
Butter lettuce or other greens such as lamb's lettuce (mâche) and endive
1 tablespoon minced chives for garnish
1 lemon for garnish
Unsalted rice crackers or melba toast rounds

Using tweezers or your fingers, pull out any small bones from fish. Cut fish into small dice with a sharp knife. Place in a medium-size bowl. Add gingerroot, onion and 3 tablespoons chives and toss to mix. Add vinegar, oil and wasabi or mustard; toss again. Season with lemon juice and soy sauce, if desired. Serve immediately. Or, if prepared ahead, cover and refrigerate up to 6 hours; remove from refrigerator 20 minutes before serving.

To serve, toss tartare with sesame seeds, then mound over lettuce leaves or other greens on a small platter. Sprinkle with 1 tablespoon chives. Cut lemon in half lengthwise, then cut crosswise into thin slices. Fan lemon slices over lettuce. Or mound tartare on 8 individual lettuce-lined plates; garnish each serving with chives and lemon slices. Serve with rice crackers or melba toast rounds. Makes 8 appetizer or first-course servings.

	kcal	carb(gm)	fat(gm)	chol(mg)	Na(mg)	iron(mg)	Ca(mg)
lavish:	175	7	9.5	37	352	.4	8
lean:	116	10	3	22	201	.7	22

CEVICHE

Lavish

♦

This is my favorite ceviche, and I've sampled hundreds. Lime juice "cooks" the firm white-fleshed fish in this South American dish; the flesh turns opaque as it stands in the acidic liquid.

8 ounces halibut or red snapper, cut in ¾-inch pieces

8 ounces sea scallops (cut in ½-inch pieces) or whole bay scallops

2½ cups lime juice

1½ cups chopped tomatoes

½ cup chopped green onions, including green tops

⅓ cup extra-virgin olive oil

1½ tablespoons *each* dry white wine and white wine vinegar

1 tablespoon jalapeño sauce or minced fresh jalapeño chile, or to taste

3 tablespoons tomato-based chili sauce

¾ cup tomato juice

1 teaspoon dried leaf oregano

1 cup shelled cooked shrimp (about 8 oz.), cut in ½-inch pieces

Salt and freshly ground pepper to taste

½ cup fresh cilantro leaves for garnish

Tortilla chips

Assemble the ceviche in glass, ceramic or stainless steel bowls. In a small bowl, toss fish and scallops in lime juice. Let stand at room temperature 3 hours, stirring occasionally. Meanwhile, in a large bowl, combine tomatoes, green onions, oil, wine, vinegar, jalapeño sauce or chile, chili sauce, tomato juice and oregano. Toss, cover loosely and let stand at room temperature.

Drain lime juice from fish and scallops; rinse fish and scallops well under running water and drain thoroughly. Add fish, scallops and shrimp to tomato mixture; toss gently. Season with salt and pepper.

If prepared ahead, cover and refrigerate up to 1 day; remove from refrigerator 20 minutes before serving.

To serve, spoon ceviche into a medium-size serving bowl or individual dishes; garnish with cilantro. Pass tortilla chips. Makes about 8 appetizer or first-course servings.

Lean

This version is refreshingly salad-like, an ideal beginning for lunch or dinner.

1 pound rock cod or scrod,
  cut in ¾-inch pieces
2½ cups lime juice
2½ cups chopped tomatoes
½ cup diced peeled jicama
¾ cup chopped green onions,
  including green tops
1 tablespoon *each* extra-virgin
  olive oil, dry white wine
  and white wine vinegar

1 tablespoon jalapeño sauce
  or minced fresh jalapeño
  chile, or to taste
1 tablespoon tomato-based
  chili sauce
½ teaspoon dried leaf oregano
Fresh lemon juice to taste
1 cup fresh cilantro leaves

Assemble the ceviche in glass, ceramic or stainless steel bowls. In a small bowl, toss fish in lime juice. Let stand at room temperature 3 hours, stirring occasionally. Meanwhile, in a large bowl, combine tomatoes, jicama, green onions, oil, wine, vinegar, jalapeño sauce or chile, chili sauce and oregano. Toss, cover loosely and let stand at room temperature.

Drain lime juice from fish; rinse fish well under running water and drain thoroughly. Add fish to tomato mixture; toss gently. Season with lemon juice. If prepared ahead, cover and refrigerate up to 1 day; remove from refrigerator 20 minutes before serving.

Just before serving, add cilantro and toss again; taste and adjust seasonings. To serve, spoon ceviche into a medium-size serving bowl or individual dishes. Makes about 8 appetizer or first-course servings.

	kcal	carb(gm)	fat(gm)	chol(mg)	Na(mg)	iron(mg)	Ca(mg)
lavish:	298	22	13	79	324	2.2	84
lean:	111	11	3	21	90	1.4	44

SQUID WITH PERNOD &
FIDDLEHEAD FERN

Lavish

♦

This is my version of a dish I tasted years ago at Browny's Seafood Broiler in Seattle. Since fiddlehead ferns are seasonal, I often substitute Chinese pea pods or the tips of slender new asparagus. The sauté juices and Pernod combine into a sauce so good you'll need plenty of crusty bread to soak up every drop.

12 fiddlehead fern tips; or 24
   Chinese pea pods or 24
   young asparagus tips (cut to
   a length of 3 inches)
3 tablespoons butter
3 tablespoons red bell pepper,
   minced
1 tablespoon minced garlic
10 ounces squid bodies
   without tentacles, cleaned,
   cut in ½" × 2" strips

Salt and freshly ground
   pepper to taste
Splash of Pernod (about 3
   tablespoons)
Additional ⅔ cup Pernod
4 rounds toasted, buttered
   French bread

Wash fiddlehead fern tips and pat them dry. If using Chinese pea pods, remove strings. If using asparagus, peel downward from tips if stalks are more than ¼ inch thick; blanch in boiling salted water 2 to 5 minutes or until barely cooked. Refresh in cold water and pat dry.

Preheat oven to 175F (80C). Warm a medium-size platter in oven. Melt 1 tablespoon butter in a large skillet over medium-low heat; add minced bell pepper and sauté until softened. Set aside for garnish. Melt remaining 2 tablespoons butter in skillet over medium-high heat, add garlic and sauté 1 minute or until soft. Add fiddlehead ferns, pea pods or asparagus. Sauté, turning frequently, 1 to 2 minutes or until vegetables turn bright green and begin to soften. Add squid strips and sauté no more than 1 minute, just until opaque; vegetables should be tender-crisp, squid hot and tender. Do not overcook squid or it will toughen. Season with salt and pepper. Add a splash of Pernod and toss to mix with squid and vegetables. Remove mixture to heated platter, cover loosely with foil and keep warm. Increase heat under skillet to high; add ⅔ cup Pernod (stand back in case it flames) and deglaze any bits clinging to skillet bottom. Reduce liquid by half; pour over squid mixture and toss again.

To serve, rearrange squid mixture on platter, wipe any sauce stains from rim, and garnish with sautéed bell pepper. Serve on individual small heated plates; eat with forks. Accompany with French bread. Makes 4 first-course servings.

Lean

The carrots in this version add body, color and flavor.

12 fiddlehead fern tips; or 24 Chinese pea pods or 24 young asparagus tips (cut to a length of 3 inches)
3 tablespoons Pernod
2 teaspoons fresh lemon juice
1 teaspoon light vegetable oil
1 tablespoon minced garlic
2 medium-size carrots, cut in 2½-inch matchsticks (about 2 cups)

10 ounces squid bodies without tentacles, cleaned, cut in ½" × 2" strips
Pinch of ground red (cayenne) pepper
Pinch of ground anise seeds
4 rounds toasted French bread

Wash fiddlehead fern tips and pat them dry. If using Chinese pea pods, remove strings. If using asparagus, peel downward from tips if stalks are more than ¼ inch thick; blanch in boiling water 2 to 5 minutes or until barely cooked. Refresh in cold water and pat dry. Mix Pernod and lemon juice in a small bowl.

Preheat oven to 175F (80C). Warm a medium-size platter in oven. Heat oil in a large non-stick skillet over medium-high heat. Add garlic and sauté 1 minute or until soft. Add carrots and fiddlehead ferns, pea pods or asparagus. Sauté, turning frequently, 1 to 3 minutes or until ferns, pea pods or asparagus turn bright green and begin to soften. Add squid strips and sauté no more than 1 minute, just until opaque; vegetables should be tender-crisp, squid hot and tender. Do not overcook squid or it will toughen. Increase heat to high, season with red pepper and anise. Add Pernod mixture and toss until combined. Serve immediately.

To serve, spoon squid mixture over toasted French bread on a heated platter or individual plates. Makes 4 first-course servings.

	kcal	carb(gm)	fat(gm)	chol(mg)	Na(mg)	iron(mg)	Ca(mg)
lavish:	329	27	14	270	373	1.9	44
lean:	223	31	3	165	234	3	89

MARINATED CHICKEN CHUNKS WITH FRESH LIME

Lavish

♦

Lime and cardamom combine to infuse the chicken with a subtle, exotic flavor. I like it as a first course or appetizer, but pianist Sheldon Steinberg (who approaches cooking almost as seriously as he does the piano) likes the lean version as a main course with a bowl of hot pasta on the side.

Lime Marinade
1 pound boneless chicken
    breasts, skin on
3 tablespoons olive oil
3 medium-size ripe tomatoes,
    seeded, cut in 1-inch pieces
½ cup sun-dried tomatoes, cut
    in small pieces
2 limes, unpeeled, cut in ½-
    inch pieces

2 tablespoons extra-virgin
    olive oil
1 tablespoon fresh lime juice,
    or to taste
Salt to taste
Butter lettuce, radicchio or
    other greens of choice
3 tablespoons 1-inch-long
    chive pieces for garnish

LIME MARINADE
½ cup fresh lime juice
2 tablespoons olive oil
1 tablespoon ground
  cardamom

1 teaspoon *each* salt and sugar
Freshly ground pepper to
  taste

Prepare Lime Marinade. Add chicken to marinade in bowl, toss to coat, cover and refrigerate 2 to 5 hours, turning occasionally. Drain chicken and pat dry. Reserve marinade.

Preheat grill or broiler. Brush skin side of chicken pieces with 3 tablespoons olive oil. Grill or broil chicken, flesh side down, 5 to 6 inches from heat source for 3 minutes. Turn over; continue to cook just until flesh is firm and juices run clear. Time will vary from 1 to 5 minutes, depending upon thickness of chicken breast; *do not overcook*. Remove chicken to a large, deep platter. Blot oil from surface of reserved marinade with paper towels. Pour marinade into a small saucepan and reduce over high heat to 2 tablespoons or until syrupy. Spoon over chicken as it cools. Cut chicken into irregular 1½-inch chunks. Add fresh tomatoes, sun-dried tomatoes and lime pieces to chicken on platter; toss to mix. Season with 2 tablespoons extra-virgin olive oil, lime juice and salt. If prepared ahead, cover and refrigerate up to 8 hours. Remove from refrigerator 15 minutes before serving; toss to mix.

To serve as a first course, arrange lettuce or other greens on 8 individual plates. Divide chicken mixture among plates; garnish with chives. To serve as an appetizer, wipe any sauce stains from rim of platter, then scatter chives over chicken. Have wooden skewers or picks handy. Makes 8 first-course or appetizer servings.

Lime Marinade: In a large glass, ceramic or stainless steel bowl, mix all ingredients.

Lean

Skinless chicken breasts steamed over a marinade are a delicious lowfat, low-calorie alternative to broiled chicken basted with olive oil.

Lime Marinade
1 pound boneless skinless
 chicken breasts, cut in 1½-
 inch chunks
½ cup water
3 (¼-inch-thick) slices red
 onion
3 medium-size ripe tomatoes,
 seeded, cut in 1-inch pieces
½ cup sun-dried tomatoes, cut
 in small pieces
2 limes, unpeeled, cut in ½-
 inch pieces
1 tablespoon extra-virgin
 olive oil

Fresh lime juice to taste
¼ cup fresh cilantro or flat-
 leaf parsley leaves
Butter lettuce, radicchio or
 other greens of choice
Cilantro or flat-leaf parsley
 sprigs for garnish

LIME MARINADE
½ cup fresh lime juice
1 tablespoon ground
 cardamom
½ teaspoon sugar
Freshly ground pepper to
 taste

Prepare Lime Marinade. Add chicken chunks to marinade in bowl, toss to coat, then cover and refrigerate 2 to 5 hours, turning occasionally. Drain chicken. Reserve marinade.

Fit a steamer rack into a medium-size skillet with a lid. Pour ½ cup water into skillet. Arrange chicken chunks on rack in a single layer and pour reserved marinade over them. Add additional water, if necessary, to bring water level to 1 inch below steamer rack. Cover and bring water to a boil over high heat. Reduce heat to medium and steam chicken pieces 2 minutes or just until opaque throughout. Remove chicken to a large, deep platter.

Pour marinade-steaming liquid into a medium-size saucepan and reduce to about 2 tablespoons or until syrupy. Spoon over chicken chunks as they cool. Separate onion slices into rings. Add onion rings, fresh tomatoes, sun-dried tomatoes and lime pieces to chicken on platter; toss to mix. Taste and add oil and lime juice, if needed. If prepared ahead, cover and refrigerate up to 8 hours (or omit fresh tomatoes and onion and refrigerate up to 24 hours; add fresh tomatoes and onion before serving). Remove from refrigerator about 15 minutes before serving.

To serve, toss with cilantro or parsley leaves. To serve as a first course, arrange lettuce or other greens on 8 individual plates. Divide chicken mixture among plates; garnish with cilantro or parsley sprigs. To serve as an appetizer, wipe any sauce stains from rim of platter, then garnish with cilantro or parsley sprigs. Have wooden skewers or picks handy. Makes 8 first-course or appetizer servings.

Lime Marinade: In a large glass, ceramic or stainless steel bowl, mix all ingredients.

	kcal	carb(gm)	fat(gm)	chol(mg)	Na(mg)	iron(mg)	Ca(mg)
lavish:	226	7	15	48	312	1.1	22
lean:	127	7	4	43	42	1.1	25

STEAK TARTARE

Lavish

♦

Steak tartare separates primitive carnivores like me from mere grillers and broilers. If you fall into the first category, (I really belong in both), be prepared to splurge and shop in a quality market for your beef. Steak tartare is usually served as an appetizer, but it's substantial enough to stand alone as a main course.

1 pound top sirloin, all fat removed
2 egg yolks
1 tablespoon plus 1 teaspoon Dijon-style mustard
1 tablespoon Worcestershire sauce
3 tablespoons tomato-based chili sauce
⅔ cup finely chopped sweet red onion
2 tablespoons extra-virgin olive oil
1 tablespoon minced capers

1 tablespoon plus 1 teaspoon good-quality vodka
4 anchovy fillets, chopped, if desired
Salt and freshly ground pepper to taste
1 tablespoon fresh lemon juice, or to taste
Additional capers for garnish
Unsalted butter, room temperature
Pumpernickel bread, thinly sliced, toasted

Cut beef in ½-inch chunks. Use a meat grinder or a food processor fitted with a metal blade to cut meat into very small pieces. If using a processor, process with about 12 (1-second) pulses, scraping down sides of work bowl as needed. Do not overprocess; meat should not be completely smooth.

Remove meat to a large bowl. Add egg yolks, mustard, Worcestershire sauce, chili sauce, onion, oil, 1 tablespoon capers and vodka, mixing to blend after each addition. Add anchovy fillets, if desired. Season with salt, pepper and lemon juice. For best flavor, prepare steak tartare as close to serving time as possible.

To serve, mound steak tartare in a medium-size bowl. Indent center of mound with a spoon and garnish with capers. Accompany with butter and toasted pumpernickel bread. Makes 8 to 10 appetizer or 4 main course servings.

VARIATION

For a sushi-like wrapped steak tartare, enclose the prepared steak tartare in sliced raw beef. Have the butcher cut 32 thin slices (about 1 lb. *total*) of fat-free beef tenderloin or fillet. (If the meat is well chilled, the butcher's slicing machine can cut it paper-thin. If slices are not paper-thin, pound them carpaccio-thin with a mallet or rolling pin.) Cut a bunch of chives in 2-inch lengths for garnish. Spoon 1 heaping tablespoon steak tartare in center of each beef slice; wrap beef slice around bottom and sides of tartare, securing chive garnish vertically between tartare and wrapping.

To serve, arrange beef rolls on a large flat platter. Makes 32 rolls (8 to 10 appetizer servings).

Lean

Before you pass up steak tartare just because it's beef, consider that certain cuts of very lean meat are as low in fat as poultry (see Note opposite). Even calorie- and cholesterol-counters can enjoy this decidedly non-classic tartare, made with water chestnuts and served with hot mustard.

1 pound lean top round steak, all fat removed
½ cup medium-fine chopped water chestnuts
1 teaspoon dry mustard
2 teaspoons Worcestershire sauce
1 tablespoon tomato-based chili sauce
⅔ cup finely chopped sweet red onion
1 teaspoon red wine vinegar
1 tablespoon minced fresh marjoram leaves or 1 teaspoon dried leaf marjoram

1 tablespoon fresh lemon juice or 1 scant teaspoon lemon syrup, see TIP, page 33 or to taste
Freshly ground pepper to taste
1 tablespoon extra-virgin olive oil
Prepared hot mustard
Pumpernickel bread, thinly sliced, toasted

Cut beef in ½-inch chunks. Use a meat grinder or a food processor fitted with a metal blade to cut meat into very small pieces. If using a processor, process with about 12 (1-second) pulses, scraping down sides of work bowl as needed. Do not overprocess; meat should not be completely smooth.

Remove meat to a large bowl. Add water chestnuts, dry mustard, Worcestershire sauce, chili sauce, onion, vinegar and marjoram, mixing to blend after each addition. Season with lemon juice or lemon syrup and pepper. For best flavor, prepare steak tartare as close to serving time as possible.

To serve, stir in oil, then mound steak tartare in a medium-size bowl. Accompany with hot mustard and toasted pumpernickel bread. Makes 8 to 10 appetizer or 4 main course servings.

Note: According to U.S.D.A. Agricultural Handbook No. 8, Science and Education Administration's series reports on Poultry (1979), Beef (1986) and Finfish and Shellfish (1987).

	kcal	carb(gm)	fat(gm)	chol(mg)	Na(mg)	iron(mg)	Ca(mg)
lavish:	203	8	12	159	249	2	24
lean:	149	8	7	85	165	1.8	17

TORTILLA-PIZZA WITH ARTICHOKE & TOMATO

Lavish

♦

Here's a fast, easy variation on the California Pizza theme that's perfect for busy cooks. Spread flour tortillas with pureed vegetables or olive, walnut or hazelnut oil, then top with your favorite ingredients (it's an ideal way to use up leftovers). Because tortillas make a crisper, thinner crust than pizza dough, have plates, forks and napkins nearby.

1 lemon
1 large artichoke
¼ cup plus 1 teaspoon olive oil
½ medium-size red onion, thinly sliced
Salt and freshly ground pepper to taste
2 (about 9-inch-diameter) flour tortillas
4 ounces Italian Fontina or Jarlsberg cheese, coarsely grated (1 cup)

8 (¼-inch-thick) slices tomato
2 tablespoons sun-dried tomatoes, cut in slivers
¼ cup fresh marjoram leaves
4 ounces Parmesan cheese, finely grated (about 1⅓ cups)
3 tablespoons extra-virgin olive oil

Fill a small bowl with cold water. Squeeze juice from lemon; add juice and juiced rinds to water. With a sharp knife, cut artichoke leaves and choke away from heart. Cut heart in 6 pieces and drop into lemon water to prevent browning. In a small saucepan, bring 2 cups salted water to a boil over high heat; add artichoke heart pieces, return to a boil, reduce heat and simmer 5 minutes or until tender. Drain artichoke pieces, then cut in ¼-inch slices. Toss with 1 teaspoon olive oil and set aside. Heat 2 tablespoons olive oil in a medium-size skillet over medium heat; add onion and sauté 5 minutes or until soft and beginning to color. Season lightly with salt and pepper; set aside.

Preheat oven to 500F (260C). Arrange tortillas on a large non-stick baking sheet; spread remaining 2 tablespoons olive oil evenly over tortillas with the back of a spoon. Arrange onion over tortillas; sprinkle half the Fontina or Jarlsberg cheese over onion. Arrange cooked sliced artichoke hearts, tomato slices and sun-dried tomatoes over cheese. Sprinkle with 2 tablespoons marjoram leaves, then with Parmesan cheese and remaining Fontina or Jarlsberg cheese. Sprinkle lightly with salt and pepper. Bake in upper third of oven 7 minutes or until tortillas begin to brown and cheese is melted. Remove from oven and drizzle with 3 tablespoons extra-virgin olive oil.

To serve, cut each tortilla-pizza in 4 wedges. Garnish with remaining 2 tablespoons marjoram leaves. Serve hot, warm or at room temperature. Makes 8 wedges (4 appetizer servings).

VARIATION

In early summer, try corn (instead of flour) tortilla-pizzas sprinkled with kernels of fresh sweet corn, chopped bell peppers, grated mild cheese, sliced red onion, sliced tomatoes and fresh basil leaves.

Lean

A little extra-virgin olive oil drizzled over these finished tortilla-pizzas adds flavor.

1 lemon
1 large artichoke
1 tablespoon fresh lemon
    juice
½ medium-size red onion,
    thinly sliced
1½ tablespoons balsamic
    vinegar or fruity red wine
3 tablespoons tomato paste
2 (about 9-inch-diameter)
    flour tortillas

1 cup asparagus tips, cooked
    tender-crisp, cut in ¾-inch
    pieces
8 (¼-inch-thick) slices tomato
2 tablespoons sun-dried
    tomatoes, cut in slivers
¼ cup fresh marjoram leaves
Freshly ground pepper to
    taste
2 tablespoons extra-virgin
    olive oil
1 lemon, cut in 4 wedges,
    seeded, for garnish

Fill a small saucepan with cold water. Squeeze juice from whole lemon; add juice and juiced rinds to water. With a sharp knife, cut artichoke leaves and choke away from heart. Cut heart in 6 pieces and drop into lemon water. Bring lemon water and artichoke pieces to a boil over high heat; reduce heat and simmer 5 minutes or until artichoke pieces are tender. Drain artichoke pieces, then cut in ¼-inch slices. Toss with 1 tablespoon lemon juice and set aside. In a covered, medium-size non-stick skillet, sweat onion over medium-low heat, stirring occasionally to prevent sticking, about 10 minutes or until soft and golden. Set aside.

Preheat oven to 500F (260C). Blend vinegar or wine and tomato paste. Arrange tortillas on a large non-stick baking sheet; spread vinegar mixture evenly over tortillas. Arrange onion over tortillas. Arrange cooked sliced artichoke hearts, asparagus tips, tomato slices and sun-dried tomatoes over onion. Sprinkle with 2 tablespoons marjoram leaves, then with pepper. Bake in upper third of oven 7 minutes or until tortillas begin to brown and tomatoes are slightly softened. Remove from oven and drizzle with oil.

To serve, cut each tortilla-pizza in 4 wedges. Sprinkle with remaining 2 tablespoons marjoram leaves. Garnish with lemon wedges. Serve hot, warm or at room temperature. Makes 8 wedges (4 appetizer servings).

	kcal	carb(gm)	fat(gm)	chol(mg)	Na(mg)	iron(mg)	Ca(mg)
lavish:	535	20	43	55	584	2.3	593
lean:	158	20	8	0	34	2.4	77

TORTILLA-PIZZA WITH SMOKED DUCK, PEAR & GARLIC

Lavish

♦

The combination of smoked duck with tender, golden pears and garlic is irresistible. Smoked duck is sold in specialty markets; if it's not available, use smoked turkey instead.

½ large underripe Anjou or
   Bartlett pear
12 garlic cloves, peeled
¼ cup olive oil
2 (about 9-inch-diameter)
   flour tortillas
1½ cups bite-size pieces of
   smoked duck (about 6 oz.)
5½ ounces fresh goat cheese,
   crumbled

Salt and freshly ground
   pepper to taste
2 tablespoons fresh sage
   leaves
2 tablespoons extra-virgin
   olive oil
Additional fresh sage leaves
   for garnish

Peel and core pear; cut in ½-inch chunks. In a small skillet, combine pear chunks, whole garlic cloves and 2 tablespoons olive oil; cook, uncovered, over medium-low heat, turning occasionally with a spatula, about 25 minutes or until pear chunks and garlic are soft and golden brown. Set aside.

Preheat oven to 500F (260C). Arrange tortillas on a large non-stick baking sheet. Spread remaining 2 tablespoons olive oil over tortillas with the back of a spoon. Divide duck pieces evenly between tortillas; scatter pear chunks, garlic and cheese over and around duck. Sprinkle lightly with salt and pepper. Tear 2 tablespoons sage leaves in bits and scatter on top. Bake in upper third of oven 7 minutes or until cheese is melted. Remove from oven and drizzle with 2 tablespoons extra-virgin olive oil.

To serve, cut each tortilla-pizza in 4 wedges; garnish with sage leaves torn in bits. Serve hot or warm. Makes 8 wedges (4 appetizer servings).

Lean

Lowfat homemade or cottage cheese replaces the lavish version's goat cheese, and just 1 tablespoon of olive oil takes the place of 6.

1 large underripe Anjou or
   Bartlett pear
20 garlic cloves, peeled
2 (about 9-inch-diameter)
   flour tortillas
1½ cups bite-size pieces of
   smoked turkey or chicken
   breast (about 6 oz.)
¾ cup lean Homemade White
   Cheese, page 31, or non-fat
   or lowfat cottage cheese

1 tablespoon fresh lemon
   juice or balsamic vinegar
2 tablespoons fresh sage
   leaves, torn in bits
1 tablespoon extra-virgin
   olive oil
Additional fresh sage leaves
   for garnish

Peel, core and halve pear; cut in ½-inch chunks. In a covered medium-size skillet, sweat pear chunks and whole garlic cloves over medium-low heat, turning occasionally with a spatula to prevent sticking, about 25 minutes or until soft and golden brown. Place about a third of the cooked pear pieces and 5 cooked garlic cloves in a small dish; mash with a fork. Set aside.

Preheat oven to 500F (260C). Arrange tortillas on a large non-stick baking sheet. Spread mashed pear-garlic mixture evenly over tortillas. Top with turkey or chicken, remaining pear pieces and garlic, then with crumbled cheese. Sprinkle with lemon juice or vinegar. Scatter 2 tablespoons sage leaves over all. Bake 7 minutes or until tortillas begin to brown. Remove tortilla-pizzas from oven and drizzle with oil.

To serve, cut each tortilla-pizza in 4 wedges; garnish with sage leaves. Serve hot or warm. Makes 8 wedges (4 appetizer servings).

	kcal	carb(gm)	fat(gm)	chol(mg)	Na(mg)	iron(mg)	Ca(mg)
lavish:	513	31	37	38	255	2.1	201
lean:	207	22	5	38	143	1.7	82

SOUPS

Eat with people who work the land and chances are you'll eat well wherever you are. From Mallorca to Mexico the ingredients may vary with local produce but the soup, like the people who make it, is always substantial.

Soup gains substance, character and flavor from prime, ripe ingredients. Kernels of sweet, field-fresh corn lend a subtle tone to Corn Chowder with Green Chiles (page 78), while Fresh Tomato Soup with Clams (page 98) delicately combines the garden with the sea.

Soup depends on the occasion and ingredients at hand, so don't be afraid to improvise. If juices saved from cooked meat or poultry or homemade stock aren't on hand, substitute canned stock that has been briefly simmered with chopped carrot, onion and celery. Making vegetable soups with vegetable stock (or even plain water) allows their own flavors to develop. But lean soups often benefit from stock and seasonings to make up for the lack of butter, egg yolks and cream.

Many soups are better lightly thickened. Lean recipes achieve this with potato, cooked grains or flour, while lavish soups often use a *roux* (flour mixed into softened butter). Beating butter, cream, or yolks into soup just before serving adds a silky texture, but even lean soups such as the corn chowder on page 80 can be finished in this way. A touch of cream or butter is all that's needed.

SUMMER SOUP WITH PEAR & AVOCADO

Lavish

♦

In a stroke of genius and desperation, columnist and cookbook author Kit Snedaker whipped this up for an unexpected lunch guest.

1½ tablespoons butter
1 small shallot, minced
Salt to taste
1 tablespoon all-purpose flour
2 cups Chicken Stock, page 15, or commercial
2 large ripe Bartlett or Anjou pears

Juice of ½ lemon
4 medium-size ripe avocados
½ cup half and half
½ cup Crème Fraîche, page 278, or whipping cream for garnish

Melt butter in a medium-size skillet or sauté pan over medium heat; add shallot and sauté 2 to 3 minutes or until soft. Season lightly with salt. Sprinkle with flour; cook, stirring, 1 minute. Add stock, increase heat to high, and bring to a boil. Reduce heat and simmer, uncovered, 10 minutes.

Peel, core and coarsely chop pears; toss with a few drops of lemon juice. Pit, peel and coarsely chop avocados; toss with a few drops of lemon juice. In a blender or a food processor fitted with a metal blade, process stock mixture, pears and avocados in 2 batches until smooth. Blend in half and half to give soup desired consistency. This soup tastes best the day it is made; it can be prepared up to 4 hours ahead, cooled, covered and refrigerated. Remove from refrigerator 15 minutes before serving and reseason with salt as needed.

To serve, spoon soup into cups or small bowls. Spoon Crème Fraîche gently over soup so it floats, or float a spoonful of (unwhipped) whipping cream in center of each portion of soup. Makes 8 servings.

TIP

Although pureed avocado and pear thicken this soup, flour in the lavish version (potato in the lean) acts as a binder to keep the soup from separating.

Lean

A little of this goes a long way. It's filling, but contains no animal fat and is rich in potassium.

1 small shallot, minced
¼ cup peeled, diced potato
2½ to 3 cups unsalted
   Chicken Stock, page 15, or
   commercial
2 large ripe Bartlett or Anjou
   pears

¼ cup fresh lemon juice, or to
   taste
2 medium-size ripe avocados
½ teaspoon curry powder
½ cup Creamy Non-fat
   Yogurt, page 22, or
   commercial, for garnish

In a medium-size saucepan, combine shallot, potato and stock. Cover and bring to a boil over high heat. Reduce heat and simmer 10 minutes. Set aside ½ cup stock. Peel, core and coarsely chop pears; toss with a few drops of lemon juice. Pit, peel and coarsely chop avocados; toss with a few drops of lemon juice. In a blender or a food processor fitted with a metal blade, process stock mixture, pears, avocados and curry powder in 2 batches until smooth. Adjust consistency with reserved ½ cup stock. Season with lemon juice. This soup tastes best the day it is made; it can be prepared up to 4 hours ahead, cooled, covered and refrigerated. Remove from refrigerator 15 minutes before serving.

To serve, spoon soup into cups or small bowls. Float a spoonful of yogurt on each portion. Makes 8 servings.

	kcal	carb(gm)	fat(gm)	chol(mg)	Na(mg)	iron(mg)	Ca(mg)
lavish:	331	16	42	75	89	2.2	61
lean:	163	19	11	4	103	1.9	63

COLD BEET BORSCHT

Lavish

♦

My mother-in-law Rosie was a talented cook. She enjoyed this magenta-colored soup as a child on her parents' produce farm in New Jersey, then served it years later to her own family in California. The recipe traveled from Russia to the United States by ship with Rosie's mother and father. A jarful makes a perfect gift, if there's any left to give away.

2 bunches (about 3 lbs.) beets
  with fresh, leafy tops
3 quarts water
3 onions (about 1½ lbs.)
  chopped medium-fine
3 garlic cloves, pressed
6 eggs, lightly beaten

5 cups dairy sour cream
⅓ cup fresh lemon juice, or to
  taste
About 1 tablespoon salt
Freshly ground pepper
1 tablespoon sugar, if desired

Trim off beet tops, leaving 1 inch of stalks attached to beets; set tops aside. Scrub beets, place in a large soup pot and add water. Bring to a boil over high heat. Reduce heat to medium-low, cover and simmer 30 to 40 minutes or until beets are tender. Pour out and reserve cooking broth; rinse grit from soup pot and return cooking broth to pot. Peel and trim beets under cold running water; coarsely grate into cooking broth in pot, rinsing grater in broth.

Trim stalks from beet tops and reserve for another use. Wash leafy tops and cut crosswise into ¼- to ½-inch-wide strips; cut strips in half crosswise. Add leaf strips and onions to soup pot. Bring to a boil over high heat; reduce heat and simmer 3 to 4 minutes or until onions are barely softened. Remove from heat; add garlic. Cool to room temperature. Blend in beaten eggs and 3 cups sour cream. Season with lemon juice, salt, pepper and sugar, if desired. If made ahead, cover and refrigerate up to 4 days; remove from refrigerator 15 minutes before serving. Stir, taste and adjust seasonings; chilled soup may need additional salt.

Serve cool borscht from a large bowl or tureen; pass remaining 2 cups sour cream in a small bowl. Or ladle soup into bowls and garnish each serving with a dollop of sour cream. Makes 24 servings.

Lean

2 bunches (about 3 lbs.) beets
  with fresh, leafy tops
3 quarts water
3 onions (about 1½ lbs.)
  chopped medium-fine
3 garlic cloves, pressed
8 ounces liquid egg
  substitute, lightly beaten

5 cups Creamy Non-fat
  Yogurt, page 22, or
  commercial
¼ cup fresh lemon juice, or to
  taste
1 tablespoon sugar or ¼ cup
  frozen concentrated orange
  juice
Freshly ground pepper

Trim beet tops, leaving 1 inch of stalks. Set tops aside. Scrub beets, place in a large soup pot and add water. Simmer covered 30 to 40 minutes or until beets are tender. Pour out and reserve cooking broth; rinse grit from soup pot and return cooking broth to pot. Peel and trim beets under cold running water; coarsely grate into cooking broth in pot.

Trim stalks from beet tops. Wash leafy tops and cut crosswise into ¼- to ½-inch-wide strips; cut strips in half crosswise. Add leaf strips and onions to soup pot. Bring to a boil over high heat; reduce heat and simmer 3 to 4 minutes or until onions are barely softened. Off heat add garlic. Cool to room temperature. Blend in egg substitute and 3 cups yogurt. Season with lemon juice, sugar or concentrated orange juice and pepper. If made ahead, cover and refrigerate up to 4 days; remove from refrigerator 15 minutes before serving. Stir, taste and adjust seasonings before serving.

Serve cool borscht from a large bowl or tureen; pass remaining 2 cups yogurt in a small bowl. Or ladle soup into bowls and garnish each serving with a dollop of yogurt. Makes 24 servings.

TIP

Cold soup usually needs reseasoning; stir, then taste and adjust seasonings before ladling into soup bowls.

	kcal	carb(gm)	fat(gm)	chol(mg)	Na(mg)	iron(mg)	Ca(mg)
lavish:	153	9	11	90	232	.8	82
lean:	64	10	.5	1	91	.8	118

GARDEN SOUP

Lavish

♦

The flavor of this soup changes with the greens used: lettuce makes it delicate and sweet, rivercress or watercress spicy, and spinach robust. When preparing greens, use only their leaves—the stalks become stringy when processed.

3 tablespoons butter
1 onion, sliced
3 medium-size carrots, peeled, coarsely chopped
1 medium-size potato, peeled, coarsely chopped
½ teaspoon salt
1 quart well-washed, packed spinach leaves or other greens of choice, such as mustard greens, beet greens, lettuce, watercress or rivercress
4 zucchini (1¼ lbs. *total*), unpeeled, trimmed, coarsely chopped

1 large tomato, peeled, coarsely chopped
1½ quarts Vegetable Stock, page 19, or water
¼ cup fresh basil or chervil leaves, chopped, or 1½ tablespoons dried leaf basil or chervil
½ cup whipping cream
Salt and freshly ground pepper to taste
½ cup unsalted butter
8 baguette (French bread) slices
¼ cup grated Parmesan cheese (about ¾ oz.)

Melt 3 tablespoons butter in a medium-size pot over medium heat. Add onion, carrots, potato and ½ teaspoon salt; cook, stirring, until onion is softened. Add spinach or other greens, zucchini, tomato and Vegetable Stock or water. Bring to a boil over high heat; reduce heat, cover and simmer 45 minutes or until vegetables are tender and breaking apart. Add basil or chervil to soup for last 2 to 3 minutes of cooking. In a blender or a food processor fitted with a metal blade, process soup in 2 or 3 batches until smoothly pureed; blend in cream. Simmer 10 minutes. Return to pot; season with salt and pepper.

Melt unsalted butter, a few tablespoons at a time, in a small skillet over medium heat; add French bread and brown on both sides. Keep warm in a low oven. Or, if preparing soup and toast ahead, cover and refrigerate separately up to 3 days.

To serve, reheat soup over low heat; reheat toast if necessary. Ladle into heated bowls and float a slice of toast in each; sprinkle cheese over toast. Or, if soup bowls are ovenproof, float toast on soup, sprinkle with cheese and broil briefly just until cheese bubbles. Serve immediately. Makes 8 servings.

Lean

4 leeks, white part only, washed well, coarsely chopped

1 quart well-washed, packed spinach leaves or other greens of choice, such as mustard greens, beet greens, lettuce, watercress or rivercress

4 zucchini (1¼ lbs. *total*), unpeeled, trimmed, coarsely chopped

1 large tomato, peeled, coarsely chopped

4 medium-size carrots, peeled

1 medium-size potato, peeled, coarsely chopped

Leafy green tops of 2 celery stalks

Scant ½ teaspoon ground cumin

Freshly ground pepper to taste

1 quart Vegetable Stock, page 19, or water

2 cups unsalted Chicken Stock, page 15, or commercial

¼ cup fresh basil leaves, chopped, or 1½ tablespoons dried leaf basil

Fresh lemon juice to taste

1 teaspoon sugar

½ teaspoon salt, if desired

8 slices French bread, toasted

3 tablespoons 1½-inch-long chive pieces for garnish

In a medium-size pot, combine leeks, spinach or other greens, zucchini, tomato, carrots, potato, celery, cumin and pepper; add Vegetable Stock or water and Chicken Stock. Bring to a boil over high heat; reduce heat, cover and simmer 20 minutes or until carrots are tender. Use tongs to remove 1 carrot; cut in matchsticks and set aside for garnish. Cover and simmer soup 25 minutes longer or until vegetables are very tender and breaking apart. Add basil to soup for last 2 to 3 minutes of cooking.

In a blender or a food processor fitted with a metal blade, process soup in 2 or 3 batches until smoothly pureed. Return to pot. Season with lemon juice and sugar; add salt, if desired. If prepared ahead, cool, cover and refrigerate up to 3 days.

To serve, reheat soup over low heat. Ladle into heated bowls; float toast in soup. Garnish with carrot matchsticks and chives. Makes 8 servings.

	kcal	carb(gm)	fat(gm)	chol(mg)	Na(mg)	iron(mg)	Ca(mg)
lavish:	298	29	17	46	474	2.7	153
lean:	185	35	2	2	267	3.6	122

SPINACH SALAD SOUP

Lavish

♦

Tender leaves from spring or summer spinach are particularly tasty in this soup. Crisp bacon bits contrast with the soup's delicate flavor and smooth texture.

⅓ pound bacon
1 tablespoon butter
1 medium-size onion, sliced
2 shallots, sliced
1 medium-size (about 8-oz.) potato, peeled, sliced
Pinch of freshly grated or ground nutmeg
1½ cups Chicken Stock, page 15, or commercial
1½ cups water
1 bunch spinach, leaves only, washed well (about 1½ quarts, loosely packed); or 1 (10-oz.) package frozen chopped spinach, thawed, squeezed dry

3 cups half and half
¼ teaspoon white pepper
About 1 teaspoon salt, or to taste
About 2 tablespoons fresh lemon juice, or to taste
3 tablespoons butter, room temperature (for hot soup only)
2 hard-cooked eggs, chopped, for garnish

In a large skillet with a lid, cook bacon over medium heat until crisp. Drain on paper towels. Crumble bacon and keep warm; set aside for garnish. Discard all but 2 tablespoons bacon drippings. Add 1 tablespoon butter to reserved 2 tablespoons drippings in skillet; add onion and shallots and cook over medium-low heat until softened but not browned. Add potato, nutmeg, stock and water. Bring to a boil over high heat; reduce heat, cover and simmer 20 minutes or until potato slices are tender and breaking apart. Add spinach for last 2 minutes of cooking.

In a blender or a food processor fitted with a metal blade, process soup in 2 or 3 batches until smoothly pureed; some green flecks will remain. Return to skillet. Stir in half and half. Season with white pepper, salt and lemon juice. If prepared ahead, cool, cover and refrigerate soup and bacon garnish separately up to 2 days.

To serve soup hot, reheat to just under a simmer, beating in 3 tablespoons butter, 1 teaspoon at a time. To serve cold, remove from refrigerator 15 minutes before serving; taste and adjust seasonings.

To serve soup hot or cold, reheat bacon garnish if necessary. Ladle soup into warmed or slightly chilled bowls. Garnish with bacon and chopped eggs. Makes 8 servings.

Lean

The addition of tarragon and extra chicken broth make this version of Spinach Salad Soup fragrant and robust; the optional cream gives it a smoother texture.

2 teaspoons light vegetable oil, if desired
5 ounces smoked turkey breast or lean boiled ham, diced
1 large onion, sliced
2 shallots, sliced
1 medium-size (about 8-oz.) potato, peeled, sliced
Generous pinch of freshly grated or ground nutmeg, or to taste
¼ teaspoon dried leaf tarragon, or to taste
3 cups unsalted Chicken Stock, page 15, or commercial

1 bunch spinach, leaves only, washed well (about 6 cups, loosely packed), or 1 (10-oz.) package frozen chopped spinach, thawed, squeezed dry
2 cups non-fat milk
1 cup Creamy Non-fat Yogurt, page 22, or commercial
3 tablespoons whipping cream, if desired
¼ teaspoon white pepper
About 1 tablespoon fresh lemon juice to taste
½ teaspoon salt, if desired
Whites of 4 hard-cooked eggs, chopped for garnish

Heat oil in a large skillet with a lid (if using a non-stick skillet, you may omit oil). Add turkey or ham and cook over medium-high heat 3 to 4 minutes or until meat is browned and becomes aromatic. Remove from skillet, drain if necessary and keep warm. Add onion and shallots to skillet; cook over medium-low heat 2 minutes, stirring to prevent sticking. Then reduce heat, cover and continue to cook, stirring occasionally to prevent sticking, until softened. Add potato, nutmeg, tarragon and stock. Bring to a boil over high heat; reduce heat, cover and simmer 20 minutes or until potato slices are tender and breaking apart.

If using fresh spinach, reserve 8 medium-size leaves for garnish; add remaining leaves (or all frozen spinach) to soup for 2 minutes of cooking.

In a blender or a food processor fitted with a metal blade, process soup in 2 or 3 batches until smoothly pureed; some green flecks will remain. Return to skillet. Stir in turkey or ham; stir in milk, yogurt and cream, if desired. Season with white pepper, lemon juice, salt, if desired, and additional tarragon or nutmeg. If prepared ahead, cover and refrigerate up to 2 days.

To serve soup hot, reheat to just under a simmer. To serve cold, remove from refrigerator 15 minutes before serving; taste and adjust seasonings.

To serve, cut reserved spinach leaves into strips. Ladle soup into warmed or slightly chilled bowls. Garnish with chopped egg whites and spinach strips. Makes 8 servings.

TIP

Slow cooking is especially useful for developing flavor in lean recipes: it caramelizes the sugar in onions, shallots and leeks and brings out their natural sweetness.

	kcal	carb(gm)	fat(gm)	chol(mg)	Na(mg)	iron(mg)	Ca(mg)
lavish:	334	10	27	129	552	1.6	140
lean:	137	12	4	23	173	1.4	177

FRESH ARTICHOKE SOUP

Lavish

♦

In winter, when artichokes are scarce, this is lavish in flavor and price —but in summer, when they're plentiful, you can eat your fill and still buy your way out of the market. Whether the soup is served hot or slightly chilled, it is a delicate essence of artichokes. For a more intense flavor, use homemade Artichoke Stock (see lean version) in place of chicken stock.

8 large artichokes
Juice and rinds of 3 lemons
6 bay leaves
15 whole allspice berries
3 tablespoons butter
2 leeks, white part only,
    washed well, sliced
¼ teaspoon salt
1½ tablespoons all-purpose
    flour

1 quart Chicken Stock, page
    15, or commercial
Pinch of ground allspice
1 cup whipping cream
Salt to taste
Pinch of white pepper
½ cup Crème Fraîche, page
    278, for garnish

In a large stock pot or deep roasting pan, bring 8 quarts water to a boil over high heat. Meanwhile, wash and trim artichokes; peel stems and reserve. Rub cut portions of artichokes with lemon rinds to prevent discoloration. Add artichokes, stems, 4 bay leaves, allspice berries, and juice and rinds of 2 lemons to boiling water. Return to a boil, reduce heat to medium, cover and simmer 45 minutes or until artichokes are tender and leaves pull out easily. Remove stems and artichokes from water; invert artichokes to drain and cool. Remove leaves and chokes from cooled artichokes. Toss 1 artichoke bottom with a few drops of lemon juice and set aside for garnish. Cut remaining artichoke hearts and stems into 1-inch chunks; toss with a few drops of lemon juice and set aside.

Melt butter in a medium-size saucepan over medium heat. Add leeks and ¼ teaspoon salt; cook 3 minutes, stirring occasionally. Reduce heat, cover and cook, stirring occasionally, 10 minutes or until leeks are soft and tender. Uncover pan, sprinkle flour over leeks and stir over medium heat 1 minute. Add 3 cups Chicken

Stock, ground allspice and remaining 2 bay leaves. Bring to a boil; reduce heat and simmer, uncovered, 10 minutes. Discard bay leaves. With a slotted spoon, remove leeks from stock.

In a blender or a food processor fitted with a metal blade, process cooked leeks with artichoke hearts and stems until smoothly pureed, then return to stock. Blend in cream. Thin to desired consistency with remaining 1 cup Chicken Stock. Season with salt, white pepper and lemon juice. If prepared ahead, cool, cover and refrigerate up to 2 days.

To serve soup hot, reheat to just under a simmer. To serve cold, remove from refrigerator 15 minutes before serving; thin with additional stock, if necessary, then taste and adjust seasonings.

Just before serving, mince reserved artichoke bottom for garnish. To serve, ladle soup into heated or slightly chilled soup bowls. Garnish each serving with a dollop of Crème Fraîche; sprinkle minced artichoke over Crème Fraîche. Makes 8 servings.

Lean

8 large artichokes
Juice and rinds of 3 lemons
6 bay leaves
15 whole allspice berries
1 quart Artichoke Stock, see
  instructions in text below
2 leeks, white part only,
  washed well, sliced
½ potato, peeled, sliced
  (about 1 cup, loosely
  packed)
Pinch of ground allspice

½ cup Enriched Non-fat Milk,
  page 22, or non-fat milk
2 tablespoons whipping
  cream, if desired
1 teaspoon salt, if desired
Pinch of white pepper
Unsalted Chicken Stock, page
  15, or commercial, if
  needed
½ cup Creamy Non-fat
  Yogurt, page 22, or
  commercial, for garnish

Cook artichokes as directed in lavish recipe, but add all 6 bay leaves to cooking liquid. Set cooking liquid aside for Artichoke Stock.

To prepare Artichoke Stock, remove leaves and chokes from cooled artichokes. Discard chokes. Add leaves to cooking liquid; boil, uncovered, 40 minutes. Strain stock and discard solids. Reduce stock over high heat to 1 quart.

Toss 1 artichoke bottom with a few drops of lemon juice and set aside for garnish. Cut remaining artichoke hearts and stems into 1-inch chunks; toss with a few drops of lemon juice and set aside. In a medium-size covered saucepan (preferably non-stick), sweat leeks over medium-low heat about 10 minutes or until softened, stirring occasionally to prevent sticking. Add potato, 3 cups Artichoke Stock and ground allspice. Bring to a boil over high heat; reduce heat to low and simmer 20 minutes or until potato is breaking apart. Strain; reserve stock and cooked potato-leek mixture.

In a blender or a food processor fitted with a metal blade, process potato-leek mixture with artichoke hearts and stems until smoothly pureed. Return puree to stock. Blend in milk. Thin to desired consistency with remaining 1 cup Artichoke Stock. Add cream, if desired. Season with lemon juice, salt, if desired, and white pepper. If prepared ahead, cool, cover and refrigerate up to 2 days.

To serve soup hot, reheat to just under a simmer. To serve cold, remove from refrigerator 15 minutes before serving; thin with Chicken Stock, if necessary. Adjust seasonings.

Just before serving, mince reserved artichoke bottom for garnish. To serve, ladle soup into heated or slightly chilled soup bowls. Garnish each serving with a dollop of yogurt; sprinkle minced artichoke over yogurt. Makes 8 servings.

	kcal	carb(gm)	fat(gm)	chol(mg)	Na(mg)	iron(mg)	Ca(mg)
lavish:	289	24	21	69	595	2.9	126
lean:	112	25	2	5	107	2.6	140

CORN CHOWDER WITH GREEN CHILES

Lavish

♦

This recipe is inspired by the corn chowder served at Mark Miller's Coyote Cafe in Santa Fe, New Mexico, and it's a great one. You can make either version up to 2 days ahead and refrigerate it.

6 green onions
5 tablespoons butter
2 large shallots, sliced (about ⅔ cup)
1 garlic clove, minced
⅔ cup diced Anaheim or other mild green chiles; or 1 (7-oz.) can diced green chiles
8 ears fresh corn (4 to 5 cups kernels and juice); or 1 (1-lb.) package frozen corn kernels, thawed

1½ quarts half and half
2 cups milk
¾ teaspoon chili powder
½ teaspoon salt
Sugar to taste
½ cup diced red bell pepper
Pinch of white pepper
⅓ cup toasted pine nuts for garnish

Chop enough green onion tops medium-fine to make ½ cup; set aside. Reserve remaining tops for another use. Slice white part of green onions. Melt 3 tablespoons butter in a large skillet or heavy saucepan over medium-high heat. When foam subsides, add shallots and sliced white part of green onions; sauté 1 minute, stirring occasionally. Add garlic and ⅓ cup diced fresh chiles and cook until soft. (Add canned chiles later, as directed.)

With a sharp, heavy knife, cut kernels from corn; set aside ½ cup. Turn knife to blunt side; scrape down sweet, milky juice from cobs. Add corn kernels (except for reserved ½ cup) and juice to chile mixture in skillet and cook over medium-high heat 1 to 2 minutes, stirring; stir in half and half, milk and chili powder. Bring to a boil over high heat; reduce heat and simmer, uncovered, 40 minutes, stirring occasionally to prevent sticking.

Meanwhile, melt remaining 2 tablespoons butter in a small skillet over medium-high heat. Add ½ cup chopped green onion tops, remaining ⅓ cup diced fresh chiles and reserved ½ cup corn kernels and sauté 1 minute; remove with a slotted spoon. Season lightly with salt and sugar and set aside. Add bell pepper to skillet and sauté about 3 minutes or just until soft (if using canned green chiles, toss 3 tablespoons chiles with pepper for last 30 seconds). Season lightly with salt and sugar, remove with a slotted spoon and set aside.

Pour corn-milk mixture into a large strainer set over a large saucepan. Place solids (and remaining canned green chiles, if used) in a blender or a food processor fitted with a metal blade. Process 1 minute or until well blended but not smooth; add to strained liquid in pan along with sautéed green onion-chile-corn mixture and sautéed bell pepper. Season with salt, sugar and white pepper.

To serve chowder, reheat to just under a simmer. Ladle into heated soup bowls. Garnish each serving with pine nuts. Makes 10 to 12 servings.

Lean

Corn juices scraped from the cobs gives this soup a field-fresh taste.

8 ears fresh corn (4 to 5 cups kernels and juice); or 1 (1-lb.) package frozen corn kernels, thawed
6 green onions
2 large shallots, sliced (about ⅔ cup)
1 garlic clove, minced
⅔ cup diced Anaheim or other mild green chiles; or 1 (7-oz.) can diced green chiles
1 quart Enriched Non-fat Milk, page 22, or non-fat milk
1 quart unsalted Chicken Stock, page 15, or commercial
1 tablespoon sugar
½ teaspoon chili powder
Pinch of white pepper
½ cup diced red bell pepper
2 tablespoons whipping cream, if desired
1½ teaspoons salt, if desired

With a sharp, heavy knife, cut kernels from corn; set aside ½ cup. Turn knife to blunt side and scrape down sweet, milky juice from cobs. Scoop kernels (except for reserved ½ cup) and juice into a medium-size bowl; set aside. Chop enough green onion tops medium-fine to make ½ cup; set aside. Reserve remaining tops for another use. Slice white part of green onions; place in a large, heavy non-stick saucepan along with shallots, garlic and ⅓ cup diced fresh chiles. (Add canned chiles later, as directed.) Cover and sweat over medium-low heat 8 to 10 minutes or until soft, stirring occasionally to prevent sticking and browning. Add corn and juice to chile mixture; cook, uncovered, over medium-high heat 1 to 2 minutes, stirring. Stir in milk, stock, sugar, chili powder and white pepper. Bring to a boil over high heat; reduce heat and cook at a bare simmer, uncovered, 40 minutes, stirring occasionally to prevent sticking.

Meanwhile, fill a medium-size saucepan with water and bring to a boil. Blanch bell pepper, reserved ½ cup corn kernels and remaining ⅓ cup diced fresh chiles 1 to 2 minutes or just until tender-crisp; blanch ½ cup chopped green onion tops for last few seconds. Remove with a strainer; set aside.

Pour corn-milk mixture into a strainer set over a large saucepan. Place solids in a blender or a food processor fitted with a metal blade. If using canned chiles, set 3 tablespoons aside; add remainder to blender or food processor. Process 1 minute or until well blended but not smooth. Add processed solids to strained liquid in saucepan. Stir in blanched vegetables and reserved 3 tablespoons canned chiles, if used. Stir in cream and salt, if desired.

To serve chowder, reheat to just under a simmer. Ladle into heated soup bowls. Makes 10 to 12 servings.

	kcal	carb(gm)	fat(gm)	chol(mg)	Na(mg)	iron(mg)	Ca(mg)
lavish:	375	28	27	75	349	1.4	223
lean:	141	25	2	2	163	1	138

CHILE PEPPER SOUP
WITH TORTILLA CHIPS

Lavish

♦

This easy-to-make soup from Michoacan, Mexico, is often served with broiled local whitefish from nearby Lake Patzcuaro. You'll find all the ingredients in Mexican or Latin American markets. The cheese should melt and string when heated.

8 or 9 dried ancho or pasilla
   chiles, stems and seeds
   removed
3 cups Chicken Stock, page
   15, or commercial
3 cups water
1 (6-oz.) can tomato paste
2 cups tomato puree (one 1-
   lb. can)
2 to 4 tablespoons fresh lime
   juice, or to taste
1½ teaspoons ground cumin
1 tablespoon crumbled dried
   epazote or dried leaf
   oregano

Salt
6 (about 7-inch-diameter)
   flour or corn tortillas
½ cup olive oil
8 ounces Mexican *queso
   ranchero* or *queso osadero*, or
   jack cheese
2 ripe avocados
2 teaspoons fresh lime juice
½ to ¾ cup dairy sour cream
   for garnish
10 lime slices for garnish

In a 3-quart saucepan, combine chiles, stock and water. Bring to a boil over high heat. Reduce heat, cover and simmer 20 minutes. Cool slightly. In a blender or a food processor fitted with a metal blade, process chiles and cooking liquid in 2 or 3 batches until smoothly pureed. Press puree through a strainer into a large sauce-pan to remove chile skins; use a spatula to scrape puree from under-side of strainer. Blend in tomato paste and tomato puree. Season with 2 to 4 tablespoons lime juice, cumin, epazote or oregano and 1 teaspoon salt. Simmer, covered, 20 minutes.

Preheat oven to 400F (205C). Brush tortillas with oil and sprinkle lightly with salt; cut in ¾-inch strips. Arrange on a baking sheet and bake 8 minutes or until crisp; set aside. Soup and tortillas can be prepared up to 3 days ahead; cool, cover tightly and refrigerate. Before serving, reheat and reseason soup.

To serve, set oven at 250F (120C). Cut cheese in ½-inch cubes. Divide cheese among 8 ovenproof soup bowls; set bowls on a baking sheet and heat 20 minutes or until cheese is melted. Pit and peel avocados, then cut in ¾-inch pieces and toss with 2 teaspoons lime juice. Arrange avocado and several tortilla strips over melted cheese in each soup bowl; ladle hot soup into bowls. Spoon sour cream into center of each bowl; arrange lime slices over sour cream. Pass remaining tortilla strips. Makes 10 servings.

Lean

8 or 9 dried ancho or pasilla chiles, stems and seeds removed

1½ quarts unsalted Chicken Stock, page 15, or commercial

1 (6-oz.) can tomato paste

2 cups tomato puree (one 1-lb. can)

2 to 4 tablespoons fresh lime juice, or to taste

1½ teaspoons ground cumin

1 tablespoon crumbled dried epazote or dried leaf oregano

1 cup fresh green peas; or 1 cup frozen green peas, thawed

6 (about 7-inch-diameter) flour or corn tortillas, cut in ¾-inch strips

1½ cups ½-inch cubes of peeled jicama or boiled potato

1 cup fresh cilantro leaves for garnish

In a 3-quart saucepan, combine chiles and stock. Bring to a boil over high heat. Reduce heat, cover and simmer 20 minutes. Cool slightly. In a blender or a food processor fitted with a metal blade, process chiles and cooking liquid in 2 or 3 batches until smoothly pureed. Press puree through a strainer into a large saucepan to remove chile skins; use a spatula to scrape puree from underside of strainer. Blend in tomato paste and tomato puree. Season with lime juice, cumin and epazote or oregano. Simmer, covered, 20 minutes.

In a small saucepan, bring 3 cups water to a boil over high heat. Add peas. Blanch fresh peas 4 minutes or until tender; blanch frozen peas 30 seconds. Drain; set aside. Preheat oven to 400F (205C). Arrange tortilla strips on a baking sheet and bake 8 minutes or until crisp; set aside.

Soup and tortillas can be prepared up to 3 days ahead; cool, cover tightly and refrigerate. Peas and jicama or potatoes can be prepared up to 2 days ahead; cool, cover tightly and refrigerate (to store jicama, see TIP, page 30).

To serve, divide peas and jicama or potatoes among heated soup bowls. Reheat and reseason soup, if needed. Arrange a few tortilla strips in each bowl. Ladle hot soup over tortillas and vegetables; garnish soup with cilantro. Pass remaining tortilla strips. Makes 10 servings.

	kcal	carb(gm)	fat(gm)	chol(mg)	Na(mg)	iron(mg)	Ca(mg)
lavish:	396	27	28	5	430	3.8	261
lean:	159	28	2	1	322	3.6	77

BREAD SOUP

Lavish

♦

This spectacular and flavorful soup is easy to prepare, and it's a complete meal. It reminds me of Na Balom, an inn and Mayan sanctuary in Chiapas, Mexico, and of the Indian cook there who prepared another delicious bread soup with her local ingredients.

3½ quarts Chicken Stock, page 15, or commercial
½ cup dried black beans, rinsed
5 (3-inch) cinnamon sticks
7 fresh thyme sprigs, bruised, or 1½ teaspoons dried leaf thyme
Freshly ground pepper to taste
6 medium-size carrots, peeled, quartered
3 medium-size potatoes, peeled, quartered
2 chayotes, peeled, cored, cut in chunks
Salt to taste

7 tablespoons olive oil
2 large onions, thickly sliced
3 large, firm tomatoes, peeled, thickly sliced
1 teaspoon sugar, or to taste
2 bananas, cut in chunks
½ cup whole blanched almonds
10 small rolls or about 10 cups torn day-old bread (14 oz. *total*)
½ cup raisins
6 hard-cooked eggs, cut in half lengthwise
3 tablespoons flat-leaf parsley leaves for garnish

In a large pot, combine stock and beans. Simmer, covered, 50 to 60 minutes or until beans are tender. Remove beans with a strainer; set aside. To broth, add cinnamon, thyme and pepper. Simmer, covered, 15 minutes. Add carrots, potatoes and chayotes; simmer 25 minutes longer or until vegetables are barely tender. Strain broth; set broth and vegetables aside separately. Discard cinnamon and thyme sprigs, if used. Season broth with salt.

Heat 3 tablespoons oil in a large skillet over medium-high heat. Season onions and tomatoes with salt and sugar. Sauté onions in oil until soft but not brown; remove from skillet. Add tomatoes and sauté until soft; remove from skillet. Add bananas and sauté just until browned; remove from skillet. Set onions, tomatoes and bananas aside separately.

Preheat oven to 400F (205C). Spread almonds on a baking sheet and toast 10 minutes or until brown; set aside. Tear rolls or bread into bite-size pieces; spread on baking sheet and toast in oven 5 minutes or until light brown. Set aside.

Layer ingredients in a deep 12-inch casserole as follows. On bottom of casserole, arrange carrots, potatoes and chayotes. Season lightly with salt. Top vegetables with toasted rolls or bread and bananas. Sprinkle with almonds and raisins; cover with onions and tomatoes. On top, arrange eggs, cut side up. Ladle broth over all; sprinkle on beans and drizzle with remaining ¼ cup oil. Bake, uncovered, 20 minutes or until hot.

To serve, garnish soup in casserole with parsley. At the table, ladle soup from casserole into heated large bowls. Makes 8 generous main-dish servings.

Lean

This flavorful version of Bread Soup has no potatoes, egg yolks or olive oil. Lemon zest and juice replace some of the salt; the tomatoes, onions and bananas are broiled or grilled, not sautéed.

3½ quarts unsalted Chicken Stock, page 15, or commercial

½ cup dried black beans, rinsed

5 (3-inch) cinnamon sticks

7 fresh thyme sprigs, bruised, or 1½ teaspoons dried leaf thyme

Zest of 1 lemon

1 teaspoon crumbled dried epazote or dried leaf thyme

Freshly ground pepper to taste

6 medium-size carrots, peeled, quartered

3 chayotes, peeled, cored, cut in chunks

Salt to taste, if desired

2 large onions, thickly sliced

3 large, firm tomatoes, peeled, thickly sliced

Fresh lemon juice to taste

2 teaspoons sugar

2 bananas, cut in chunks

¼ cup whole blanched almonds

10 small rolls or about 10 cups torn day-old bread (14 oz. *total*)

¼ cup raisins

Whites of 6 hard-cooked eggs, cut in half lengthwise

3 tablespoons flat-leaf parsley leaves for garnish

In a large pot, combine stock and beans. Simmer, covered, 50 to 60 minutes or until beans are tender. Remove beans with a strainer; set aside. To broth, add cinnamon, thyme, lemon zest, epazote or thyme and pepper. Simmer, covered, 15 minutes. Add carrots and chayotes; simmer 25 minutes longer or until vegetables are barely tender. Strain broth; set broth and vegetables aside separately. Discard cinnamon and thyme sprigs, if used. Season broth with salt, if desired.

While vegetables are simmering, preheat broiler or grill. Broil or grill sliced onions 5 to 6 inches from heat source 5 minutes on each side or until soft and lightly browned. Broil or grill tomatoes 3 minutes on each side or until soft. Season onions and tomatoes with a few drops of lemon juice, salt, if desired, and sugar. Broil or grill bananas about 4 minutes or just until browned. Set onions, tomatoes and bananas aside separately.

Preheat oven to 400F (205C). Spread almonds on a baking sheet and toast 10 minutes or until brown; set aside. Tear rolls or bread into bite-size pieces; spread on baking sheet and toast 5 minutes or until light brown. Set aside.

Layer ingredients in a deep 12-inch casserole as follows. On bottom of casserole, arrange carrots and chayotes. Season lightly with salt, if desired. Top vegetables with toasted rolls or bread and bananas. Sprinkle with almonds and raisins; cover with onions and tomatoes. On top, arrange egg whites, rounded sides up. Ladle broth over all; sprinkle on beans. Bake, uncovered, 20 minutes or until hot.

To serve, garnish soup in casserole with parsley. At the table, ladle soup from casserole into heated large bowls. Makes 8 generous main-dish servings.

	kcal	carb(gm)	fat(gm)	chol(mg)	Na(mg)	iron(mg)	Ca(mg)
lavish:	590	68	25	207	655	5.2	176
lean:	361	54	7	2	435	3.9	142

MIDDLE-EASTERN GRAIN
& BEAN SOUP WITH MINT
Ashe-Joe

Lavish

♦

Don't let the laundry list of ingredients put you off—this hearty soup is simple to make. Ali Assar serves it at his Los Angeles restaurant, Javan. The soup is traditionally topped with kashk, *but yogurt is easier to find and similar in flavor and texture. If you do want to use* kashk, *look in a Middle Eastern market, where you'll also find dried mint sold inexpensively in bulk.*

½ cup barley
About 4 quarts water
1 bunch spinach, leaves only, washed well (about 1½ quarts, loosely packed)
½ bunch flat-leaf parsley, leaves only, washed well
1 bunch green onions, green tops only, coarsely chopped
⅓ cup dried mint
⅓ cup plus 2 tablespoons light vegetable oil

4 garlic cloves, sliced
1 medium-size onion, sliced
½ cup dried red beans or kidney beans, rinsed
¼ cup white rice
½ teaspoon ground turmeric
1 tablespoon coarse salt, or to taste
Freshly ground pepper to taste
½ cup lentils, rinsed
1 cup mild yogurt or kashk for garnish

Rinse barley 3 or 4 times or until water is clear. Cover with about 2 cups water and soak overnight, then drain barley and discard water. In a large stock or soup pot, bring 4 quarts water to a boil over high heat; add barley, reduce heat and simmer, uncovered, 30 minutes. Add spinach, parsley and green onion tops; simmer 10 minutes.

While barley is cooking, pick through dried mint to remove stems. Place mint in a small saucepan. Cover with ⅓ cup oil. Over low heat, steep mint in oil 30 minutes. Set aside. Heat remaining 2 tablespoons oil in a medium-size skillet over medium heat; add garlic and sauté until soft and golden. Remove from skillet and set aside. Add sliced onion to oil in skillet and sauté until golden. Add onion along with oil in skillet to soup; add beans, rice, turmeric, salt and several grindings of pepper. Simmer gently, uncovered, stirring occasionally to prevent sticking, 1½ hours or until soup is reduced and thickened. Stir in lentils; cook over low heat 45 minutes, stirring occasionally. Stir in sautéed garlic and mint with oil; simmer 30 minutes longer, stirring frequently. Soup will be thick. If prepared ahead, cool, cover and refrigerate up to 3 days. Reheat soup before serving, adding more liquid as necessary and stirring often to prevent sticking.

To serve, ladle soup into heated bowls. Garnish each serving with 1 tablespoon yogurt or kashk. Makes 16 main-dish servings.

Lean

½ cup barley
2 quarts unsalted Chicken Stock, page 15, or commercial
2 quarts unsalted Beef Stock, page 16, or commercial
1 bunch spinach, leaves only, washed well (about 1½ quarts, loosely packed)
1 bunch flat-leaf parsley, leaves only, washed well
4 large green onions, green tops only, coarsely chopped
4 garlic cloves, sliced
½ medium onion, sliced
½ cup dried red beans or kidney beans, rinsed

¼ cup white rice
2 teaspoons ground turmeric
Freshly ground pepper to taste
½ cup lentils, rinsed
⅓ cup dried mint
¼ cup fresh lemon juice
2 tablespoons sugar or ¼ cup frozen concentrated apple juice
1 tablespoon salt, if desired
1 cup Creamy Non-fat Yogurt, page 22, or commercial, for garnish
Additional dried mint for garnish

Rinse barley 3 or 4 times or until water is clear. Cover with about 2 cups water and soak overnight, then drain barley and discard water. In a large stock or soup pot, bring Chicken Stock and Beef Stock to a boil over high heat. Add barley, reduce heat and simmer, uncovered, 30 minutes. Add spinach, parsley and green onion tops; simmer 10 minutes.

In a covered medium-size skillet, sweat garlic over medium heat until soft, stirring occasionally to prevent sticking. Remove from skillet and set aside; add sliced onion to skillet and sweat until soft, stirring occasionally to prevent sticking. Add onion to soup along with beans, rice, turmeric, and several grindings of pepper. Simmer gently, uncovered, stirring occasionally to prevent sticking, 1½ hours or until soup is reduced and thickened. Stir in lentils; cook over low heat 45 minutes, stirring occasionally.

Pick through ⅓ cup dried mint to remove stems. Add garlic and mint to soup; season with lemon juice, sugar or concentrated orange juice and salt, if desired. Simmer 30 minutes longer, stirring as needed to prevent sticking. Taste and adjust seasonings. If prepared ahead, cool, cover and refrigerate up to 3 days. Reheat before serving, adding more water or stock as necessary and stirring often to prevent sticking.

To serve, ladle soup into heated bowls. Garnish each serving with 1 tablespoon yogurt and few crumbled mint leaves. Makes 16 main-dish servings.

	kcal	carb(gm)	fat(gm)	chol(mg)	Na(mg)	iron(mg)	Ca(mg)
lavish:	139	15	7	3	476	1.8	57
lean:	115	18	1	2	137	2.2	70

WINTER SQUASH & FISH CHOWDER

Lavish

♦

This is a serious whole-meal soup. I love the chowder's delicate, mellow flavor and its quiet undertone of spice. Baking and slow sautéing bring out the squash and onion's sweetness. If you want to serve the chowder as a first course, you'll only need 1¼ pounds of fish.

3 cups (about 2½ pounds) cooked, peeled winter squash (such as butternut, acorn or banana squash or pumpkin, when available), cut in ½-inch cubes

3 cups Fish Stock, page 18, commercial fish stock or bottled clam juice, see TIP, page 97

1½ cups diced peeled potato

2½ pounds sea bass fillets

1 tablespoon butter

1 tablespoon light cooking oil

1 medium-size onion, chopped

3 cups milk

1 cup whipping cream

½ teaspoon ground nutmeg

¼ teaspoon ground allspice

2 teaspoons light brown sugar

1 tablespoon fresh lemon juice

Salt to taste

Ground white pepper to taste

⅓ cup coarsely chopped chives for garnish

Preheat oven to 350F (175C). Rub cut squash with a little cooking oil and place, cut side down, on a foil-lined shallow baking sheet. Or bake small squashes whole. Bake until tender. Cooking time will vary from 45 minutes to 1¼ hours depending on size and shape of squash. Cool, remove seeds, then cut and measure squash.

Bring Fish Stock to a boil, add potatoes, reduce heat and simmer just until tender, about 10 minutes. Remove potatoes and set aside. Poach fish in same stock, covered, over low heat until barely cooked, 3 to 6 minutes or until flesh in thickest part of fillets is opaque but still moist. Place fish on plate and remove skin and bones, if any; cover loosely.

In a large skillet melt butter in oil over medium-low heat and add onion. Cook, slowly stirring, until onion is translucent. Add 1 cup cooked squash, Fish Stock, milk and cream. Use a slotted spoon to remove solids from chowder to a food processor fitted with a metal blade; add ½ cup diced cooked potato. Process with 3 or 4 one-second pulses or until solids are broken up but still have some texture. Stir solids back into soup. Add nutmeg, allspice, brown sugar and lemon juice. Taste and season with salt and white pepper.

Bring to a boil, reduce heat and simmer about 10 minutes, stirring occasionally. Add fish, remaining 1 cup cooked diced potato and remaining 2 cups cooked diced squash to soup; taste and adjust seasonings. Stir gently while reheating chowder to a simmer.

To serve, ladle chowder into heated bowls and garnish each serving with chopped chives. Makes 8 servings.

Lean

The secret to this soup's earthy taste lies in baking the squash, slowly cooking the onion, and in using double-strength stock. The squash and potato puree make a natural, flavorful thickener. With such loving care, lavish enrichments aren't even missed.

3 cups (about 2½ pounds) cooked, peeled winter squash (see lavish introduction), cut in ½-inch cubes

3 cups double-strength Fish Stock, page 18, commercial fish stock or bottled clam juice, see TIP, opposite

1½ cups diced peeled potato

2½ pounds cod, or fish fillets of choice, see TIP, page 115

1 medium-size onion, chopped

3 cups non-fat milk

½ teaspoon ground nutmeg

¼ teaspoon ground allspice

1 tablespoon light brown sugar

2 tablespoons fresh lemon juice

Salt, if desired

Ground white pepper to taste

⅓ cup coarsely chopped chives for garnish

Preheat oven to 350F (175C). Rub cut squash with a little cooking oil and place, cut side down, on a foil-lined shallow baking sheet. Or bake small squashes whole. Bake until tender. Cooking time will vary from 45 minutes to 1¼ hours depending on size and shape of squash. Cool, remove seeds, then cut and measure squash.

Bring Fish Stock to a boil, add potatoes, reduce heat and simmer uncovered until just tender, about 10 minutes. Remove potatoes and set aside. Poach fish in same stock at a bare simmer, over low heat until flesh is just opaque, 3 to 6 minutes. Place fish on plate and remove skin and bones, if necessary. Break fish into large chunks.

In a large pot cook onion slowly over low heat, stirring frequently, until onion is translucent. Use a slotted spoon to remove onion to a food processor fitted with a metal blade. Add ½ cup reserved cooked potato, 1 cup squash and 1 cup milk. Process with 3 or 4 one-second pulses or until solids are a textured but not smooth puree. Stir vegetable solids back into pot. Add remaining milk, fish stock, nutmeg, allspice, brown sugar and lemon juice.

Bring to a boil, reduce heat and simmer about 10 minutes, stirring occasionally. Add fish, remaining 1 cup cooked diced potato and remaining 2 cups cooked diced squash to soup; taste and adjust seasonings with salt, if used, and white pepper. Bring chowder to a simmer for just one minute.

To serve, ladle chowder into heated bowls and garnish each serving with chopped chives. Makes 8 servings.

TIP

Frozen unsalted fish stock is available in selected markets. Bottled clam juice may be used in place of stock, but some brands have a high sodium content. When reduced, they have a pronounced flavor that will change the chowder's delicate taste.

	kcal	carb(gm)	fat(gm)	chol(mg)	Na(mg)	iron(mg)	Ca(mg)
lavish:	418	21	20	121	398	1.4	198
lean:	248	21	2	68	168	1.5	183

FRESH TOMATO SOUP WITH CLAMS

Lavish

♦

The ocean and the garden meet here. Although the recipe calls for fresh tomatoes, you can use canned ones with good results.

24 fresh hard-shell clams,
  such as littleneck or
  cherrystone
2½ tablespoons olive oil
3 tablespoons butter
2 garlic cloves, sliced
3 flat-leaf parsley sprigs
1 bay leaf, crumbled
1 medium-size onion, sliced
2 shallots, sliced
5 tablespoons all-purpose
  flour
2 pounds ripe tomatoes,
  peeled, coarsely chopped, or
  1 (28-oz.) can tomatoes
  with their juice
2 tablespoons tomato paste
3 cups Fish Stock or Chicken
  Stock, pages 18 or 15, or
  commercial

Bouquet Garni
1 cup whipping cream
Salt and sugar to taste
Chopped fresh fennel or flat-
  leaf parsley leaves for
  garnish

BOUQUET GARNI
4 fresh thyme sprigs, bruised,
  or ½ teaspoon dried leaf
  thyme
3 fresh fennel sprigs, bruised,
  or ¼ teaspoon fennel seeds
1 garlic clove, unpeeled,
  halved
2 bay leaves, crumbled
5 flat-leaf parsley sprigs

Scrub clams, place in a large pot and cover with salted water. Let stand 1 hour or more to let clams release grit and sand; then drain and rinse clams. Place 1½ tablespoons oil, 1 tablespoon butter, garlic, parsley sprigs and bay leaf in a large, heavy pot. Cook over medium heat about 3 minutes or until garlic is softened. Add drained clams, cover and cook over medium-high heat until pot begins to steam. Reduce heat and steam 5 to 7 minutes or just until all shells open. Discard any clams that do not open. Remove clams from pot with tongs; remove clams from shells and set aside. Strain clam cooking liquid; measure 1 cup and set aside.

Melt remaining 2 tablespoons butter in remaining 1 tablespoon oil in a medium-size saucepan over medium-low heat. Add onion and shallots; cook, stirring occasionally, 15 minutes or until softened but not brown. Sprinkle flour over onion mixture; stir over medium heat 1 minute. Add fresh or canned tomatoes, tomato paste, stock, reserved 1 cup strained clam cooking liquid and Bouquet Garni; stir, partially cover pan and simmer 30 minutes. Discard Bouquet Garni. In a blender or a food processor fitted with a metal blade, process soup in 2 or 3 batches until smoothly pureed. Press puree through a strainer into saucepan; use a spatula to scrape puree from underside of strainer. Stir in cream and clams. Season with salt and sugar. Reheat to just under a simmer before serving.

To serve, ladle soup into heated bowls. Garnish with fennel or parsley leaves. Makes 8 servings.

Bouquet Garni: Tie all ingredients in a piece of washed cheesecloth.

Lean

24 fresh hard-shell clams, such as littleneck or cherrystone
2 garlic cloves, sliced
3 flat-leaf parsley sprigs
1 bay leaf, crumbled
½ cup dry white wine
1 medium-size onion, sliced
2 shallots, sliced
1 medium-size (about 6-oz.) potato, peeled, sliced
2 pounds ripe tomatoes, peeled, coarsely chopped, or 1 (28-oz.) can tomatoes with their juice
2 tablespoons tomato paste

3 cups Fish Stock or Chicken Stock, pages 18 or 15, or commercial
Bouquet Garni, page 98
½ cup Enriched Non-fat Milk, page 22, or non-fat milk
2 tablespoons fresh lemon juice, or to taste
1 tablespoon sugar, or to taste
½ cup Creamy Non-fat Yogurt, page 22, or commercial, for garnish
Chopped fresh fennel or flat-leaf parsley leaves for garnish

Scrub clams, place in a large pot and cover with salted water. Let stand 1 hour or more to let clams release grit and sand; then drain and rinse clams. Place garlic, parsley sprigs, bay leaf and wine in a small saucepan. Bring to a boil over medium heat; reduce heat and simmer, uncovered, 15 minutes. Then pour mixture into a large, heavy pot. Add drained clams, cover and cook over medium-high heat until pot begins to steam. Reduce heat and steam 5 to 7 minutes or just until all shells open. Remove clams from pot with tongs; remove clams from shells and set aside. Strain clam cooking liquid; measure 1 cup and set aside.

In a covered medium-size non-stick skillet, sweat onion, shallots and potato over medium-low heat 15 minutes or until onion and shallots are softened but not brown, stirring occasionally to prevent sticking. Transfer onion mixture to a medium-size saucepan. Add fresh or canned tomatoes, tomato paste, stock, reserved 1 cup strained clam cooking liquid and Bouquet Garni. Stir, partially cover pan and simmer 30 minutes. Discard Bouquet Garni. In a blender or a food processor fitted with a metal blade, process soup in 2 or

3 batches until smoothly pureed. Press puree through a strainer into saucepan, use a spatula to scrape puree from underside of strainer. Stir in milk and clams. Season with lemon juice and sugar. Reheat to just under a simmer before serving.

To serve, ladle soup into heated bowls. Spoon 1 tablespoon yogurt into center of each bowl and garnish with fennel or parsley leaves. Makes 8 servings.

	kcal	carb(gm)	fat(gm)	chol(mg)	Na(mg)	iron(mg)	Ca(mg)
lavish:	333	13	21	65	366	13.1	74
lean:	188	18	1	11	125	13.1	120

CHICKEN SOUP WITH HERBAL MATZO BALLS

Lavish

♦

The fragrant matzo balls in this main course soup dish are not what our family calls "bullets." Beaten egg whites and herbs make them light.

2 (3-lb.) chickens, cut up
1½ quarts Chicken Stock,
 page 15 or commercial, or
 water
1 onion, sliced
16 medium-size carrots,
 peeled
Leafy green tops of 3 celery
 stalks; or 1 lovage sprig
1 teaspoon poultry seasoning
3 large fresh thyme sprigs,
 bruised, or 1 teaspoon dried
 leaf thyme
2 teaspoons salt, or to taste
4 whole black peppercorns

Herbal Matzo Balls
1½ cups fresh green peas; or
 frozen green peas, thawed

HERBAL MATZO BALLS
1 cup matzo meal
¾ teaspoon salt
Pinch of white pepper
3 tablespoons minced fresh
 herbs of choice
4 large eggs, separated
¼ cup chicken fat, melted
¼ cup chicken broth (reserved
 from soup), cooled

Pull off excess fat from chicken. Rinse chicken in cold water. Set breasts aside. Arrange remaining chicken parts, including necks, in a large soup pot. Add stock or water to barely cover. Add onion, carrots, celery or lovage, poultry seasoning, thyme, salt and peppercorns. Simmer, covered, 20 minutes. Add chicken breasts, pushing them down into broth. Cover and simmer 10 to 12 minutes longer. Taste broth and adjust seasonings.

Using tongs, remove chicken necks from broth; discard. Remove remaining chicken and carrots, place on a warm platter, cover and keep warm. Strain broth; discard solids. Skim fat from broth. Return chicken and carrots to broth. Prepare Herbal Matzo Balls. Just before serving, add peas to soup; simmer 5 minutes for fresh peas, 1 minute for frozen peas.

Serve hot soup in heated bowls. Arrange 1 or 2 pieces of chicken, 2 carrots and 3 matzo balls in each bowl. Use a slotted spoon to retrieve peas from bottom of pot; sprinkle over chicken. Ladle hot broth over all and serve immediately. Makes 8 main-dish servings.

Herbal Matzo Balls: In a medium-size bowl, mix matzo meal, salt, white pepper and herbs. In a small bowl, lightly blend egg yolks, chicken fat and broth with a fork; stir into dry ingredients. Beat egg whites until they hold soft peaks. Fold half the whites into matzo meal mixture to lighten it, then fold in remaining whites. Refrigerate 30 minutes or until firm. In a large, wide pot, bring 4 quarts lightly salted water to a boil. Working quickly, use a spoon and moistened hands to form walnut-size balls of dough. Drop matzo balls into boiling salted water; cover and simmer 15 minutes. Makes 24 matzo balls.

Lean

It's the cook's choice, but a little salt makes the matzo balls more flavorful, and longer cooking time develops the flavor of the broth.

4 (about 1-lb.) whole chicken breasts, split, bone in
3 pounds additional chicken parts, such as necks, backs and wings
1½ quarts unsalted Chicken Stock, page 15, or commercial
1 onion, sliced
16 medium-size carrots, peeled
Leafy green tops of 3 celery stalks; or 1 lovage sprig
Zest of 1 lemon, studded with 1 whole clove
1 teaspoon poultry seasoning
3 large fresh thyme sprigs, bruised, or 1 teaspoon dried leaf thyme
Salt to taste, if desired

4 whole black peppercorns
Herbal Matzo Balls
¾ cup fresh green peas; or frozen green peas, thawed

HERBAL MATZO BALLS
1 cup unsalted matzo meal
¼ teaspoon salt, if desired
Pinch of white pepper
3 tablespoons minced fresh herbs of choice
½ teaspoon grated lemon zest
4 egg whites
½ cup chicken broth (reserved from soup), cooled
About 4 quarts lightly salted water or unsalted Chicken Stock, page 15, or commercial

Discard skin and fat from chicken breasts, then rinse chicken breasts in cold water and set aside. In a large pot, combine remaining chicken parts, stock, onion, carrots, celery or lovage, lemon zest, poultry seasoning, thyme, salt, if desired, and peppercorns. Simmer, covered, 50 minutes. Add chicken breasts, pushing them down into broth; simmer 10 to 12 minutes longer. Taste broth and adjust seasonings. Using tongs, remove chicken breasts and carrots from broth; cool, cover and refrigerate. Strain broth; discard solids. Cool broth uncovered; cover and refrigerate until fat congeals. Remove fat; return chicken breasts and carrots to broth. Prepare Herbal Matzo Balls. Reheat soup; add peas and simmer 5 minutes for fresh peas, 1 minute for frozen peas.

Serve hot soup in heated bowls. Arrange 1 chicken-breast half, 2 carrots and 3 matzo balls in each bowl. Use a slotted spoon to retrieve peas from bottom of pot; sprinkle over chicken. Ladle hot broth over all and serve immediately. Makes 8 main-dish servings.

Herbal Matzo Balls: In a medium-size bowl, mix matzo meal, salt, if desired, white pepper, herbs and lemon zest. In another bowl, beat 2 egg whites until frothy; in a third bowl, beat remaining 2 egg whites until they hold soft peaks. Quickly stir broth and the frothy egg whites into dry ingredients. Fold 1 large spoonful of softly beaten egg whites into matzo meal mixture to lighten it, then fold in remaining whites. Refrigerate 30 minutes or until firm. In a large, wide pot, bring about 4 quarts lightly salted water or stock to a boil. Working quickly, use a spoon and moistened hands to form walnut-size balls of dough. Drop matzo balls into boiling salted water or stock; cover and simmer 15 minutes. Makes 24 matzo balls.

	kcal	carb(gm)	fat(gm)	chol(mg)	Na(mg)	iron(mg)	Ca(mg)
lavish:	594	26	32	305	1246	12	100
lean:	394	28	10	123	192	2.7	98

SPICED CABBAGE & BEEF SOUP

Lavish

♦

Thanks to an old friend, Mollie Golvin (and to her mother, who brought this recipe over from Poland), we've enjoyed the simplest and best borscht ever for 30 years. I've added lemon zest studded with a clove or two, but the soup is equally good in its pure and original form.

2 bunches beets with fresh, leafy tops (about 3 lbs. *total*)
2 quarts water or Beef Stock, page 16, or commercial
3 pounds beef short ribs
1½ to 2 pounds red or green cabbage, cut in ½-inch-wide strips
2 onions, quartered
4 carrots, peeled, sliced
4 garlic cloves, pressed
2 whole cloves

6 (½" × 2") strips lemon zest
2 tablespoons coarse salt
Freshly ground pepper to taste
½ cup fresh lemon juice, or to taste
Sugar to taste
4 medium-size boiling potatoes, peeled
Dairy sour cream for garnish
¼ cup chopped flat-leaf parsley leaves for garnish

Trim off beet tops, leaving 1 inch of stalks attached to beets. Wash and coarsely chop leaves; set aside. Scrub beets, place in a large soup pot, add water or stock and bring to a boil over high heat. Reduce heat to medium-low, cover and simmer 30 to 40 minutes or until beets are tender. Strain and reserve cooking broth; rinse grit from soup pot and return broth to soup pot.

Peel and trim beets under cold running water. Coarsely grate beets into cooking broth in pot, rinsing grater in broth. Add short ribs, cabbage, onions, carrots and garlic. Stick cloves into lemon zest and add to broth with chopped beet tops, salt and pepper. Bring to a boil, reduce heat, cover and simmer 1½ to 2 hours or until meat is tender and falling off bones. Remove lemon zest with cloves. If desired, pull meat from bones; return meat to soup. Cool soup slightly and skim off fat. Reseason with additional salt, lemon juice and sugar. If prepared ahead, cool, cover and refrigerate up to 3 days; soup improves when reheated.

Thirty minutes before serving, boil potatoes in salted water over medium-low heat just until tender; cut in large chunks. Reheat soup to just below a simmer.

To serve, cut potatoes in half and arrange in heated large soup bowls. Ladle hot soup over potatoes; top each serving with a dollop of sour cream and sprinkle with parsley. Makes 8 to 10 main-dish servings.

Lean

Somewhere along the line, beef has gotten itself a bad reputation. It's true that some cuts are fairly fatty, so here we substitute lean stewing meat for short ribs and take time to chill the broth, then lift off the fat. The result is a lowfat, richly flavored soup that makes a meal when served with crusty rye bread.

2 bunches beets with fresh, leafy tops (about 3 lbs. *total*)
1 quart unsalted Beef Stock, page 16, or commercial
1 quart unsalted Chicken Stock, page 15, or commercial
3 pounds center-cut beef shank, bone in, fat removed
1½ to 2 pounds red or green cabbage, cut in ½-inch-wide strips
2 onions, quartered
4 carrots, peeled, sliced
4 garlic cloves, pressed
2 whole cloves

3 (½ " × 2") strips lemon zest
Freshly ground pepper to taste
½ cup fresh lemon juice, or to taste
2 tablespoons sugar or frozen concentrated orange juice, or to taste
2 medium-size boiling potatoes, peeled
½ cup Creamy Non-fat Yogurt, page 22, or commercial, for garnish
¼ cup chopped flat-leaf parsley leaves for garnish

Trim off beet tops, leaving 1 inch of stalks attached to beets. Wash and coarsely chop leaves; set aside. Scrub beets; place in a large soup pot, add stocks and bring to a boil over high heat. Reduce heat to medium-low, cover and simmer 30 to 40 minutes or until beets are tender. Strain and reserve cooking broth; rinse grit from soup pot and return broth to pot.

Peel and trim beets under cold running water. Coarsely grate beets into cooking broth in pot, rinsing grater in broth. Add beef shank, cabbage, onions, carrots and garlic. Stick cloves into lemon zest and add to broth with chopped beet tops and pepper. Bring to a boil; reduce heat, cover and simmer 1½ to 2 hours or until meat is tender and falling off bones. Remove lemon zest with cloves.

Strain broth into a medium-size bowl. Cool, cover and refrigerate broth and solids (meat and vegetables) separately. When broth is chilled, remove solidified fat from surface. Reheat broth and gently mix in meat and vegetables. Season with pepper, lemon juice and sugar or concentrated orange juice. If prepared ahead, cool, cover and refrigerate up to 3 days; soup improves when reheated.

Thirty minutes before serving, boil potatoes in water over medium-low heat just until tender; cut in chunks. Reheat soup to just below a simmer.

To serve, cut potatoes in half and arrange in heated large soup bowls. Ladle hot soup over potatoes; top each serving with a dollop of yogurt and sprinkle with parsley. Makes 8 to 10 main-dish servings.

	kcal	carb(gm)	fat(gm)	chol(mg)	Na(mg)	iron(mg)	Ca(mg)
lavish:	973	37	73	163	1792	6.3	139
lean:	561	33	19	153	569	8.3	153

MAIN COURSES &
MAIN COURSE
SALADS

"But what's for *dinner*?" we silently wonder as we nibble our appetizers and bide our time. If dinner is drama, it builds toward the main course.

Whether you serve Spicy Chicken with Cumin & Lime (page 146) or Lettuce-Wrapped Rock Cod with Carrot Sauce (page 124), careful cooking is the secret to success: the chicken must be moist and tender, the Carrot Sauce a delicate complement to the succulent fish. Tempting textures and flavors like these are easy to produce in your kitchen with the help of a few simple techniques and methods.

When food is cooked with high heat (broiled, browned or sautéed), the protein and sugars break down, interact and form a delicious crust. That's why foods marinated with a trace of sugar brown faster than those without it. Bits of crust left in the pan can be combined with stock or wine and herbs to make a simple, tasty sauce; the wine sauce in Golden Chicken in Port Sauce with Prunes & Garlic (page 142), for example, has more flavor because the pan is deglazed after the chicken has been sautéed. And browned bits of meat fortify the rich-tasting sauce of lean or lavish Braised Beef with Green Chiles & Orange (page 168).

Because high temperatures toughen meat by chemically changing the protein, sautéed, grilled and broiled poultry,

red meats and fish all require close attention. Some authorities believe quick searing over high heat seals in meat juices and flavor; others disagree. For me, the magic word here is "quick." Cook foods over high heat *just* until browned; if sautéing is followed by braising, reduce the heat as soon as the meat, poultry or fish is seared.

Another way to produce moist, tender chicken and fish is to steam it—just until done. Even steaming isn't foolproof, though; it's possible to overcook very lean meat with gentle, moist heat and end up with something dry, rubbery and inedible. Once again, careful timing is critical. Lettuce-Wrapped Rock Cod with Carrot Sauce (page 124), for example, steams inside its wrapper as it bakes; the cooking time is calculated according to the thickness of the wrapped fillet to ensure succulent fish. The cooking times suggested in this chapter should produce juicy, tender results, but keep in mind that you may need to adjust them to suit your particular oven or range.

Braising combines sautéing or browning with moist-heat cooking. The food is quickly browned (in fat or oil, if the dish is a lavish one), then simmered in liquid, covered, at a low temperature on top of the range or in the oven. In Braised Beef with Green Chiles & Orange (page 168), (lavish) brisket or (lean) round roast slowly cooks in a flavorful sauce until tender.

All lean dishes in this chapter are prepared with methods and ingredients that lower fats, salt and sugar. For instance, when browning food for lean recipes, I omit almost all the usual butter or oil; instead, I rub a small amount of oil into a skillet or use a non-stick pan. This technique cuts calories and allows a "browned" flavor to develop without risk of scorching. Attention to such details means that even red meat can be lean eating: try Pork with Red Cabbage & Apples (page 154) and the braised beef mentioned above. But because seafood and poultry lend themselves most readily to lean/lavish cooking, fish and chicken entrées account for most of the recipes in this chapter.

Finally, it's my experience that freezing meat, poultry and fish gives them a slightly mealy texture. For the best results, use fresh—small details make a big difference.

FISH IN LEMON-GINGER SAUCE

Lavish

♦

Years ago, a Chinese friend visiting Tomi Kuwayama Haas' family in New York broke tradition by adding garlic and sherry to their miso sauce. The Kuwayamas liked the new version so much that they gave up the old. Now the recipe has been changed again, this time with the juice of California lemons.

4 bunches (about 24) green onions
2 tablespoons peanut oil
¼ cup light miso (soybean paste)
2 tablespoons plus 2 teaspoons soy sauce
2 teaspoons sugar

¼ cup dry sherry
1 tablespoon plus 1 teaspoon grated fresh gingerroot
2 garlic cloves, minced
¼ cup fresh lemon juice
3 pounds fish fillets of choice, such as catfish, halibut or yellowtail, see TIPS, page 115

Trim all but 1 inch of tops from green onions; cut enough green tops lengthwise in 4-inch slivers to make ¾ cup. Cover with ice water and refrigerate for garnish. (Reserve remaining green tops for another use.) Slice white parts of onions lengthwise into 4-inch slivers. In a medium-size skillet, combine oil and slivered white parts of onions; cook over medium heat, stirring, just until onions are softened. Set aside in a small bowl.

In a separate small bowl, blend miso, soy sauce, sugar, sherry, gingerroot, garlic and lemon juice; mixture will be thick.

Coat both sides of each fish fillet with miso mixture. In a large, shallow skillet with a lid, arrange fillets so thinnest portions overlap. Spoon sautéed green onions over fillets. Spoon remaining miso mixture, if any, over onions. Cover and bring to a simmer over medium heat. Then reduce heat and simmer gently until fillets are opaque but still moist in center; allow 8 to 10 minutes for each 1 inch of thickness (adjust cooking time accordingly for thinner or thicker fillets). When testing, remove lid carefully so condensed steam inside it does not drip down onto fish and dilute sauce.

To serve, pat slivered green onion tops dry with paper towels. Serve fillets in skillet, strewn with green onion tops. Or arrange fillets on a heated platter; spoon sautéed green onions from skillet around fillets, then pour sauce over top. Sprinkle with onion tops. Makes 8 servings.

Lean

4 bunches (about 24) green onions
1 tablespoon *each* light miso (soybean paste), soy sauce and thawed frozen concentrated orange juice
Grated zest of 1 orange
2 tablespoons dry sherry
1 tablespoon plus 1 teaspoon grated fresh gingerroot

2 garlic cloves, minced
¼ cup fresh lemon juice
Grated zest of 1 lemon
3 pounds lean top fillets of yellowfin or bluefin tuna or other fillets of choice, see TIPS, opposite

Fit a deep serving dish into a large steamer or heavy pot with a tight-fitting lid. If not using a steamer, invert a plate or set a rack in pot; add enough water to come halfway up inverted plate. Serving dish with fish will rest on plate. Allow 1½ to 2 inches around sides of dish to let steam circulate. (Cooking time depends on the size of the dish in relation to the size of the pot; the more steam builds up and circulates, the faster the fish will cook.)

Trim all but 1 inch of tops from green onions; reserve tops for another use. Slice white parts of onions lengthwise into 4-inch slivers. Cover ¾ cup of the slivered onions with ice water; refrigerate for garnish. Make a bed of remaining slivered onions in a deep serving dish. In a small bowl, blend miso, soy sauce, concentrated orange juice, orange zest, sherry, gingerroot, garlic, lemon juice and lemon zest.

Coat both sides of each fish fillet with miso mixture. Arrange fillets over onions in serving dish with thinnest portions overlapping. Spoon remaining miso mixture, if any, over fillets. Place serving dish in steamer, cover and steam fillets until flesh is opaque but still moist in center; allow 20 to 25 minutes for each 1 inch of thickness (adjust cooking time accordingly for thinner or thicker fillets). When testing, remove lid carefully so condensed steam inside it does not drip down onto fish and dilute sauce.

To serve, pat refrigerated slivered green onions dry with paper towels. Spoon cooking juices over fillets and sprinkle with slivered green onions. Makes 8 servings.

TIPS

Choose the freshest fish you can find; it will have a more succulent texture than frozen fish. Available varieties vary from region to region. Lavish choices include catfish, halibut, swordfish, yellowtail or salmon; among lean choices are flounder or sole, cod (Boston scrod), sea bass, red snapper, pike and yellowfin or bluefin tuna. This recipe also works well with fish steaks.

A hot dish will be easier to remove from the steamer if you support it with a cheesecloth sling. Before cooking, center the dish on a piece of cheesecloth that's long enough to hang over the rim of the steamer on either side when the dish is placed inside the steamer. Use the ends of the cloth as ''handles'' to lift the dish in and out of the steamer.

	kcal	carb(gm)	fat(gm)	chol(mg)	Na(mg)	iron(mg)	Ca(mg)
lavish:	288	7	17	98	592	2.1	78
lean:	175	5	2.4	63	221	.9	76

GRILLED FISH WITH SWEET RED PEPPER & TOMATO SAUCE

Lavish

♦

Necessity is the mother of invention. I set out to make tomato sauce one day, but found too few tomatoes and substituted sweet red peppers. The result has become one of my favorite sauces.

Sweet Red Pepper & Tomato
  Sauce
2 tablespoons *each* butter and
  olive oil
3 pounds halibut steaks or
  fillets, about 1 inch thick
Salt and freshly ground
  pepper to taste
3 tablespoons flat-leaf parsley
  leaves for garnish

SWEET RED PEPPER & TOMATO
SAUCE
2 tablespoons butter
1 tablespoon olive oil

6 shallots or 1 medium-size
  onion, coarsely chopped
2 large tomatoes, coarsely
  chopped
5 large red bell peppers,
  seeded, coarsely chopped
Leafy green tops of 2 celery
  stalks
2 garlic cloves, unpeeled,
  halved
1 teaspoon dried leaf thyme
Salt and freshly ground
  pepper to taste
Pinch of sugar
¼ cup whipping cream

Prepare Sweet Red Pepper & Tomato Sauce. Ignite coals and burn just until flame is gone and ashes are white; or preheat broiler.

Melt butter in oil in a small saucepan over low heat. Brush mixture over both sides of each piece of fish. Grill or broil fish 5 inches from heat source, turning once, until flesh is opaque but still moist in center; allow 8 to 10 minutes total cooking time for each 1 inch of thickness. Season with salt and pepper.

To serve, reheat sauce over low heat. Arrange fish on a heated platter and nap each piece with a spoonful of sauce. Garnish with whole parsley leaves. Pass additional sauce in a heated bowl. Makes 8 servings.

Sweet Red Pepper & Tomato Sauce: In a large skillet with a lid, melt butter in oil over medium heat. Add shallots or onion; sauté until soft. Add tomatoes, bell peppers, celery and garlic. Stir to mix; season with thyme, salt, pepper and sugar. Reduce heat to medium-low, cover and simmer, stirring occasionally, 20 minutes or until peppers are soft. Spoon mixture into a blender or a food processor fitted with a metal blade and process until pureed. With the back of a wooden spoon, press sauce through a strainer into a small saucepan. Add cream and simmer 5 minutes. Taste and adjust seasonings. If prepared ahead, cover and refrigerate up to 2 days. Makes about 3 cups.

Lean

Sea bass or cod is a tasty lowfat substitute for halibut in this recipe. If the fish pieces are ½ inch thick or less, grill or broil them on just one side so they don't dry out (see TIP, page 173).

3 pounds sea bass or cod
fillets or steaks, about 1
inch thick
1 quart non-fat milk
Sweet Red Pepper & Tomato
Sauce
Freshly ground pepper to
taste
3 tablespoons finely diced red
or yellow bell pepper for
garnish
2 tablespoons flat-leaf parsley
leaves for garnish

SWEET RED PEPPER & TOMATO
SAUCE
1 teaspoon olive oil
6 shallots or 1 medium-size
onion, coarsely chopped

2 large tomatoes, coarsely
chopped
5 large red bell peppers,
seeded, coarsely chopped
Leafy green tops of 2 celery
stalks
2 garlic cloves, unpeeled,
halved
1 teaspoon dried leaf thyme
Freshly ground pepper to
taste
Pinch of sugar
3 tablespoons unsalted Fish
Stock, page 18, or
commercial *or* bottled clam
juice, if desired
1 tablespoon fresh lemon
juice, or to taste

Place fish in a large, deep bowl; cover with milk. Cover bowl and refrigerate 2 to 6 hours, turning fish occasionally. Meanwhile, prepare Sweet Red Pepper & Tomato Sauce. Ignite coals and burn just until flame is gone and ashes are white; or preheat broiler.

To cook, pat fish dry. Then grill or broil 5 inches from heat source, turning once, until flesh is opaque but still moist in center; allow 8 to 10 minutes total cooking time for each 1 inch of thickness. Season with pepper.

To serve, reheat sauce over low heat. Arrange fish on a heated platter and nap each fillet at one end with a little sauce. Scatter bell pepper and whole parsley leaves over fillets. Pass additional sauce in a heated bowl. Makes 8 servings.

Sweet Red Pepper & Tomato Sauce: Rub oil over bottom of a large skillet with a lid. Add shallots and cook over medium-low heat until translucent, stirring occasionally. Add tomatoes, bell peppers, celery and garlic. Stir to mix; season with thyme, pepper and sugar. Increase heat until mixture bubbles, then reduce heat to medium-low, cover and simmer, stirring occasionally, 20 minutes or until peppers are soft. Spoon mixture into a blender or a food processor fitted with a metal blade and process until pureed. With the back of a wooden spoon, press sauce through a strainer into a small saucepan. Add stock, if necessary, to thin sauce to desired consistency. Season with lemon juice; taste and adjust seasonings. If prepared ahead, cover and refrigerate up to 24 hours. Makes about 3 cups.

	kcal	carb(gm)	fat(gm)	chol(mg)	Na(mg)	iron(mg)	Ca(mg)
lavish:	234	0	10	60	368	1.5	50
lean:	161	0	2	67	15	.6	55
(for 3 tablespoons sauce)							
lavish:	46	3	4	9	85	.5	11
lean:	16	3	0	0	3	.5	8

COLD MARINATED SOLE WITH RAISINS & PINE NUTS

Lavish

♦

Here's an ideal make-ahead alternative to poached salmon for the buffet table. It's my version of a traditional Venetian dish served at Al Graspo de Uva's restaurant, tucked away under the Rialto bridge.

2¼ cups *each* dry white wine and Japanese rice vinegar
Pinch of ground cloves
7 whole allspice berries
3 bay leaves
⅓ cup olive oil
4 medium-size onions (about 1½ lbs. *total*), thinly sliced

Salt and freshly ground pepper to taste
¾ cup all-purpose flour
8 (about 6-oz.) sole fillets
Additional olive oil
½ cup *each* toasted pine nuts and seedless golden raisins

In a covered medium-size saucepan, simmer wine, vinegar, cloves, allspice berries and bay leaves for 20 minutes. Remove from heat; set aside. Remove bay leaves and set aside for garnish.

Heat ⅓ cup oil in a large skillet over medium-low heat; add onions and cook about 15 minutes or until soft but not brown, stirring occasionally. Season onions lightly with salt and pepper, then remove them from skillet with a slotted spoon and set aside on a plate. Dredge fillets in flour and shake off excess. Sauté fillets in skillet 1 minute on each side in a little olive oil or until lightly browned and opaque in center, adding more oil as needed. Remove to a platter. Season lightly with salt and pepper.

Arrange a layer of fish in a deep, non-reactive platter. Scatter some onions, pine nuts and raisins over fish. Repeat layers, spooning marinade over each layer. Top with onions, pine nuts and raisins. Marinade will almost reach top layer of fish. Cover and refrigerate at least 24 hours or up to 2 days.

Remove fish from refrigerator 30 to 45 minutes before serving. Fan reserved bay leaves over fish as garnish. Makes 8 servings.

Lean

8 (about 6-oz.) sole fillets
3 cups non-fat milk
2¼ cups *each* dry white wine
   and Japanese rice vinegar
Pinch of ground cloves
7 whole allspice berries
3 bay leaves

4 medium-size onions (about
   1½ lbs. *total*), thinly sliced
   crosswise
¼ cup all-purpose flour
Freshly ground pepper
2 tablespoons extra-virgin
   olive oil
¼ cup *each* toasted pine nuts
   and seedless golden raisins

Place fish in a large, deep bowl; cover with milk. Cover bowl and refrigerate 2 to 6 hours, turning fish occasionally.

In a medium-size (covered) saucepan, bring wine, vinegar, cloves, allspice berries and bay leaves to a simmer for 20 minutes. Remove from heat; set aside. Remove bay leaves; set aside for garnish.

Place onions in a medium-size non-stick skillet with a lid, cover and sweat over medium-low heat about 15 minutes or until soft, stirring occasionally to prevent sticking. Set onions aside on a plate.

Preheat broiler. Pat fillets dry. Dust tops of fillets with flour; shake off excess. Broil on top side only 5 inches from heat source 5 minutes or until lightly browned and opaque in center; separate flesh with a fork to test. Remove to a platter; lightly season with pepper and drizzle with 2 tablespoons extra-virgin olive oil.

Choose a deep glass, ceramic or stainless steel platter to hold fish and marinade. Arrange a layer of fish in a deep, non-reactive platter. Scatter some onions, pine nuts and raisins over fish. Repeat layers, gently spooning marinade over each layer of fish. Top with onions, pine nuts and raisins. Cover and refrigerate at least 24 hours or up to 2 days.

Remove fish from refrigerator 30 to 45 minutes before serving. Fan reserved bay leaves over fish as garnish. Makes 8 servings.

	kcal	carb(gm)	fat(gm)	chol(mg)	Na(mg)	iron(mg)	Ca(mg)
lavish:	470	27	20	96	398	2.4	69
lean:	297	17	8	96	175	1.5	78

HOMESTYLE FISH FILLETS

Lavish

♦

My mother-in-law Rosie, a slapdash genius of a cook, soaked her fish as long as time permitted. An all-day soak with an occasional poke to dunk any exposed portions works best, but even a half-hour milk bath produces delicious results. In either case, the fish is moist and delicate inside its crisp crust. To convert the dish from homestyle to company-style, present it with Sweet Red Pepper & Tomato Sauce.

8 (about 5-oz.) catfish fillets or other white-fleshed fish fillets of choice, such as halibut, cod or red snapper, ½ to ¾ inch thick
1 quart milk
3 cups unseasoned fine dry bread crumbs

16 fennel or basil sprigs or other herb sprigs of choice
Salt and freshly ground white pepper to taste
¼ cup unsalted butter
Sweet Red Pepper & Tomato Sauce, if desired, page 116

Butter a rimmed baking pan that is large enough to hold fish fillets without overlapping. Then place fillets in a large, deep bowl and cover with milk. Cover bowl and refrigerate 30 minutes to 8 hours, turning fish occasionally.

Preheat oven to 500F (260C). Spread bread crumbs on a small platter. Drain excess milk from fish fillets, but do not pat dry. Coat fillets on both sides with bread crumbs; shake off excess. Arrange fillets in baking pan without overlapping. Slip an herb sprig or several herb leaves under each fillet. Season fillets with salt and white pepper; dot with ¼ cup butter. (At this point, you may loosely cover fish and refrigerate up to 6 hours. Return to room temperature before baking.) Bake, uncovered, 8 to 10 minutes or until flesh in thickest part of fillets is opaque but still moist in center.

To serve unsauced fillets, arrange on a heated large platter and garnish with remaining 8 herb sprigs. To serve fillets with Sweet Red Pepper & Tomato Sauce, reheat sauce to just under a simmer. Spoon heated sauce onto heated individual plates; set fillets over sauce. Nap one end of each fillet with sauce; garnish with an herb sprig. Makes 8 servings.

Lean

8 (about 5-oz.) boneless sole fillets or other white-fleshed fish fillets of choice, such as cod, red snapper or sea bass, ½ to ¾ inch thick
1 quart non-fat milk
1½ cups *each* unsalted fine dry bread crumbs and wheat germ

16 fennel or basil sprigs or other herb sprigs of choice
Freshly ground white pepper to taste
Lean Sweet Red Pepper & Tomato Sauce, if desired, page 118
8 lemon wedges for garnish

Place fillets in a large, deep bowl; cover with milk. Cover bowl and refrigerate 30 minutes to 8 hours, turning fish occasionally.

Preheat oven to 500F (260C). Choose a rimmed non-stick baking pan that is large enough to hold fish fillets without overlapping. Drain excess milk from fish, but do not pat dry. Toss bread crumbs and wheat germ in a small bowl. Dip fillets into crumb mixture to coat both sides; shake off excess. Arrange fillets in baking pan without overlapping. Slip an herb sprig or several herb leaves under each fillet. Season with white pepper. (At this point, you may loosely cover fish and refrigerate up to 6 hours. Return to room temperature before baking.) Bake, uncovered, 8 to 10 minutes or until flesh in thickest part of fillets is opaque but still moist in center.

To serve, reheat Sweet Red Pepper & Tomato Sauce to just under a simmer. Spoon sauce onto heated individual plates; set fillets over sauce. Nap one end of each fillet with sauce; garnish with an herb sprig and a lemon wedge. Makes 8 servings.

Without sauce:

	kcal	carb(gm)	fat(gm)	chol(mg)	Na(mg)	iron(mg)	Ca(mg)
lavish:	345	14	19	116	232	2.7	103
lean:	197	5	3	94	133	1	57

LETTUCE-WRAPPED ROCK COD
WITH CARROT SAUCE

Lavish

♦

The delicate tastes of tarragon, white fish and carrots mingle deliciously. The flavor of the sauce depends on the carrots' sweetness. If you can, sample the carrot crop before buying; if necessary, add a pinch of sugar to the finished sauce.

Carrot Sauce
3 heads lettuce with large leaves, such as romaine, Boston or iceberg
8 (about 6-oz.) rock cod fillets or other white-fleshed fish fillets of choice, see TIP, page 115
Salt and freshly ground white pepper to taste
1 tablespoon chopped fresh tarragon leaves or 1 teaspoon dried leaf tarragon
3 tablespoons unsalted butter
½ cup Crème Fraîche, page 278, or dairy sour cream for garnish
8 tarragon sprigs for garnish

CARROT SAUCE
1½ cups Fish Stock, page 18, or commercial; or ¾ cup bottled clam juice plus ¾ cup Chicken Stock, page 15 or commercial
1 pound carrots, peeled, cut in chunks
2 tablespoons unsalted butter
3 shallots, sliced
2 tablespoons fresh tarragon leaves or 2 teaspoons dried leaf tarragon
¼ cup half and half
½ cup Fish Stock or Chicken Stock, pages 18 or 15 or commercial, for thinning
Salt, sugar and fresh lemon juice to taste

Butter a shallow baking dish that is large enough to hold wrapped fish fillets without overlapping. Prepare Carrot Sauce and set aside.

Remove 24 large outer lettuce leaves and 16 smaller ones for fillers; wash and drain. In a large pot, bring 3 quarts salted water to a boil over high heat. Blanch lettuce leaves in boiling water 30 seconds to 2 minutes or until wilted, pressing leaves under water with a slotted spoon (cooking time depends on thickness of leaves). Remove leaves from pot with tongs; place on clean dishtowels to drain, spreading leaves out. Cut out tough stem portions of leaves.

Preheat oven to 350F (175C). Season fish lightly with salt and white pepper. Arrange each fillet on 3 overlapping lettuce leaves. Sprinkle tarragon leaves evenly over fillets. Slip bits of butter under fillets. Wrap lettuce leaves around fillets, filling in with smaller leaves, if necessary. Turn packets over and arrange in buttered baking dish, seam side down. Measure lettuce-wrapped fillets; bake, uncovered, 12 minutes for each inch of thickness.

To serve, reheat sauce over low heat. Arrange lettuce-wrapped fillets on a heated platter or on individual plates. Nap each packet with Carrot Sauce at one end; garnish each with 1 tablespoon Crème Fraîche or sour cream and a tarragon sprig. Pass remaining sauce. Makes 8 servings.

Carrot Sauce: In a medium-size saucepan, bring 1½ cups Fish Stock to a boil. Add carrots; reduce heat, cover and simmer until tender. Drain; set carrots and broth aside separately. Melt butter in a medium-size skillet over medium heat; add shallots and sauté until soft. Add reserved broth to skillet and reduce by half over medium-high heat. In a blender or a food processor fitted with a metal blade, process carrots, shallot mixture and tarragon 1 minute or until tarragon leaves fleck sauce. Add half and half; process just to blend. Remove sauce to a small saucepan; reheat, adding additional stock to thin sauce, if desired. Season with salt, sugar and a few drops of lemon juice. Makes about 3½ cups.

Lean

If you have leftover Carrot Sauce, mix it with fresh or frozen green peas to give that old favorite, peas and carrots, a bright new look and taste.

Carrot Sauce
3 heads lettuce with large
   leaves, such as romaine,
   Boston or iceberg
8 (about 6-oz.) rock cod fillets
   or other white-fleshed fish
   fillets of choice, see TIP,
   page 115
1½ tablespoons fresh lemon
   juice
2 teaspoons grated fresh
   gingerroot
2 tablespoons chopped fresh
   tarragon leaves or 2
   teaspoons dried leaf
   tarragon
8 tarragon sprigs for garnish

CARROT SAUCE
2 cups unsalted Fish Stock,
   page 18; or 1 cup bottled
   clam juice plus 1 cup
   unsalted Chicken Stock,
   page 15, or commercial

1 pound carrots, peeled, cut
   in chunks
4 shallots, sliced
2 tablespoons fresh tarragon
   leaves or 2 teaspoons dried
   leaf tarragon
1 tablespoon Creamy Non-fat
   Yogurt, page 22, or
   commercial; or 1 tablespoon
   whipping cream
½ to 1 cup unsalted Chicken
   Stock or Fish Stock, pages
   15 or 18, or commercial, for
   thinning; or ½ to 1 cup
   carrot juice, see TIP,
   opposite
Pinch of sugar
Fresh lemon juice to taste

Choose a shallow non-stick baking dish large enough to hold wrapped fillets without overlapping. Prepare Carrot Sauce and set aside. Following directions opposite, blanch, drain and trim 24 large outer lettuce leaves and 16 smaller ones for fillers.

Preheat oven to 350F (175C). Sprinkle both sides of each fillet with lemon juice. Arrange each fillet on 3 overlapping lettuce leaves. Scatter ginger and tarragon leaves evenly over fillets. Wrap lettuce leaves around fillets, filling in with smaller leaves, if necessary. Turn packets over and arrange in baking dish, seam side down. Measure lettuce-wrapped fillets; bake, uncovered, 12 minutes for each inch of thickness.

To serve, reheat sauce over low heat. Arrange lettuce-wrapped fillets on a heated platter or on individual plates. Nap each packet with sauce at one end; garnish each with a tarragon sprig. Pass remaining sauce. Makes 8 servings.

Carrot Sauce: In a medium-size saucepan, bring 2 cups Fish Stock to a boil. Add carrots and shallots, reduce heat, cover and simmer until tender. Drain; set vegetables aside and return broth to saucepan. Reduce by half over medium-high heat. In a blender or a food processor fitted with a metal blade, process cooked vegetables, reduced broth and tarragon 1 minute or until tarragon leaves fleck sauce. Add yogurt or cream and process just to blend. Remove sauce to a small saucepan; reheat, adding additional stock to thin sauce, if desired. Season with sugar and a few drops of lemon juice. Makes about 3½ cups.

TIPS

Bottled clam juice is high in sodium.

Most commercially bottled fresh carrot juices are so strong-tasting that they overwhelm this delicate sauce. But if you have a home juice extractor, you can produce a delicate-flavored juice which can be used in place of stock for thinning the Carrot Sauce.

	kcal	carb(gm)	fat(gm)	chol(mg)	Na(mg)	iron(mg)	Ca(mg)
lavish:	377	8	18	117	192	2.1	89
lean:	227	8	1	84	86	2.1	75

RENÉ FRACHEBOUD'S PRAWNS WITH ONION & RED PEPPER PUREE

Lavish

♦

At restaurant La Cassolette in Carouge, an 18th-century Swiss village, Chef René Fracheboud turns out an amazing assortment of fresh, pure dishes for his patrons. Here is one he shared.

½ cup light vegetable oil
2 sweet white onions,
   coarsely chopped
Salt and freshly ground
   pepper to taste
1 large red bell pepper,
   seeded, coarsely chopped

Juice of ½ lemon
6 extra-large prawns (about
   12 oz. *total*), shelled,
   deveined
1 tablespoon minced parsley
   for garnish

Heat 3 tablespoons oil in a medium-size skillet over medium heat. Add onions and sauté about 15 minutes or until soft and beginning to color. Season with salt and pepper. In a blender or a food processor, process onions until pureed. Scrape onions into a small saucepan; keep warm in a hot waterbath, stirring occasionally.

In a small saucepan filled with boiling salted water, blanch bell pepper 3 minutes. Drain; puree in a blender or a food processor, then press through a strainer into saucepan. Whisk in lemon juice over low heat, then slowly whisk in remaining 5 tablespoons oil; season with salt and pepper. Set sauce in a hot waterbath to keep warm; whisk as needed to keep sauce from separating.

Season prawns with salt and pepper. Arrange prawns on a rack in a large, flat-bottomed pan or steamer with a lid, cover tightly and steam 30 seconds to 2 minutes or just until prawns turn opaque and pink.

To serve, spoon onion puree into center of 2 heated plates. Spoon red pepper sauce carefully around onion puree. Arrange 3 prawns on each plate as a bridge across white and red sauces. Scatter parsley in cluster between prawns. Makes 2 servings.

Lean

½ teaspoon vegetable oil, if not using a non-stick skillet
2 sweet white onions, coarsely chopped
Freshly ground pepper to taste
1 large red bell pepper, seeded, coarsely chopped
Juice of ½ lemon

Pinch of sugar
1½ tablespoons extra-virgin olive oil
6 extra-large prawns (about 12 oz. *total*), shelled, deveined
1 tablespoon minced parsley for garnish

Rub vegetable oil into bottom and sides of a medium-size skillet (or use a non-stick skillet and omit oil). Add onions, cover and cook over low heat 20 minutes or until soft and beginning to color, stirring occasionally to prevent sticking. In a blender or a food processor fitted with a metal blade, process onions until pureed. With a rubber spatula, scrape onions into a small saucepan; keep warm in a hot waterbath, stirring occasionally.

In a small saucepan filled with boiling water, blanch bell pepper 3 minutes. Drain; puree in a blender or a food processor fitted with a metal blade, then press through a strainer into saucepan. Whisk in lemon juice and sugar over low heat. Slowly whisk in olive oil. Set sauce in a hot waterbath to keep warm; whisk as needed to keep sauce from separating.

Set a rack in a large, flat-bottomed pan or steamer with a lid. Arrange prawns on rack, cover tightly and steam 30 seconds to 2 minutes or just until prawns turn opaque and pink; cooking time depends on size of prawns.

To serve, spoon onion puree into center of 2 heated plates. Spoon red pepper sauce carefully around onion puree. Arrange 3 prawns on each plate as a bridge across white and red sauces. Scatter parsley in clusters between prawns. Makes 2 servings.

	kcal	carb(gm)	fat(gm)	chol(mg)	Na(mg)	iron(mg)	Ca(mg)
lavish:	693	14	53	277	568	5.2	122
lean:	312	13	14	277	335	5.3	119

SEAFOOD PASTA WITH SAFFRON

Lavish

♦

This is lavish and worth it for a big splurge. Rotelle lend themselves to catching up sauce, but so do fusilli, penne and even macaroni. Cook the pasta al dente *allowing some bite to remain; overcooked pasta is mushy.*

12 fresh mussels
1 garlic clove, cut in half
1 tablespoon olive oil
Handful flat-leafed parsley
1 cup good quality white
  vermouth
Salt, for pasta water
3 tablespoons olive oil, for
  pasta water
1 pound spinach rotelle pasta,
  or spinach pasta of choice
12 large shrimp (about 1-
  pound unshelled), shelled,
  deveined, and cleaned
Salt to taste
Ground white pepper
3 tablespoons olive oil

4 ounces fresh wild
  mushrooms (morels,
  chanterelles, porcini or
  shiitake), or ordinary
  mushrooms, cleaned and
  cut into ¼-inch pieces
10 to 12 ounces sea scallops,
  cut into 1½-inch chunks
2 shallots, finely chopped
1 small garlic clove, minced
1 tablespoon olive oil
3 cups Fish Stock, page 18, or
  commercial stock, see TIP,
  page 133
2 cups whipping cream
Pinch saffron stems
¼ cup whole flat-leaf parsley
  leaves for garnish

Preheat oven to 200F (95C). Scrub mussels (see page 98, method for scrubbing clams). Soften garlic in 1 tablespoon olive oil over medium-low heat in a heavy-bottomed pot. Add handful of parsley, ½ cup vermouth and mussels. Cover and cook over medium-high heat until vermouth boils. Reduce heat to low, and steam 5 to 7 minutes or just until all mussel shells open. Discard any mussels that do not open. Use tongs to remove mussels in their shells to plate. Cover loosely and place in warm oven. Strain mussel juice into Fish Stock.

Fill a large pot ⅔-full with cold water, bring to a boil and add salt and 3 tablespoons olive oil. Add pasta and cook according to directions. Place 4 pasta bowls or large soup bowls in oven to warm.

Heat 2 tablespoons olive oil in a large sauté pan over high heat. Sauté mushrooms about 2 minutes. Sauté scallops 30 seconds on each side. Sauté shrimp 1 minute on each side, or just until they become pink. Don't wash the sauté pan. NOTE: After cooking mushrooms, scallops and shrimp remove each to a large platter, season lightly with salt and pepper, loosely cover and place in warm oven.

Cook shallots and garlic in sauté pan in 1 tablespoon olive oil for about 5 minutes over medium-low heat until they soften and begin to color. Add Fish Stock and remaining ½ cup vermouth, increase heat to high and reduce sauce to about 2 cups. Blend in cream, continue to cook over medium heat, stirring, about 4 minutes, reducing sauce by about ½ cup. Add saffron, and season with salt and pepper.

To serve, drain pasta and divide among heated bowls. Arrange scallops and shrimp over pasta. Scatter mushrooms over seafood and spoon sauce over all. Arrange 3 mussels in their shells over sauce on each bowl. Sprinkle with parsley. Makes 4 servings.

Lean

This pasta's delicate sauce depends on the reduction of good fish stock, on high quality saffron and on the mushrooms. The dish is worth the effort and cost; the flavor is lovely. Potato starch gives the sauce body, but if you prefer a natural sauce (I do), leave it out. Thick, even fish fillets are best for poaching.

12 fresh hard-shell clams, such as littleneck or cherrystone
1 garlic clove, cut in half
Handful flat-leafed parsley
6 cups Fish Stock, page 18, or commercial stock, see TIP, opposite
4 ounces wild mushrooms (morels, chanterelles, porcini, shiitake), or ordinary mushrooms, cleaned and cut into ¼-inch pieces
Salt if desired or lemon juice
10 to 12 ounces cod or sea bass fillets

10 to 12 ounces salmon fillets
1 pound spinach (green) rotelle pasta, or spinach pasta of choice
2 shallots, finely chopped
1 small garlic clove, minced
2 teaspoons olive oil
1 tablespoon potato starch, optional
¼ cup white vermouth
2 tablespoons lemon juice
Pinch saffron stems
1 cup flat-leaf parsley leaves, loosely packed

Preheat oven to 200F (95C). Scrub clams, see page 98. Place garlic, a handful of parsley and ½ cup water in a heavy-bottomed pot. Add clams, cover and cook over medium-high heat until water boils. Reduce heat and steam 5 to 7 minutes or just until all clam shells open. Discard any that do not open. Use tongs to remove clams in their shells to plate. Cover loosely and place in oven. Strain clam juice into Fish Stock.

In a shallow pan with a lid, bring stock to a boil, reduce heat and simmer mushrooms 2 to 5 minutes (time depends on kind of mushrooms) until softened. Drain, salt if desired or sprinkle with a few drops of lemon juice; loosely cover and place in oven. Poach fish in stock, covered, over low heat until barely cooked, 3 to 6 minutes, turning if liquid does not cover, or until flesh in thickest part of fillets is opaque but still moist. Place on plate, remove skin and bones, if necessary, from fish, cover loosely and place in warm oven. Over high heat reduce stock to 3 cups.

Fill a large pot with water, bring to a boil and add salt, if desired. Add pasta and cook according to directions. Place 4 pasta bowls or large soup bowls in oven to warm.

Meanwhile in a medium-size sauté pan, cook shallots and garlic in olive oil for about 5 minutes over medium-low heat until they soften and begin to color. If desired for thickness sprinkle potato starch over mixture, and continue to cook, stirring, for 2 minutes. Remove pan from heat and add 1 cup stock, stirring until blended and smooth. Blend in remaining stock, vermouth and lemon juice, return to heat and simmer 5 minutes until smooth and slightly thickened. Add saffron and salt if desired. Just before serving, mix 1 cup parsley leaves into sauce.

To serve, drain pasta and divide between 4 heated bowls. Gently separate fish into 2-inch chunks and arrange over pasta. Scatter mushrooms over fish and spoon sauce over all. Arrange 3 clams in their shells on each dish. Makes 4 servings.

TIP

Frozen unsalted fish stock is available in selected markets. Bottled clam juice may be used in place of stock, but some brands have a high sodium content. When reduced, they have a pronounced flavor.

	kcal	carb(gm)	fat(gm)	chol(mg)	Na(mg)	iron(mg)	Ca(mg)
lavish:	1060	46	66	380	945	8.1	245
lean:	522	40	9	73	191	4.2	100

COLD STEAMED CHICKEN BREASTS WITH HERBAL SAUCE

Lavish

♦

The garden, some leftover homemade mayonnaise, and unexpected company produced this favorite, which, despite the title, I sometimes serve hot.

4 (about 1-lb. each) whole chicken breasts, split, bone in
Salt and freshly ground white pepper to taste
2 large onions, thickly sliced
2 handfuls fresh herbs, such as rosemary, thyme, basil, tarragon, marjoram, chives or a mixture, bruised
1 cup good-quality dry white vermouth
Herbal Sauce
8 herb sprigs, see choices above, for garnish

Cherry tomatoes for garnish

HERBAL SAUCE
Reserved strained cooking broth
⅔ cup finely chopped well-washed spinach leaves
⅓ cup minced fresh herbs, see choices at left
2 cups Mayonnaise, page 23, or commercial
Salt and freshly ground pepper to taste

Season chicken on both sides with salt and white pepper. Make a bed of onions in a wide pot with a lid. Cover with bruised herbs. Arrange chicken breasts in a single layer over herbs, skin side up and with thin, bony portions overlapping. Sprinkle chicken with some of the vermouth, then pour remaining vermouth around chicken and cover pot. Bring vermouth to a boil over high heat. Reduce heat to medium-low and steam chicken 8 to 10 minutes or until juices run clear when meat is pierced to bone in thickest portion. Remove pot from heat and let stand, covered, 5 minutes longer. Remove chicken with tongs to a platter; spoon a little broth over each piece. Cover loosely. Strain remaining broth into a small saucepan, pressing down on solids to extract all liquid; use liquid in Herbal Sauce.

To serve, remove skin and bones from chicken with a sharp knife. Cut each portion crosswise in 3 pieces. Arrange chicken on individual plates; nap with Herbal Sauce and garnish with herb sprigs and cherry tomatoes. Pass remaining sauce. Makes 8 servings.

Herbal Sauce: Reduce strained broth in saucepan over medium-high heat to ½ cup. Add spinach and set aside. Blanch minced herbs in boiling water 30 seconds. Rinse in cold water; drain and squeeze dry with paper towels. Place Mayonnaise, herbs and broth-spinach mixture in a blender or a food processor fitted with a metal blade; process until sauce is blended but green flecks remain. Season with salt and pepper. Makes 3 cups.

Lean

4 (about 1-lb. each) whole chicken breasts, split, bone in

Freshly ground white pepper to taste

2 large onions, thickly sliced

1 medium-size carrot, peeled, cut in large chunks

2 handfuls fresh herbs, such as rosemary, thyme, basil, tarragon, marjoram, chives or a mixture, bruised

2 cups good-quality dry white vermouth

Herbal Sauce, if desired

4 cherry tomatoes, cut in half, for garnish

8 herb sprigs, see choices at left, for garnish

HERBAL SAUCE
1 shallot, minced

Reserved strained cooking broth (about 2 cups)

½ cup Japanese rice vinegar

¼ cup extra-virgin olive oil

2 carrot chunks (reserved from steaming), minced

Whites of 2 hard-cooked eggs, diced

3 tablespoons minced fresh herbs, see choices at left

1 teaspoon minced capers

Season chicken with white pepper. Make a bed of onions, carrots and herbs in a wide pot with a lid. Top with chicken, skin side up with bony portions overlapping. Sprinkle with vermouth; pour remaining vermouth around chicken and cover pot. Bring to a boil, reduce heat and steam 8 to 10 minutes or until juices run clear when meat is pierced to bone in thickest portion. Let stand off heat, covered, 5 minutes. Remove chicken to platter, moisten with a little broth and loosely cover. Strain remaining broth into saucepan saving 2 carrot chunks for sauce. Extract all liquid and prepare Herbal Sauce. If made ahead, cool, cover and refrigerate up to one day. Remove from refrigerator 20 minutes before serving.

To serve, remove skin and bones from chicken. Cut each portion crosswise in 3 pieces. Arrange on a platter garnished with tomatoes and herb sprigs. Stir sauce; spoon 1 tablespoon over each portion. Pass remaining sauce. Makes 8 servings.

Herbal Sauce: Add shallot to strained broth and reduce to ½ cup over medium-high heat. Off heat add vinegar, oil, carrot and egg whites. Blanch minced herbs in boiling water 30 seconds, rinse in cold water, drain and squeeze dry. Stir herbs and capers into sauce; let stand 30 minutes to blend flavors. Makes about 2 cups.

TIP

For moist, tender chicken, steam small (6-oz.) half-breasts about 8 minutes over medium-low heat, larger ones 10 minutes. Then remove from heat and let stand, covered, 5 minutes—or a minute or two longer if you like your chicken a bit more cooked. Chicken is cooked when meat near bone in thickest portion is done to your liking, or when the juices run clear (at about 165F, 75C). If you practice a bit, you can determine the proper cooking time simply by pressing the meat with your finger. Chicken that is firm with some give will have faintly pink meat near the bone. If it's firm with little give, the meat is not pink at all, but is still tender. Chicken that is very firm is overcooked, rubbery and dry. Remember: You can always add to the cooking time if you must, but you can't take it away.

	kcal	carb(gm)	fat(gm)	chol(mg)	Na(mg)	iron(mg)	Ca(mg)
lavish:	587	4	48	123	396	1.7	37
lean:	317	6	11	91	293	1.4	43

CHICKEN WITH TWO CHEESES
& FRESH SAGE

Lavish

♦

Sage leaves tucked beneath chicken skin bring back memories of Jerry's childhood in Malibu. The herb grows wild in the Malibu hills.

2 (about 1-lb. each) whole chicken breasts, split, bone in
4 (about 8-oz. each) whole chicken legs with thighs attached
8 ounces ripe Camembert cheese, room temperature
10 ounces fresh goat cheese

16 fresh sage leaves, washed, dried; or 1½ teaspoons dried leaf sage
3 tablespoons olive oil
1 teaspoon salt
Freshly ground pepper to taste
½ cup fresh lemon juice
Sage sprigs for garnish

Using your forefinger, gently separate skin from flesh on each chicken piece, making a large pocket. Cut each cheese into 8 equal portions. Insert cheeses under chicken skin, pressing down on skin to form an even layer of cheese beneath. Slip 2 sage leaves under skin of each piece. Arrange chicken on a deep platter. In a small bowl, whisk together oil, salt, pepper and lemon juice; pour over chicken and turn to coat. (At this point, you may loosely cover chicken and refrigerate up to 1 day. Return to room temperature before grilling.)

Ignite coals and burn just until flame is gone and ashes are white; or preheat broiler. Grill or broil chicken 5 to 6 inches from heat source, skin side last, breasts 5 minutes on each side, legs 8 minutes on each side or until juices run clear when chicken is pierced to the bone. If cooked in batches, loosely cover cooked pieces and keep warm in a low oven until all is cooked.

To serve, arrange chicken on a heated platter; garnish with sage sprigs. Makes 8 servings.

Lean

4 (about 1-lb. each) whole
  chicken breasts, split,
  boned, skinned
1 cup fresh lemon juice
24 fresh sage leaves, washed,
  dried; or 2 teaspoons dried
  leaf sage
1 cup unsalted fine dry bread
  crumbs
Freshly ground pepper

8 ounces lowfat, low-sodium
  Swiss cheese such as Swiss
  Delicat, divided in 8 equal
  portions
½ cup lowfat cottage cheese,
  divided in 8 portions
8 sun-dried tomatoes, slivered
Lean Sweet Red Pepper &
  Tomato Sauce, page 118, if
  desired
Sage sprigs for garnish

Place chicken breasts and lemon juice in a shallow glass or ceramic dish. Cover and refrigerate, turning occasionally, 2 to 4 hours.

Preheat oven to 375F (190C). Blot chicken with paper towels. Place each breast half between sheets of plastic wrap and flatten with a mallet or rolling pin to about ⅓ inch. Tear 8 sage leaves into small pieces; scatter on flattened chicken breasts (or season chicken with 1 teaspoon dried sage). Mince remaining 16 sage leaves and toss with crumbs in a small bowl; or toss remaining 1 teaspoon dried sage with crumbs. Season chicken with pepper. Place a portion of each cheese and an eighth of the sun-dried tomatoes in center of each breast; roll to enclose filling. Dip in reserved lemon juice, then in crumb mixture. Arrange, seam side down, in a shallow non-stick baking dish. Bake, uncovered, 20 minutes or until meat is opaque throughout.

To serve, arrange chicken on a heated platter; nap each piece with Sweet Red Pepper & Tomato Sauce, if desired. Garnish with sage sprigs.

	kcal	carb(gm)	fat(gm)	chol(mg)	Na(mg)	iron(mg)	Ca(mg)
lavish:	474	3	32	152	973	1.7	306
lean:	378	18.5	13	121	250	2.2	308

LEMON CHICKEN

Lavish

♦

Natural juices from the chicken, lemon and vegetables combine into a tangy gravy. The secret to making this gravy is to seal the casserole well, cook it over low, even heat, and let it stand (no peeking) for 15 minutes. Try to use a pot or casserole that can go to the table.

2 tablespoons butter
1 teaspoon light vegetable oil
1 (3-lb.) chicken, cut up
Salt and ground pepper
½ cup fresh lemon juice (save lemon rinds)
3 large onions, thickly sliced
8 medium-size carrots, peeled

12 small (about 1½-inch-diameter) whole thin-skinned potatoes, unpeeled, about 1 lb.
Leafy green tops of 3 celery stalks
Chopped flat-leaf parsley leaves for garnish

In a large, heavy pot or heatproof casserole with a tight-fitting lid, melt butter in oil over medium-high heat. Add chicken pieces and brown on all sides; remove with tongs to a platter. Season with salt, pepper and lemon juice.

Make a bed of half the onions in pot. Arrange chicken pieces skin side up, over onions; place breasts on top.

Top chicken evenly with remaining onions; pour juices from platter over all. Rub carrots and potatoes with cut lemon rinds; arrange over onions. Poke celery down into chicken. Sprinkle vegetables lightly with salt. Seal pot tightly with foil, then cover with lid.

Bring juices to a boil, then immediately reduce heat and simmer 40 minutes. Remove from heat and let stand, sealed, 15 minutes. Uncover and serve. Flavor and texture are best when chicken is first cooked, but it may be prepared 1 day ahead, then cooled, covered and refrigerated. To reheat, bring to room temperature, cover tightly with foil and place in a 300F (150C) oven 30 minutes or until hot.

Garnish with parsley. Serve from pot onto heated plates; use a long spoon or ladle to reach the natural gravy in bottom of pot. Makes 4 servings.

Lean

2 (about 1-lb. each) whole chicken breasts, split, bone in
1¼ cups fresh lemon juice
½ teaspoon olive oil, if not using a non-stick pot
Freshly ground pepper
1 cup dry white wine
Finely grated zest of 2 lemons
12 fresh sage leaves, minced, or 1 teaspoon dried leaf sage
3 large onions, cut in ½-inch-thick slices
8 medium-size carrots, peeled, parboiled 15 min.
About 1 pound small potatoes, peeled, parboiled 15 min.
Leafy green tops of 3 celery stalks
Chopped flat-leaf parsley leaves for garnish

Remove skin and fat from chicken breasts. Place chicken in a shallow dish, pour ½ cup lemon juice over it, cover loosely and refrigerate 2 hours, turning occasionally. Pat chicken dry with paper towels.

Rub a large heavy pot with a tight-fitting lid with oil. Lightly brown chicken breasts flesh side only over high heat; remove with tongs to a platter. Season with pepper. Deglaze pot with wine, scraping up browned bits. Over high heat, reduce wine to ⅓ cup. Off heat mix lemon zest, sage and remaining ¾ cup lemon juice into reduced wine. Pour into a small bowl. Make a bed of onions in pot. Sprinkle half the zest-wine mixture over onions. Arrange carrots and potatoes over onions. Place chicken breasts, flesh side up, over vegetables. Poke celery down into center of chicken. Sprinkle remaining zest-wine mixture and juices from platter over chicken. Seal pot tightly with foil, and cover with lid.

Bring juices to a boil; reduce heat and simmer 15 to 20 minutes. Let stand off heat, sealed, 8 minutes. Uncover and serve. Chicken breasts are best served when first cooked; they become dry when re-heated.

To serve, garnish chicken and vegetables with parsley. Serve from
pot onto heated plates; use a long spoon or ladle to reach the natural
gravy at bottom of pot. Makes 4 servings.

	kcal	carb(gm)	fat(gm)	chol(mg)	Na(mg)	iron(mg)	Ca(mg)
lavish:	652	49	27	160	733	4	111
lean:	550	54	6	144	229	3.6	128

GOLDEN CHICKEN IN PORT SAUCE WITH PRUNES & GARLIC

Lavish

♦

*Garlic is delicious cooked with fruit; I particularly like it stewed with
prunes.*

24 or more large, firm garlic
 cloves, peeled
2½ cups Chicken Stock, page
 15, or commercial
5 medium-size carrots, peeled,
 cut in chunks
2 medium-size onions, cut in
 chunks
1 cup packed dried pitted
 prunes
1½ tablespoons *each* butter
 and light vegetable oil

2 (3-lb. each) chickens, cut up
Salt and freshly ground
 pepper to taste
2 garlic cloves, minced
2½ tablespoons all-purpose
 flour, browned if desired,
 see page 11
2 cups port wine
¼ cup chopped flat-leaf
 parsley leaves for garnish

In a small saucepan filled with boiling water, blanch whole garlic
cloves 5 minutes; drain. In a medium-size saucepan, simmer
blanched garlic cloves in stock 40 minutes or until garlic is tender.
With a slotted spoon, carefully remove garlic to a plate. Add carrots,
onions and ⅓ cup prunes to stock; cover and simmer 20 minutes
or until carrots are tender. Dice enough carrot to make ½ cup; set

aside for garnish. To make sauce, in a blender or a food processor fitted with a metal blade, process remaining carrots, onions and cooked prunes with stock in 2 or 3 batches until pureed. Set aside.

Melt butter in oil in a large skillet over medium-high heat. Add chicken pieces and brown on all sides; remove with tongs to a large platter. Season chicken with salt and several grindings of pepper. Add minced garlic to skillet and cook over low heat 1 minute or until soft. Sprinkle flour over garlic and stir 1 minute. Add port, increase heat to medium-high and deglaze skillet, scraping up any browned bits from skillet bottom. Add prune sauce and bring to a boil. Reduce heat and simmer gently, stirring occasionally, 10 minutes. Taste and adjust seasonings. Set aside.

Preheat oven to 375F (190C). Spoon a thin layer of sauce over bottom of a large, shallow ovenproof casserole. Arrange chicken pieces (except breasts), skin side up, over sauce; leave space for breasts. Stir juices from platter into sauce. Spoon a little sauce over reserved breasts; spoon remainder of sauce over chicken in casserole. Arrange whole garlic cloves and remaining ⅔ cup prunes around and over chicken. Bake, uncovered, 15 minutes. Add chicken breasts, spooning sauce over them. Continue to bake, uncovered, 15 to 20 minutes longer or until juices run clear when chicken is pierced to the bone in thickest portion. Let stand 5 minutes before serving.

To serve, sprinkle chicken with parsley and reserved diced carrot. Serve from casserole onto heated plates. Makes 8 servings.

Lean

24 or more large, firm garlic cloves, peeled

2½ cups unsalted Chicken Stock, page 15, or commercial

5 medium-size carrots, peeled, cut in chunks

2 medium-size onions, cut in chunks

½ cup packed dried pitted prunes

4 (about 1¼-lb.) whole chicken breasts, split, bone in

½ teaspoon vegetable oil, if not using a non-stick skillet

Freshly ground pepper to taste

2 garlic cloves, minced

2½ tablespoons all-purpose flour, browned if desired, see page 11

⅓ cup balsamic vinegar or red wine vinegar

2 cups port wine

¼ cup flat-leaf chopped parsley leaves for garnish

In a small saucepan filled with boiling water, blanch whole garlic cloves 5 minutes; drain. In a medium-size saucepan, simmer blanched garlic cloves in stock 40 minutes or until garlic is tender. With a slotted spoon, carefully remove garlic to a plate. Add carrots, onions and ⅓ cup prunes to stock; cover and simmer 20 minutes or until carrots are tender. Dice enough carrot to make ½ cup; set aside for garnish. To make sauce, in a blender or a food processor fitted with a metal blade, process remaining carrots, onions and cooked prunes with stock in 2 or 3 batches until pureed.

Remove skin and fat from chicken breasts. Rub a large skillet with oil (or use a non-stick skillet and omit oil). Add chicken breasts and lightly brown over medium heat. Remove with tongs to a platter; season with several grindings of pepper. Add minced garlic to skillet and cook over low heat 1 minute or until soft. Sprinkle flour over garlic and stir 1 minute. Add vinegar and port, increase heat to medium-high and deglaze skillet, scraping up any bits of chicken and garlic that cling to skillet bottom. Add prune sauce and bring to a boil; reduce heat and simmer gently, stirring occasionally, 10 minutes.

Preheat oven to 350F (175C). Spoon a thin layer of sauce over bottom of a large, shallow ovenproof casserole. Arrange chicken pieces over sauce. Blend juices from platter into remaining sauce; spoon sauce over chicken. Arrange whole garlic cloves and remaining prunes around and over chicken. Bake, uncovered, 20 to 25 minutes or until juices run clear when chicken is pierced to the bone in thickest portion. Let stand 5 minutes before serving.

To serve, sprinkle chicken with parsley and reserved diced carrot. Serve from casserole onto heated plates. Makes 8 servings.

	kcal	carb(gm)	fat(gm)	chol(mg)	Na(mg)	iron(mg)	Ca(mg)
lavish:	720	39	29	177	363	5.6	93
lean:	520	29	6	168	192	4.1	90

SPICY CHICKEN WITH CUMIN & LIME

Lavish

♦

Great for large groups and picnics, this dish reheats well (it can be made a day ahead) and is equally delicious hot or at room temperature.

2 (3-lb. each) chickens, cut up
½ cup fresh lime juice
¼ cup olive oil
1½ teaspoons salt
1 teaspoon dry mustard
1½ tablespoons chili powder
⅛ teaspoon cayenne
1 teaspoon ground cumin
1½ teaspoons paprika

2 large garlic cloves, minced
Freshly ground black pepper
¼ cup unseasoned fine dry
    bread crumbs
Additional paprika to taste
Fresh cilantro leaves for
    garnish
8 lime wedges for garnish

Remove all fat from chicken. Arrange chicken, skin side down, in a glass or ceramic baking dish large enough to hold pieces without overlapping. In a small bowl, mix lime juice, oil, salt, mustard, chili powder, red pepper, cumin, ½ teaspoon paprika, garlic and black pepper. Pour over chicken; cover and refrigerate at least 4 hours or up to 24 hours, turning chicken pieces occasionally. Return to room temperature.

Preheat oven to 375F (190C). Arrange chicken, skin side up, in 2 (9" × 13") baking dishes or ovenproof casseroles. Sprinkle with bread crumbs. Spoon marinade over bread crumbs; sprinkle with additional paprika to taste. Remove chicken breasts, leaving space for them in baking dishes. Bake chicken, uncovered, 25 minutes. Add chicken breasts; baste all chicken pieces. Continue to bake, uncovered, 20 minutes longer or until juices run clear when chicken is pierced to the bone in thickest portion.

Chicken can be assembled (ready to bake) or baked up to 1 day ahead, then covered and refrigerated. Return to room temperature before baking or reheating.

Serve chicken hot or at room temperature, either in baking dishes or on a large platter. Garnish with cilantro leaves and lime wedges. Makes 8 servings.

Lean

When chicken skin is peeled away, so are calories. Here, increased seasonings and citrus juices make salt and more olive oil unnecessary.

4 (about 1-lb. each) whole chicken breasts, split, bone in
⅔ cup fresh lime juice
¼ cup frozen concentrated orange juice
1½ teaspoons dry mustard
3 tablespoons chili powder
⅛ teaspoon cayenne
1½ teaspoons *each* ground cumin and paprika

3 large garlic cloves, minced
Freshly ground black pepper
¼ cup wheat germ
2 tablespoons olive oil
Additional paprika to taste
Fresh cilantro leaves for garnish
8 lime wedges for garnish

Remove skin and fat from chicken. Arrange in a glass or ceramic baking dish large enough to hold pieces without overlapping. In a small bowl, mix lime and concentrated orange juice, mustard, chili powder, red pepper, cumin, ½ teaspoon paprika, garlic and black pepper. Pour over chicken; cover and refrigerate at least 4 hours or up to 24 hours, turning chicken pieces occasionally. Return to room temperature.

Preheat oven to 350F (175C). Arrange chicken, flesh side up, in 2 (9″ × 13″) baking dishes. Spoon marinade over chicken. Sprinkle with wheat germ, oil and additional paprika to taste. Bake, uncovered, 20 minutes or until juices run clear when chicken is pierced to the bone in thickest portion.

Chicken can be prepared or baked up to 1 day ahead, then covered and refrigerated. Bring to room temperature before baking or serving. (Reheated baked chicken breasts become dry and stringy.)

Serve chicken in baking dishes or on a large platter. Garnish with cilantro leaves and lime wedges. Makes 8 servings.

	kcal	carb(gm)	fat(gm)	chol(mg)	Na(mg)	iron(mg)	Ca(mg)
lavish:	456	5.5	23	146	417	3.4	38
lean:	308	10	9	119	133	2.3	40

BRAISED PORK WITH FOUR SPICES

Lavish

◆

Cardamom seeds, when taken from their pods and crushed with a mortar and pestle, become intensely aromatic. Because this dish has decided flavors and textures, I often serve it with simple accompaniments: boiled new potatoes, coarse country bread to mop up the sauce, and a green salad.

2 tablespoons butter
2 tablespoons peanut oil
4 bunches (about 24) green onions, cut in 2-inch lengths
2 garlic cloves, minced
Salt to taste
8 (about 8-oz.) pork chops, at least 1 inch thick
½ teaspoon ground red (cayenne) pepper
1½ teaspoons ground mace
1 tablespoon ground cinnamon

10 cardamom seeds, crushed, or 1½ teaspoons ground cardamom
8 medium-size tomatoes (about 2¼ lbs. *total*), peeled, seeded
2 tablespoons all-purpose flour
Pinch of sugar
½ cup Crème Fraîche, page 278, or dairy sour cream
3 tablespoons flat-leaf parsley leaves for garnish

Melt 1 tablespoon butter in 1 tablespoon oil in a large skillet over medium heat. Add green onions and cook 6 to 8 minutes or until softened; stir in garlic for last minute. Make a bed of cooked green onion-garlic mixture in a wide ovenproof casserole with a lid, large enough to hold chops without overlapping. Season onions lightly with salt.

Season pork chops with salt and red pepper. In a small bowl, blend mace, cinnamon and cardamom. Press spices into both sides of chops; reserve any remaining spices. Melt remaining 1 tablespoon butter in remaining 1 tablespoon oil in skillet over medium-high heat; add pork chops and brown on both sides. Arrange chops over green onions in casserole.

Preheat oven to 300F (150C). Coarsely dice tomatoes, add to skillet and cook over medium-high heat 3 to 4 minutes or until soft and juicy, scraping up any browned bits of meat from skillet bottom. Sprinkle tomatoes with flour and season with reserved spices, salt and a pinch of sugar, if needed. Cook, stirring, 1 minute longer. Spoon over chops.

Bake, covered, 1 to 1½ hours; liquid in casserole should be at a bare simmer. A fast simmer will toughen meat, so check and adjust oven temperature as needed. Pork is cooked when juices run clear when meat is pierced with fork. With a slotted spoon, remove chops and onions to a heated platter; cover loosely with foil and keep warm. Pour cooking liquid into a small saucepan and reduce over medium heat until thickened. Remove from heat, blend in Crème Fraîche or sour cream and reheat to just below a simmer. Taste and adjust seasonings.

To serve, spoon sauce onto a heated large platter. Arrange chops over sauce; garnish with parsley. Makes 8 servings.

Lean

Boneless pork braised in this four-spice sauce makes a hearty stew to serve over rice or pasta. Because the dish can be eaten without a knife, it is ideal for buffets.

4 bunches (about 24) green
  onions, cut in 2-inch
  lengths
2 garlic cloves, minced
2 pounds boneless pork loin,
  about 1½ inches thick,
  trimmed of all fat
Pinch of ground red (cayenne)
  pepper
1½ teaspoons ground mace
1 tablespoon ground
  cinnamon
10 cardamom seeds, crushed,
  or 1½ teaspoons ground
  cardamom

½ teaspoon olive oil, if
  desired
8 medium-size tomatoes
  (about 2¼ lbs. *total*), peeled,
  seeded
2 tablespoons all-purpose
  flour
1 tablespoon frozen
  concentrated apple juice
2 tablespoons fresh lemon
  juice
3 tablespoons flat-leaf parsley
  leaves for garnish

In a covered medium-size non-stick saucepan, sweat green onions and garlic over medium heat 6 to 8 minutes or until soft, stirring occasionally to prevent sticking. Make a bed of cooked green onion-garlic mixture in a large ovenproof casserole.

Cut pork into eight 3- to 4-inch chunks. Season with red pepper. In a small bowl, mix mace, cinnamon and cardamom. Press spices into all sides of meat; reserve any remaining spices. Rub a heavy non-stick saucepan with oil, if desired. Heat pan over medium-high heat; add pork and brown on all sides. Set aside.

Preheat oven to 300F (150C). Coarsely dice tomatoes, add to saucepan and cook over medium-high heat 3 to 4 minutes or until soft and juicy, scraping up any browned bits of meat from pan bottom. Add reserved spices, sprinkle with flour and cook, stirring, 1 minute longer. Taste and season with concentrated apple juice and lemon juice.

Spoon half the tomatoes over green onion mixture in casserole; arrange browned pork chunks over tomatoes. Spoon remaining tomatoes over pork. Bake, covered, 1 hour; liquid in casserole should be at a bare simmer. A fast simmer will toughen meat, so check and adjust oven temperature as needed. Pork is cooked when juices run clear when meat is pierced with a fork. With a slotted spoon, remove pork and onions to a heated large dish; cover loosely with foil and keep warm. Pour cooking liquid into a small saucepan and reduce over medium heat until thickened.

To serve, toss pork and onions in sauce until well coated. Spoon into a heated large serving dish or deep platter. Garnish with parsley. Makes 8 servings.

	kcal	carb(gm)	fat(gm)	chol(mg)	Na(mg)	iron(mg)	Ca(mg)
lavish:	544	9	46	116	374	2	47
lean:	327	10	16	107	94	2.3	27

PORK WITH RED CABBAGE & APPLES

Lavish

♦

For a smoky, outdoor taste, I sometimes finish the cabbage and ribs in our barbecue-smoker and increase the roasting (smoking) time to an hour or so, just long enough to heat the meat and cabbage thoroughly.

1 pound sliced bacon, cut in
    ½-inch pieces
2 tablespoons butter
2 medium-size onions,
    chopped
2½ pounds red cabbage,
    thinly sliced
2 tart apples, peeled, cored,
    cut in ½-inch chunks

1 tablespoon red wine vinegar
1 quart dry red wine
5 pounds pork back ribs
Salt and freshly ground
    pepper to taste
Paprika to taste
3 tablespoons flat-leaf parsley
    leaves for garnish

In a large skillet, cook bacon over medium heat until crisp. Drain on paper towels; discard all but 2 tablespoons of the drippings. Melt butter in reserved 2 tablespoons drippings; add onions and sauté 10 minutes or until soft. Add cabbage and toss to coat with fat; then cook over medium-high heat, stirring, 5 minutes. Stir in drained cooked bacon, apples, vinegar and wine. Bring to a boil over high heat; reduce heat, partially cover and simmer 30 minutes.

Meanwhile, in a large pot, cover pork ribs with water and bring to a boil over high heat. Reduce heat and simmer, uncovered, 30 minutes or until meat begins to pull away from bones. Remove ribs from pot with tongs; drain ribs.

With a slotted spoon, arrange cabbage mixture in 1 or 2 large, shallow glass, ceramic or stainless steel ovenproof casseroles or baking pans. Season with salt and pepper; set aside. Reduce liquid remaining in skillet by half over medium-high heat; set aside for basting.

Preheat oven to 375F (190C). Season both sides of ribs with salt, pepper and paprika. Arrange over cabbage. Spoon some of the reduced cooking liquid over pork ribs. (At this point, you may cover and refrigerate up to 1 day. Return to room temperature before roasting.)

Roast ribs, uncovered, basting occasionally, 30 to 40 minutes or until browned and tender when pierced with a fork. Present ribs and cabbage in casserole, garnished with parsley; serve on heated plates. Makes 8 servings.

Lean

This oven-braised pork marinates in a spiced cabbage and wine broth for a full day to develop flavor.

2 medium-size onions,
  chopped
2 garlic cloves, minced
½ cup diced lean ham
1 cup unsalted Chicken Stock,
  page 15, or commercial
2½ pounds red cabbage,
  thinly sliced
2 tart apples, peeled, cored,
  cut in ½-inch chunks
5 whole cloves
1 teaspoon *each* ground
  nutmeg and ground allspice

3 tablespoons *each* red wine
  vinegar and frozen
  concentrated apple juice
3 to 4 cups dry red wine
3½ pounds boneless pork
  loin, at least 1 inch thick,
  trimmed of all fat
½ teaspoon olive oil
All-purpose flour
Freshly ground pepper to
  taste
3 tablespoons flat-leaf parsley
  leaves for garnish

In a large non-stick pot, cook onions and garlic, uncovered, over medium-low heat about 12 minutes, stirring occasionally. Add ham; continue to cook, stirring, about 3 minutes longer or until onions are soft. Add stock and bring to a boil; reduce heat, cover and simmer 10 minutes. Add cabbage, apples, cloves, nutmeg, allspice, vinegar and concentrated apple juice to pot; toss to mix. Add enough wine to bring liquid to about halfway up cabbage. Bring liquid to a boil over high heat; reduce heat, cover and simmer 30 minutes. Cool uncovered. Drain cabbage mixture, reserving liquid; cover and refrigerate cabbage mixture. Arrange uncooked pork in a glass or ceramic dish; spoon cooled cabbage liquid over pork. Cover and refrigerate at least 24 hours or up to 2 days, turning pork occasionally.

Preheat oven to 325F (165C). Arrange cabbage mixture in a glass, ceramic or stainless steel casserole. Rub a medium-size non-stick skillet with ½ teaspoon oil. Lift pork from cabbage liquid, blot dry, dust lightly with flour and season with pepper. Heat skillet over medium-high heat; add pork and brown on all sides. Bury pork in cabbage mixture. Pour cabbage liquid into skillet; deglaze skillet over high heat, scraping up browned bits. Reduce liquid by half;

add to cabbage and pork in casserole. Cover and bake 1½ hours or until cabbage is hot and pork is tender and no longer pink in center.

To serve, arrange pork and cabbage on a heated large, deep platter. Spoon cooking juices over pork and cabbage or serve juices separately in a heated gravy boat. Garnish pork and cabbage with parsley. Serve on heated plates. Makes 8 servings.

	kcal	carb(gm)	fat(gm)	chol(mg)	Na(mg)	iron(mg)	Ca(mg)
lavish:	1072	17	73	227	1051	5.1	169
lean:	545	23	20	139	392	3.5	112

LAMB IN MUSTARD-THYME SAUCE

Lavish

♦

Beautiful and elegant enough for a formal party, this lamb in a rich, piquant sauce is served on a bed of buttered spinach and crowned with diced cooked carrot. For a simpler version, serve the lamb over hot buttered pasta, or as a stew with steamed carrots, potatoes and fresh peas.

1 tablespoon *each* butter and vegetable oil
1 leek, white part only, washed well, cut in chunks
1 large onion, cut in chunks
5 pounds boned lamb from shoulder chops, cut 1 inch thick
Reserved lamb bones from chops
7 cups Chicken Stock, page 15, or commercial
3 carrots, peeled, cut in half
Leafy green tops of 4 celery stalks
10 flat-leaf parsley sprigs
7 fresh thyme sprigs, bruised, or 1½ teaspoons dried leaf thyme

2 bay leaves
7 whole black peppercorns
¼ cup butter
¼ cup all-purpose flour
2 tablespoons Dijon-style mustard
2 tablespoons fresh thyme leaves, bruised, or 2 teaspoons dried leaf thyme
2 tablespoons fresh lemon juice
1½ teaspoons sugar
1⅓ cups whipping cream
Salt to taste
8 servings hot blanched spinach, well drained, buttered (4 to 5 bunches spinach)

Melt 1 tablespoon butter in oil in a large, heavy pot over medium-high heat. Add leek and onion; cook 15 to 20 minutes or until soft and lightly browned, stirring occasionally. Place lamb, bones, stock, carrots, celery, parsley, thyme sprigs (or 1½ teaspoons dried thyme), bay leaves and peppercorns in pot. Bring to a simmer over medium-high heat; immediately reduce heat, cover and simmer 40 to 50 minutes or until lamb is tender, checking frequently to maintain a gentle simmer. Remove lamb to a large saucepan, cover loosely and keep warm. Dice enough carrot to make ½ cup and set aside for garnish. Strain stock into a small, deep bowl, pressing out as much liquid as possible; discard solids. Degrease stock, then pour into a saucepan and reduce to 2½ cups over high heat.

Melt ¼ cup butter in a small saucepan over low heat. Sprinkle in flour and cook 1 minute, stirring. Add reduced stock, a little at a time, stirring with a whisk until smooth and thickened. Stir in mustard, bruised thyme leaves (or 2 teaspoons dried thyme), lemon juice, sugar and cream. Simmer gently over low heat 10 minutes, stirring occasionally. Season with salt. Add sauce to lamb and reheat to a bare simmer. If prepared ahead, cool, cover tightly and refrigerate up to 2 days or freeze up to 2 months.

To serve, reheat lamb and sauce. Make a bed of hot buttered spinach on heated individual plates or a large platter. With a slotted spoon, arrange lamb over spinach; spoon sauce over lamb. Garnish with warmed diced carrot. Makes 8 servings.

Lean

Tender lamb in a tangy mustard-thyme sauce contrasts deliciously with deep green spinach.

4 pounds boned leg of lamb, trimmed of all fat, cut in 1-inch chunks
2 or 3 lamb bones
7 cups unsalted Chicken Stock, page 15, or commercial
2 leeks, white part only, washed well, cut in chunks
1 large onion, cut in chunks
3 large carrots, peeled, cut in chunks
Leafy green tops of 3 celery stalks
8 flat-leaf parsley sprigs
6 fresh thyme sprigs, bruised, or 1 teaspoon dried leaf thyme

2 bay leaves
7 whole black peppercorns
2 tablespoons fresh thyme leaves, bruised, or 2 teaspoons dried leaf thyme
1 cup Creamy Non-fat Yogurt, page 22, or mild commercial
3 tablespoons all-purpose flour
1½ tablespoons Dijon-style mustard
1½ tablespoons fresh lemon juice
1 teaspoon sugar
8 servings hot blanched spinach, well drained (4 to 5 bunches spinach)

In a large, heavy pot, combine lamb, bones, stock, leeks, onion, carrots, celery, parsley, thyme sprigs (or 1 teaspoon dried thyme), bay leaves and peppercorns. Bring to a simmer over high heat; then reduce heat, cover and simmer gently 40 to 45 minutes or until lamb is tender, checking frequently to maintain a gentle simmer. Remove lamb to a medium-size bowl or platter. Dice enough carrot to make ½ cup; set aside for garnish. Strain stock into a large, deep bowl, pressing out as much liquid as possible. Discard solids. Add cooked lamb to stock; cool, then cover and refrigerate. When stock is well chilled, remove fat from surface. Strain stock into a large skillet; reserve lamb. Add bruised thyme leaves (or 2 teaspoons dried thyme) to stock; reduce to 2 cups over high heat. Remove from heat; pour into a small saucepan.

In a small saucepan, whisk yogurt and flour together until blended. Slowly simmer 5 minutes over low heat. Stir in mustard, lemon juice and sugar. Blend in a little reduced stock, then stir mixture into stock in saucepan. Over low heat, cook at a bare simmer 5 minutes, whisking occasionally. Taste and adjust seasonings, if necessary. Combine lamb and sauce in a large saucepan. If prepared ahead, cool, cover tightly and refrigerate up to 2 days.

To serve, reheat lamb and sauce. Make a bed of hot spinach on heated individual plates or on a large platter. With a slotted spoon, arrange lamb over spinach; spoon sauce over lamb. Garnish with warmed diced carrot. Makes 8 servings.

	kcal	carb(gm)	fat(gm)	chol(mg)	Na(mg)	iron(mg)	Ca(mg)
lavish:	850	15	73	208	400	5.6	227
lean:	413	16	17	159	368	8.4	261

VEAL SCALOPPINE WITH FRESH PLUM SAUCE

Lavish

♦

A sumptuous dish with beautiful colors and delicate contrasting flavors.

Fresh Plum Sauce
1½ tablespoons *each* butter
  and light vegetable oil
1 pound (about 12 pieces)
  veal for scaloppine,
  pounded to a thickness of
  ¼ inch
All-purpose flour
Salt and freshly ground
  pepper to taste
½ cup dry white vermouth
2 tablespoons unsalted butter,
  cut in small pieces
12 slender asparagus spears,
  cut to a length of 5 inches,
  blanched (see page 37),
  heated

FRESH PLUM SAUCE
1½ teaspoons *each* butter and
  light vegetable oil, such as
  safflower
2 shallots, minced
1 garlic clove, minced
2 pounds large ripe plums,
  pitted, coarsely chopped
Pinch of ground allspice
2 tablespoons whipping
  cream
¼ teaspoon salt
2 teaspoons Dijon-style
  mustard
1½ tablespoons plum
  preserves

Prepare Fresh Plum Sauce and keep warm. Melt 1½ tablespoons butter in oil in a large, heavy skillet over medium-high heat until butter foams. Dust veal with flour and shake off excess; quickly sauté veal slices 1 minute or less on each side or just until lightly browned. As veal is browned, remove to a heated platter, season with salt and pepper, cover loosely and keep warm until all veal has been cooked. Deglaze skillet with vermouth, scraping up browned bits. Reduce liquid to ¼ cup; blend into Fresh Plum Sauce. Then remove sauce from heat and whisk in 2 tablespoons butter, a piece at a time.

To serve, spoon a 5-inch circle of sauce on each of 4 heated plates. Fan 3 asparagus spears over sauce on each plate, positioning tips of asparagus on unsauced portion of plate. Arrange 3 overlapping veal slices over stalk ends of asparagus. Spoon a ribbon of sauce across veal slices. Makes 4 servings.

Fresh Plum Sauce: Melt butter in oil in a medium-size, heavy saucepan over medium-high heat. Add shallots and garlic; sauté 1 to 2 minutes or until soft. Add plums and allspice. Reduce heat to medium-low, cover and cook, stirring occasionally, 10 to 12 minutes or until plums begin to soften and become juicy; plums will be only partly cooked. Puree plum mixture in a blender or a food processor fitted with a metal blade. Press puree through a strainer back into a medium-size saucepan. Stir in cream and salt; reduce sauce by a third. Blend in mustard and preserves. Finish sauce with reduced vermouth and butter as directed above. Makes 2 cups.

Lean

To keep costs and calories down, you can substitute thinly sliced turkey breast for the veal in this recipe. The flavor and texture are somewhat different, but the dish is still strikingly colorful and tasty.

Fresh Plum Sauce
½ teaspoon light vegetable oil
1 pound (about 12 pieces) veal for scaloppine, pounded to a thickness of ¼ inch; or 1 pound turkey breast, cut in 12 slices and pounded to a thickness of ¼ inch
Freshly ground pepper to taste
½ cup dry white vermouth
12 slender asparagus spears, cut to a length of 5 inches, blanched (see page 37), heated

FRESH PLUM SAUCE
2 shallots, minced
1 garlic clove, minced
2 pounds large ripe plums, pitted, coarsely chopped
1½ teaspoons dry mustard
¼ teaspoon ground allspice
1 tablespoon balsamic vinegar or red wine vinegar
1½ tablespoons plum preserves

Prepare Fresh Plum Sauce and keep warm. Rub a large, heavy non-stick skillet with oil, then set over medium-high heat. Blot moisture from veal or turkey with a paper towel, then quickly sauté 1 minute or less on each side or just until lightly browned. As meat is browned, remove to a heated platter, season with pepper, cover loosely and keep warm until all meat has been cooked. Deglaze skillet with vermouth, scraping up browned bits. Reduce liquid to ¼ cup; blend into Fresh Plum Sauce.

To serve, spoon a 5-inch circle of sauce on each of 4 heated plates. Fan 3 asparagus spears over sauce on each plate, positioning tips on unsauced portion of plate. Arrange 3 overlapping meat slices over stalk ends of asparagus. Spoon a ribbon of sauce across meat slices. Makes 4 servings.

Fresh Plum Sauce: In a covered medium-size, heavy non-stick saucepan, sweat shallots and garlic over medium-low heat about 5 minutes or until soft, stirring occasionally to prevent sticking. Stir in plums, mustard and allspice. Cover and cook, stirring occasionally, 10 to 12 minutes or until plums begin to soften and become juicy; plums will be only partly cooked. Puree plum mixture in a blender or a food processor fitted with a metal blade. Press puree through a strainer back into a medium-size saucepan to remove plum skins. Stir in vinegar; reduce sauce by a third. Blend preserves into sauce, then add reduced vermouth as directed above. Taste and adjust seasonings. Makes about 2 cups.

	kcal	carb(gm)	fat(gm)	chol(mg)	Na(mg)	iron(mg)	Ca(mg)
lavish:	546	43	31	132	310	4.2	49
lean:	327	39	3	94	65	2.5	38

BEEF WITH LIME & DRIED RED PEPPER SAUCE

Lavish

♦

Cook this roast beef as you like it—rare, medium or well done. When sliced, arranged on a pretty platter and napped with spicy sauce, it's a handsome buffet dish. For a picnic, dip the sliced beef in sauce, then tuck into pita bread with butter lettuce, fresh corn kernels and chopped tomato.

2 (2-lb. each) beef loin triangle tip roasts, trimmed of all fat
Grated zest of 2 large limes
¼ cup fresh lime juice
¼ cup tequila or dry cocktail sherry
1 teaspoon ground coriander
¼ teaspoon red pepper flakes
1 teaspoon salt
All-purpose flour

½ cup *each* Chicken Stock and Beef Stock, pages 15 and 16, or commercial
3 tablespoons currant jelly
¼ cup fresh cilantro leaves, chopped
1 teaspoon unsalted butter
2 tablespoons Crème Fraîche, page 278, or whipping cream
Additional fresh cilantro leaves for garnish

Place roasts in a large glass, ceramic or stainless steel bowl. In a small bowl, combine lime zest, lime juice, tequila or sherry, coriander, red pepper flakes and salt. Pour marinade over roasts; turn roasts several times to coat. Cover loosely; let stand at room temperature 4 hours or refrigerate overnight, turning occasionally. Drain and pat dry; reserve marinade.

Preheat oven to 325F (165C). Dust roasts lightly with flour. Place, fat sides up, on a rack over a large, shallow baking pan. Roast, uncovered, 45 minutes for medium (35 minutes for rare, 50 to 55 minutes for well-done). Place roasts on a heated large platter and cover loosely. Sprinkle 1 tablespoon flour over fat in roasting pan. Set pan over medium-high heat; pour in stocks and reserved marinade and deglaze pan, scraping up browned bits. Strain, if desired; pour into a small saucepan. Add jelly and stir over low heat until blended. Add ¼ cup cilantro, increase heat to medium-high and reduce sauce by a third or until slightly thickened. Beat in butter, ½ teaspoon at a time. Remove from heat; blend in Crème Fraîche or cream. Unsliced beef roasts and sauce can be prepared 1 hour ahead, covered loosely and served at room temperature. If meat and sauce are served at room temperature, omit butter from sauce.

To serve, cut roasts across the grain into thin slices. Arrange beef slices, slightly overlapping, on a heated or room-temperature large platter. Spoon sauce down center of slices and garnish with cilantro. Pass any additional sauce separately in a small bowl. Makes 8 servings.

Lean

Great for a hearty dinner or a cold salad, sliced over greens and dressed with the sauce.

4 pounds boneless top round steak, cut 1 inch thick, or 4 pounds flank steak, trimmed of all fat
Grated zest of 2 limes
½ cup fresh lime juice
¼ cup tequila or dry cocktail sherry
1 teaspoon ground coriander
½ teaspoon *each* ground cumin and dry mustard
¼ teaspoon red pepper flakes
½ cup *each* unsalted Chicken Stock and unsalted Beef Stock, pages 15 and 16, or commercial
1½ tablespoons currant jelly
¼ cup fresh cilantro leaves, chopped
Additional fresh cilantro leaves for garnish

Place steak in a large glass, ceramic or stainless steel bowl. In a small bowl, combine lime zest, lime juice, tequila or sherry, coriander, cumin, mustard and red pepper flakes. Pour marinade over steak; turn steak several times to coat. Cover and let stand at room temperature 4 hours or refrigerate overnight, turning occasionally.

Preheat broiler. Drain steak, reserving marinade, and thoroughly blot dry (a damp steak will steam, not broil). Broil 5 inches from heat source 3 minutes on each side for medium; adjust cooking times as desired for rare or well-done meat. Use tongs to lift steak to a cutting board; let stand 5 minutes before slicing. Over medium-high heat, deglaze broiler pan with stocks and reserved marinade, scraping up browned bits. Pour stock mixture into a small saucepan. Add jelly and stir over low heat until blended. Add ¼ cup cilantro and reduce sauce by half. If prepared ahead, cover sauce and un-sliced steak and refrigerate up to 1 day. Return to room temperature before serving (do not reheat steak).

To serve, carve steak on the diagonal across the grain into thin slices. Arrange sliced steak on a heated or room-temperature medium-size platter. Garnish platter with cilantro. Pass sauce separately in a small bowl. Makes 8 servings.

	kcal	carb(gm)	fat(gm)	chol(mg)	Na(mg)	iron(mg)	Ca(mg)
lavish:	416	6.5	29	106	344	3.1	18
lean:	262	4	11	99	82	3.6	12

BRAISED BEEF WITH GREEN CHILES & ORANGE

Lavish

♦

Braised beef is a perfect make-ahead dish; as it stands in the refrigerator, the sauce's flavor soaks in. Be sure to chill the meat thoroughly before carving it—it slices beautifully, but only when cold.

4 fresh mild green chiles or canned whole roasted green chiles
10 (¼" × 4") strips orange zest
1 tablespoon duck, goose or bacon fat
1 tablespoon *each* peanut oil and butter
4½ pounds beef brisket
½ cup fresh orange juice
3 garlic cloves, pressed
Salt to taste
2 teaspoons ground coriander

1¼ pounds ripe tomatoes, quartered
3 medium-size onions, quartered
Handful of fresh cilantro
Beef Stock, page 16, or commercial, if necessary
3 tablespoons Crème Fraîche, page 278, or whipping cream
¼ cup *each* diced tomato and fresh cilantro leaves for garnish
2 bay leaves, crumbled

If using fresh chiles, preheat broiler. Place chiles on foil; place under broiler and char on all sides, turning with tongs as needed. Enclose chiles tightly in a plastic bag and let stand until cool enough to handle. Remove and discard skins, stems and seeds; set chiles aside. Cover orange zest strips with cold water and bring to a boil; drain. Repeat; set zest aside.

Preheat oven to 300F (150C). In a large, heavy pot with ovenproof handles, heat fat, oil and butter over medium-high heat; add brisket and brown on all sides. Remove meat; discard fats. Pour orange juice into pot and deglaze, scraping up browned bits. Remove from heat. Rub brisket with garlic, salt and 1 teaspoon coriander. Return brisket to pot. Add remaining ground coriander, 5 orange zest strips, and bay leaves to sauce; arrange quartered tomatoes, onions, a handful of cilantro and roasted fresh or canned chiles over and around brisket. Cover pot tightly with foil, then with lid. Bake 2-½ hours or until brisket is very tender. Uncover, turn meat over and cool to room temperature, basting occasionally.

Remove meat from sauce, cover and refrigerate. With a slotted spoon, remove chiles from sauce and set aside. Strain sauce into a deep saucepan, pressing hard on solids to remove as much liquid as possible; discard solids. You should have about 3 cups liquid; if necessary, add enough stock to make 3 cups. Refrigerate sauce until well chilled, then remove fat from surface. In a blender or a food processor fitted with a metal blade, process reserved chiles with about ½ cup sauce until pureed; return to sauce. Slice chilled meat across the grain, arrange in a shallow ovenproof casserole and top evenly with ½ cup sauce. (At this point, you may cover and refrigerate up to 3 days.)

Bring sliced meat to room temperature; spoon sauce in casserole up over meat. Cover tightly with foil and heat in a 300F (150C) oven 30 to 40 minutes. Pour remaining sauce into a small saucepan. Add remaining 5 orange zest strips to sauce and reduce over high heat to about 2 cups or until slightly thickened. Remove from heat; whisk in Crème Fraîche or cream. Taste and adjust seasonings; pour into a heated small serving bowl.

To serve, garnish brisket in casserole with diced tomato and ¼ cup cilantro. Accompany with heated sauce. Makes 8 to 10 servings.

Lean

4 fresh mild green chiles or
  canned whole roasted green
  chiles
20 (¼″ × 4″) strips orange
  zest
½ teaspoon olive oil
4½ pounds lean top round
  roast, trimmed of all fat
1 cup fresh orange juice
1 tablespoon balsamic vinegar
  or red wine vinegar
3 or 4 garlic cloves, pressed

2 teaspoons ground coriander
2 bay leaves, crumbled
3 medium-size onions,
  quartered
1¼ pounds ripe tomatoes,
  quartered
Handful of fresh cilantro
Unsalted Beef Stock, page 16,
  or commercial, if necessary
¼ cup fresh cilantro leaves for
  garnish

Roast and peel fresh chiles and blanch orange zest strips as directed on page 168. Set aside.

Preheat oven to 300F (150C). Rub bottom of a large, heavy non-stick pot with ovenproof handles with oil. Add roast and brown on all sides over medium-high heat. Remove roast to a platter. With a paper towel, blot grease from pot, leaving browned bits in pot. Pour ½ cup orange juice and vinegar into pot and deglaze over medium heat, scraping up browned bits. Remove from heat. Rub garlic and 1 teaspoon coriander into roast; return to pot. Sprinkle remaining 1 teaspoon coriander, 5 orange zest strips, bay leaves, onions, tomatoes, a handful of cilantro and roasted fresh or canned chiles over and around roast. Cover pot tightly with foil, then with lid. Bake 2½ hours or until roast is very tender. Uncover, turn meat over and cool to room temperature, basting occasionally.

Remove meat from sauce; cover and refrigerate. With tongs, remove chiles from sauce and set aside. Strain sauce into a deep saucepan, pressing hard on solids to remove as much liquid as possible. You should have about 3 cups liquid; if necessary, add enough stock to make 3 cups. Refrigerate sauce until well chilled, then remove fat from surface. In a blender or a food processor fitted with a metal blade, process reserved chiles with remaining ½ cup orange juice until pureed; stir into sauce. Slice chilled roast across the grain and arrange in a shallow ovenproof casserole. Pour sauce into a small saucepan, add 5 orange zest strips and reduce over high heat to about 2½ cups or until slightly thickened. Taste and adjust seasonings; then spoon over sliced meat. (At this point, you may cover and refrigerate up to 3 days; bring to room temperature and spoon sauce in casserole up over meat before continuing.) Cover casserole tightly with foil and bake in a 300F (150C) oven 30 to 40 minutes or until heated through.

To serve, garnish roast in casserole with remaining 10 orange zest strips and ¼ cup cilantro leaves. Makes 8 to 10 servings.

	kcal	carb(gm)	fat(gm)	chol(mg)	Na(mg)	iron(mg)	Ca(mg)
lavish:	415	9	37	105	369	2.5	9
lean:	204	10	6	70	74	3.7	29

GRILLED FISH & POTATO SALAD

Lavish

♦

In Portofino, there's an inexpensive (and wonderful) trattoria facing the harbor. We found the restaurant, lost its name and now have only the memory of grilled local fish and garden-sweet potatoes tossed together in a salad.

1 pound halibut fillets or other fish fillets of choice (see TIP, page 115), about 1 inch thick
2 tablespoons olive oil
Salt and freshly ground pepper to taste
12 ounces small (about 1½-inch-diameter) red thin-skinned potatoes, unpeeled, boiled until tender

3 tablespoons *each* drained capers and minced flat-leaf parsley
½ cup fruity extra-virgin olive oil
4 lemon wedges for garnish

Ignite coals and burn just until flame is gone and ashes are white; or preheat broiler.

Remove any small bones from fish fillets with tweezers. Rub both sides of fish with 2 tablespoons olive oil. Grill or broil fish 5 inches from heat source, turning once, until flesh is opaque but still moist in center; allow 8 to 10 minutes total cooking time for each 1 inch of thickness (see TIP, opposite). Season fish lightly with salt and pepper and break into bite-size pieces.

Cut warm potatoes into bite-size pieces and place in a medium-size salad bowl. Add fish, capers and parsley; toss gently. Add extra-virgin olive oil and toss again. Taste; add more salt and pepper, if needed. Serve warm.

Wipe down sides of bowl after tossing salad. Serve from salad bowl onto individual plates; garnish each plate with a lemon wedge. Makes 4 servings.

Lean

1 pound cod or sea bass fillets
  (see TIP, page 115), about 1
  inch thick
Freshly ground pepper
12 ounces small (about 1½-
  inch-diameter) red thin-
  skinned potatoes, unpeeled,
  boiled until tender

3 tablespoons sun-dried
  tomatoes, slivered
¼ cup minced flat-leaf parsley
2 tablespoons fruity extra-
  virgin olive oil
1 tablespoon plus 1 teaspoon
  fresh lemon juice
1 teaspoon Dijon-style
  mustard

Ignite coals and burn just until flame is gone and ashes are white; or preheat broiler.

Remove any small bones from fish fillets with tweezers. Grill or broil fish 5 inches from heat source, turning once, until fish is opaque but still moist in center; allow 8 to 10 minutes total cooking time for each 1 inch of thickness (see TIP). Season fish with pepper and break into bite-size pieces.

Cut warm potatoes into bite-size pieces and place in a salad bowl with fish, sun-dried tomatoes and parsley; toss gently. Blend oil, lemon juice and mustard and add to fish mixture; toss again. Taste and adjust seasonings. Serve warm.

Wipe down sides of bowl after tossing salad. Serve from salad bowl onto individual plates. Makes 4 servings.

TIP

Fish fillets or steaks over ½ inch thick can be turned halfway through the estimated grilling or broiling time; the flesh can then be separated with a fork to test doneness. Pieces under ½ inch thick should be broiled or grilled on one side only to prevent the flesh from overcooking and breaking apart.

	kcal	carb(gm)	fat(gm)	chol(mg)	Na(mg)	iron(mg)	Ca(mg)
lavish:	555	20	41	47	268	2.1	44
lean:	253	20	8	60	9	1.4	54

GINGERED GARDEN SALAD WITH CHICKEN

Lavish

♦

You can substitute fresh sweet peas, artichoke hearts, sugar peas or any favorite seasonal salad ingredients for the vegetables suggested below; those with delicate flavors work best. With hot, crusty rolls and butter, this salad is an easy one-dish lunch or supper.

Dressing
1 (about 1¼-lb.) head iceberg lettuce, washed, dried, torn in large bite-size pieces
1 large bunch arugula, washed, dried, torn in large bite-size pieces
2 large ripe tomatoes, peeled, seeded, juiced, cut in chunks (about 2 cups)
2 yellow bell peppers, seeded, thinly sliced
1 cup sun-dried tomatoes, cut in slivers
Kernels cut from 6 ears cooked fresh corn; or about 3 cups frozen corn kernels, thawed, drained
6½ cups diced cooked chicken
4 hard-cooked eggs, diced
1 small red onion, thinly sliced (you may use more or less onion, to taste)

½ cup fresh basil leaves, thinly sliced, or ¼ cup fresh marjoram leaves; or 3 tablespoons dried leaf basil or 2 tablespoons dried leaf marjoram

DRESSING
3 tablespoons minced onion
⅓ cup minced celery
¼ cup grated fresh gingerroot
⅓ cup Japanese rice vinegar
3 tablespoons *each* fresh lemon juice and soy sauce
2 tablespoons water
1 tablespoon sugar
¾ teaspoon salt
Freshly ground pepper to taste
¾ cup safflower oil
1 teaspoon Oriental sesame oil

Prepare Dressing. Layer all remaining ingredients in a large salad bowl. Toss with two-thirds of Dressing. Taste and adjust seasonings; add more Dressing to taste.

Lettuce and arugula can be washed, dried, loosely wrapped in kitchen towels and refrigerated up to 1 day ahead. Chicken and whole eggs can be prepared up to 1 day ahead, covered and refrigerated. Tomatoes, bell peppers, sun-dried tomatoes and corn can be prepared 4 hours ahead, covered and left at room temperature. Just before serving, dice eggs and slice onions and basil.

Serve salad at room temperature on individual plates. Makes 8 servings.

Dressing: Place all ingredients except oils in a blender or a food processor fitted with a metal blade. Process until sugar and salt are dissolved and onion and celery are pureed. Add oils; process until blended. Whisk just before using. Makes 2 cups.

Lean

Dressing
1 (about 1¼-lb.) head iceberg
   lettuce, washed, dried, torn
   in large bite-size pieces
1 large bunch arugula,
   washed, dried, torn in large
   bite-size pieces
2 large ripe tomatoes, peeled,
   seeded, juiced, cut in
   chunks (about 2 cups)
2 yellow bell peppers, seeded,
   thinly sliced
1 cup sun-dried tomatoes, cut
   in slivers
Kernels cut from 3 ears
   cooked fresh corn; or about
   1½ cups frozen corn
   kernels, thawed, drained
1½ cups diced peeled jicama
6½ cups diced cooked
   chicken breast, all skin and
   fat removed
6 hard-cooked egg whites,
   diced

1 small red onion, thinly
   sliced (you may use more or
   less onion, to taste)
½ cup fresh basil leaves,
   thinly sliced, or ¼ cup fresh
   marjoram leaves; or 3
   tablespoons dried leaf basil
   or 2 tablespoons dried leaf
   marjoram

DRESSING
3 tablespoons minced onion
⅓ cup minced celery
¼ cup grated fresh gingerroot
⅓ cup Japanese rice vinegar
3 tablespoons *each* fresh
   lemon juice and soy sauce
2 teaspoons sugar
Freshly ground pepper to
   taste
½ teaspoon Oriental sesame
   oil

Prepare Dressing. Layer all remaining ingredients in a large salad bowl. Toss with two-thirds of Dressing; taste and adjust seasonings. Add additional Dressing to taste.

Lettuce and arugula can be washed, dried, loosely wrapped in kitchen towels and refrigerated up to 1 day ahead. Chicken and whole eggs can be prepared 1 day ahead, covered and refrigerated. Tomatoes, peppers, sun-dried tomatoes and corn can be prepared 4 hours ahead, covered and left at room temperature. Just before serving, dice egg whites and slice onions and basil.

Serve salad at room temperature on individual plates. Makes 8 servings.

Dressing: Place all ingredients in a blender or a food processor fitted with a metal blade. Process until sugar is dissolved and onion and celery are pureed. Whisk just before using. Makes 1¼ cups.

	kcal	carb(gm)	fat(gm)	chol(mg)	Na(mg)	iron(mg)	Ca(mg)
lavish:	642	28	43	258	768	4.7	131
lean:	310	23	5	96	566	3.4	123

PASTA, SPINACH & CHICKEN SALAD

Lavish

♦

Spinach is tender and small-leafed in spring and early summer—good seasons to serve this salad. I sometimes replace part of the chicken with cooked shrimp. You can vary the proportions to suit your taste.

2 pounds small pasta shells (conchiglie) or spirals (fusilli), cooked al dente, rinsed, drained well

3 tablespoons extra-virgin olive oil

2 (3-lb. each) chickens, poached (see page 20), boned, skinned cut in bite-size pieces (7 to 8 cups cooked meat)

2 large (about 1-lb. each) bunches spinach, leaves only, washed, dried, torn in bite-size pieces

¾ cup chopped pancetta or ham

1 cup finely chopped green onions, including green tops

⅓ cup Dijon-style mustard

¾ cup fresh lemon juice

1½ to 2 cups extra-virgin olive oil

Salt and freshly ground pepper to taste

Toss cooked pasta in a large bowl with 3 tablespoons oil. Add chicken, spinach, pancetta or ham and green onions; toss again. In a small bowl, blend mustard and lemon juice. Pour 1½ cups oil over salad and toss to coat ingredients. Add mustard-lemon juice mixture and toss again. Season with salt and pepper; add remaining ½ cup oil if needed for flavor and texture.

Pasta, chicken, spinach and pancetta or ham can be prepared 1 day ahead, wrapped separately and refrigerated. Bring ingredients to room temperature, prepare green onions and toss salad with dressing just before serving.

Serve salad from a very large salad bowl onto individual plates. Makes 12 servings.

Lean

I sometimes replace the tarragon in this salad with chopped fresh oregano or marjoram. If you use marjoram, you'll need only 2 tablespoons fresh leaves. Although pasta soaks up lemon juice, the salad will taste tangy.

2 pounds small pasta shells (conchiglie) or spirals (fusilli), cooked al dente, rinsed, drained well
4 pounds chicken breasts, poached, boned, skinned, cut in bite-size pieces (7 to 8 cups cooked meat)
2 large (about 1-lb.) bunches spinach, leaves only, washed, dried, torn in bite-size pieces
½ cup 1½-inch-long matchsticks of red bell pepper
½ cup 1½-inch-long matchsticks of yellow bell pepper

1 cup finely chopped green onions, including green tops
¼ cup fresh tarragon leaves, chopped, or 2 teaspoons dried leaf tarragon
2 tablespoons Dijon-style mustard
¾ to 1 cup fresh lemon juice
½ cup unsalted Chicken Stock, page 15, or commercial, reduced to 2 tablespoons syrup (see page 14)
½ cup fruity extra-virgin olive oil
Red pepper flakes to taste

Put cooked pasta in a large bowl. Add chicken, spinach, red and yellow bell peppers, green onions and fresh tarragon, if used. Toss to mix. In a small bowl, mix mustard, 1 cup lemon juice, stock syrup and dried tarragon, if used. Pour oil over salad and toss to coat ingredients. Add mustard-lemon juice mixture and toss again. Season with red pepper flakes. Taste and adjust seasonings; add more lemon juice, if needed.

Chicken, spinach, bell peppers and stock can be prepared 1 day ahead, wrapped separately or covered and refrigerated. Bring ingredients to room temperature, cook pasta, prepare green onions and tarragon, and toss salad with dressing just before serving. (You can't cook the pasta in advance and refrigerate it—it would stick together in a lump, since it's not tossed with oil as in the lavish version.)

Serve salad from a very large salad bowl onto individual plates. Makes 12 servings.

	kcal	carb(gm)	fat(gm)	chol(mg)	Na(mg)	iron(mg)	Ca(mg)
lavish:	662	27	48	95	348	4.8	113
lean:	456	29	15	121	232	4.8	119

COLD SLICED MEAT WITH GUATEMALAN MARINADE

Lavish

♦

Gladys Castillo, a Los Angeles caterer and fine cook, turns sliced leftover meat, poultry or fish into a new dish by spooning this simple marinade over it. When the meat is chopped instead of sliced, the dish is called salipan. *Gladys serves* salipan *over hot or cold pasta.*

1 pound sliced leftover meat, poultry or fish, with fat, bones and skin removed
⅓ cup orange juice
3 tablespoons *each* fresh lemon juice and extra-virgin olive oil

Salt and freshly ground black pepper to taste
⅓ cup *each* fresh mint and cilantro leaves, chopped
3 green onions, sliced
2 large tomatoes, peeled, seeded, chopped

Arrange sliced meat, poultry or fish on a deep glass, ceramic or stainless steel platter. In a small bowl, mix orange juice, lemon juice and oil; season with salt and pepper. Spoon marinade over meat, poultry or fish, then sprinkle with mint, cilantro, green onions and tomatoes. Cover loosely and let stand at room temperature 1 hour. Serve at room temperature from platter. Makes 4 servings.

Lean

This version is almost identical to the lavish dish, and every bit as good. Use leftover lean meat, breast of chicken or turkey, or fish. Reduce the olive oil to 2 teaspoons and omit the salt.

	kcal	carb(gm)	fat(gm)	chol(mg)	Na(mg)	iron(mg)	Ca(mg)
lavish:	368	6	22	101	211	4.2	23
lean:	215	2	6	96	85	1.4	24

COLD BEEF & GARLIC SALAD

Lavish

♦

We raised our family in Los Angeles on Chrysanthemum Lane, where our neighbor Sasha Shorr used to straddle the tiny street to stop my car and boom in his Russian accent, "Judy, you have dinner yet?" Whether or not I had, I always answered "no," because I knew that Sasha (who cooked for his auberge in Belgium before he came to California) was about to share a leftover treat from his cooking class. He served this salad as a one-course meal with hot French bread and sweet butter.

Dressing
About 5 cups ½-inch cubes of cooked beef brisket (3 lbs. uncooked)
2 pounds boiling potatoes, boiled, peeled, cut in ½-inch dice
8 hard-cooked eggs, coarsely chopped
2 bunches (about 12) green onions, finely sliced
½ cup flat-leaf parsley leaves, coarsely chopped
Salt and freshly ground pepper to taste

Fresh lemon juice and Dijon-style mustard to taste
1 small head *each* romaine lettuce and Boston or butter lettuce, washed, dried, torn in bite-size pieces

DRESSING
1½ cups Mayonnaise, page 23, or commercial
¼ cup Dijon-style mustard
5 garlic cloves, pressed
½ cup *each* fresh lemon juice and extra-virgin olive oil

Prepare Dressing. Toss beef, potatoes, eggs, green onions and parsley in a large salad bowl. Add Dressing; toss salad until ingredients are well coated. Season with salt, pepper, lemon juice and mustard. Cover and refrigerate at least 3 hours or until flavors are blended. Return salad to room temperature. Just before serving, gently toss salad with lettuce.

Serve salad from bowl onto large individual plates. Makes 8 servings.

Dressing: In a small bowl, mix all ingredients until blended. Makes about 2¾ cups.

Lean

Dressing
About 5 cups ½-inch cubes of
   cooked top round roast (3
   lbs. uncooked)
1 cup ½-inch cubes of boiled,
   peeled potatoes
Whites of 10 hard-cooked
   eggs, coarsely chopped
2 bunches (about 12) green
   onions, finely sliced
½ cup *each* flat-leaf parsley
   and fresh tarragon leaves,
   coarsely chopped
Freshly ground pepper to
   taste
1 small head *each* romaine
   lettuce and Boston or butter
   lettuce, washed, dried, torn
   in bite-size pieces

2 cups watercress leaves
3 large, firm red bell peppers,
   roasted (see directions for
   chiles on page 168), peeled,
   cut in bite-size pieces

DRESSING
1¼ cups Creamy Non-fat
   Yogurt, page 22, or
   commercial
⅓ cup Mayonnaise, page 23,
   or commercial
2 tablespoons Dijon-style
   mustard
¼ cup balsamic vinegar or
   sherry wine vinegar
5 garlic cloves, pressed

Prepare Dressing. Toss beef, potatoes, egg whites, green onions, parsley and tarragon in a large salad bowl. Add Dressing and toss salad until ingredients are well coated; season with pepper. Cover and refrigerate at least 3 hours or until flavors are blended. Return salad to room temperature. Just before serving, gently toss salad with lettuce, watercress and roasted bell peppers.

Serve salad from bowl onto large individual plates. Makes 8 servings.

Dressing: In a small bowl, whisk together all ingredients until blended. Makes about 2 cups.

	kcal	carb(gm)	fat(gm)	chol(mg)	Na(mg)	iron(mg)	Ca(mg)
lavish:	912	28	75	376	466	4.7	83
lean:	337	13	16	82	259	4.2	131

VEGETABLES, LEGUMES, GRAINS & SALADS

Most people consider vegetables and salads no more than well-behaved escorts to the main course, necessary but merely tolerated. I think they deserve special attention, and an increasing number of home cooks, chefs and restaurant diners agree.

Today, cooks take ideas and ingredients from all over the world and use them to create exciting salads and vegetable dishes—a giant leap beyond the virtuously boiled-to-death victuals so common in years past! Now we might blanch tiny green beans (*haricots verts*), season them with exotic spices, and toss in a French-Chinese-Japanese stir-fry with cèpes and shiitake mushrooms. Or they might be sautéed to tender-crisp perfection French style, then lightly dressed with vinaigrette and served warm on a bed of lamb's lettuce, with poached prawns and a cool, thin slice of foie gras tucked into the greens.

Whatever the cooking style or seasoning, recipes in this chapter build on the pure flavors of fresh ingredients. Most of these dishes are simple, with lean and lavish versions often differing only slightly—so to assure delicious results, use the very best produce you can find. In Lia's Rice, Leek & Asparagus Custard (page 204), for example, success depends on developing (by sweating or sautéing) the delicate essence of leek and asparagus. Sautéed Tomatoes & Spinach (page 196) gain texture, flavor and color from deep green spinach tossed with fragrant ripe tomatoes and crunchy, sweet kernels of newly husked corn.

Even if prime produce is unavailable, what's at hand can often be revived. Cottony market tomatoes can make a

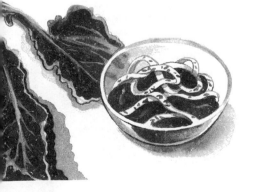

fresh-tasting salad even in winter when tossed with a few drops of lemon juice, a little salt (if you use it), a pinch of sugar, some extra-virgin olive oil and thinly sliced sweet red onion. Listless green beans or carrots perk up with the same treatment (with or without the olive oil and onion); if you're cooking lean, try a few drops of lemon and concentrated apple juice as natural seasoners. Freshly grated nutmeg pairs well with green beans, while tarragon, ginger and cumin enhance carrots. You'll discover your own favorite combinations with a little experimentation.

Vinegars can be delicious seasoners for vegetables; use the suggestions in this chapter as guides. Delicately flavored and textured lettuces such as limestone or lamb's lettuce (mâche) are often enhanced by a mild vinegar such as light white wine or Japanese rice vinegar; assertive greens such as arugula, spinach and the cresses, taste best with robust red wine vinegars. When you experiment, remember that several vinegars can be combined in a dressing or sauce, with or without citrus juices.

Pungent oils make good seasoners too. Walnut and hazelnut oils are often so strong that just a few drops are sufficient. If more than a few drops are needed—for a dressing, perhaps—try mixing about one part walnut or hazelnut oil with two parts of a light salad oil such as canola or safflower. Nut oils nicely flavor milder oils, often balancing their taste perfectly.

Olive oils vary greatly in flavor and can be ideal for seasoning salads and vegetables all by themselves. Warm Potato Salad (page 226), for example, has an unforgettable aroma and taste when dressed with a fruity, full-bodied extra-virgin olive oil. Experiment with fine extra-virgin olive oils from Greece, Italy and France; California has some good ones, too.

Whether seasoned with herbs, vinegar or oil, vegetables can be cooked in a variety of ways; roasting and grilling are often overlooked, but well worth trying. Roasted Japanese Eggplants with Hot Cheese (page 222) are crispy outside, melting-soft inside; Grilled Basted Vegetables (page 200) gain a subtle, smoky flavor from cooking over coals. Served warm or at room temperature, either dish makes an ideal accompaniment to a simple main course.

Of course, vegetable dishes and salads can also star at dinner. Tempting choices such as Lia's Rice, Leek & Asparagus Custard (page 204) and Gingered Garden Salad with Chicken (page 174) will satisfy the heartiest appetite, and lighter dishes in this chapter can be combined to create delicious, filling vegetarian meals.

CREAMY CORN WITH BASIL

Lavish

♦

The reduced cream that coats the sweet corn kernels gives this dish a sumptuous, silky quality, yet the corn still tastes garden-fresh.

2 tablespoons butter
1 small white onion, minced (about ⅔ cup)
1 garlic clove, minced
1 large red bell pepper, seeded, chopped
Salt and freshly ground pepper to taste

Pinch of sugar
Kernels cut from 4 ears fresh corn; or 2 cups frozen corn kernels, thawed
¼ cup whipping cream
1 cup loosely packed fresh basil leaves

Melt butter in a large skillet over medium-high heat. Add onion and garlic; sauté until soft. Add bell pepper; season lightly with salt, pepper and sugar. Cook, stirring, 5 minutes or until pepper is limp. Add corn and cream and cook 1 minute or until sauce is thickened. As corn cooks, slice basil leaves, setting aside 2 tablespoons for garnish. Toss remaining sliced basil leaves with vegetables as they finish cooking, then taste and adjust seasonings. Serve immediately in a heated serving bowl, garnished with reserved 2 tablespoons sliced basil leaves. Makes 4 servings.

Lean

The creamy texture of this version comes from peeled tomatoes and their reduced juices, but you can also enrich the dish with a tablespoon or two of cream, if you like.

1 teaspoon olive oil
2 shallots, minced
1 garlic clove, minced
2 medium-size tomatoes, peeled, seeded, chopped
Freshly ground pepper to taste
Pinch of sugar

1 teaspoon fresh lemon juice
1 cup loosely packed fresh basil leaves
Kernels cut from 4 ears fresh corn; or 2 cups frozen corn kernels, thawed
2 tablespoons whipping cream, if desired

Rub a large skillet with oil. Add shallots and garlic and cook over medium-low heat about 12 minutes or until soft, stirring frequently. Add tomatoes; season lightly with pepper, sugar and lemon juice. Cook, stirring, 3 to 4 minutes or until sauce has thickened to the consistency of sour cream. Meanwhile, slice basil leaves, setting aside 2 tablespoons for garnish. Add remaining sliced basil leaves, corn and cream, if desired, to tomato mixture; cook 1 minute, stirring to mix vegetables. Taste and adjust seasonings. Serve immediately in a heated serving bowl, garnished with reserved 2 tablespoons sliced basil leaves. Makes 4 servings.

	kcal	carb(gm)	fat(gm)	chol(mg)	Na(mg)	iron(mg)	Ca(mg)
lavish:	186	21	11	36	75	1.5	43
lean:	141	25	5	8	28	1.8	34

WARM BEETS WITH ONIONS & MARJORAM

Lavish

♦

Beets are usually pickled or served plain with butter, if they're not over-looked altogether. Nothing wrong with pickled or buttered beets, but for a change, contrast their sweetness with tart tomatoes, crunchy onions and chopped herbs.

6 small beets without tops
  (about 12 oz. *total*)
1 large firm yellow or red
  tomato, seeded, juiced
3 sweet white onions, thinly
  sliced crosswise

¼ cup extra-virgin olive oil
Salt and freshly ground black
  pepper to taste
Pinch of sugar
1½ tablespoons chopped fresh
  marjoram or tarragon leaves

Scrub beets, place in a saucepan and cover with water. Bring to a boil; reduce heat, cover and simmer 30 to 40 minutes or until tender. Peel and trim under cold running water, then cut into bite-size chunks.

While beets are cooking, cut tomato in ¼-inch-wide strips. Separate onion slices into rings. In a large bowl, toss warm cooked beets, tomato and onion rings with oil. Season with salt, pepper and sugar. Serve warm or at room temperature, not chilled.

Just before serving, toss vegetables with 1 tablespoon marjoram or tarragon. Then spoon into a serving bowl and sprinkle with re-maining ½ tablespoon marjoram or tarragon. Makes 4 servings.

Lean

6 small beets without tops (about 12 oz. *total*)
1 large firm yellow or red tomato, seeded, juiced
3 sweet white onions, thinly sliced crosswise
1 tablespoon extra-virgin olive oil
2 teaspoons Japanese rice vinegar
Freshly ground pepper to taste
Pinch of sugar
2 tablespoons chopped fresh marjoram or tarragon leaves

Scrub beets, place in a saucepan and cover with water. Bring to a boil; reduce heat, cover and simmer 30 to 40 minutes or until tender. Peel and trim beets under cold running water, then cut into bite-size chunks.

While beets are cooking, cut tomato in ¼-inch strips. Separate onion slices into rings. In a large bowl, toss warm cooked beets, tomato and onion rings with oil. Season with vinegar, pepper and sugar. Serve warm or at room temperature, not refrigerated.

Just before serving, toss vegetables with 1½ tablespoons marjoram or tarragon. Then spoon into a serving bowl and sprinkle with remaining ½ tablespoon marjoram or tarragon. Makes 4 servings.

	kcal	carb(gm)	fat(gm)	chol(mg)	Na(mg)	iron(mg)	Ca(mg)
lavish:	181	13	14	0	107	1.3	39
lean:	92	13	4	0	47	1.4	41

TENDER GREENS WITH GARLIC

Lavish

♦

As winter ends, delicate young greens spring from the earth. But you don't have to wait for the seasons to change to enjoy these fresh and simple flavors; today's greenhouse owners fly sweet, small-leafed greens right into local markets all year long.

4 unpeeled roasted garlic
   cloves, page 26, for garnish
2 large (about 1-lb. each)
   bunches greens, such as
   spinach, chard or dandelion
   greens, leaves only, washed
   well

1 raw garlic clove, cut in half
2 tablespoons butter
3 tablespoons olive oil
Salt and freshly ground white
   pepper to taste

Roast 1 head of garlic as directed for Roasted Garlic Heads with Rosemary (lavish), page 26, but omit rosemary. Set aside 4 roasted cloves for garnish and keep warm; use remaining roasted garlic as desired.

Place greens with whatever water clings to them (no other water is needed) in a large saucepan with a tight-fitting lid. Cover and cook over high heat, stirring once or twice, about 1 minute or just until leaves are wilted but still bright green. Drain very well, pressing down on greens with paper towels to dry them.

Rub a medium-size skillet with cut raw garlic clove; leave garlic clove in skillet. Add butter and oil and set over medium-high heat; sauté garlic until it turns golden and butter-oil mixture begins to color. Discard garlic. Increase heat to high, add drained greens and stir 30 seconds or just until greens are hot and well coated with butter and oil. Serve immediately on a heated platter, topped with warm roasted garlic cloves. Makes 4 servings.

Lean

4 unpeeled roasted garlic
  cloves, page 26, for garnish
2 large (about 1-lb. each)
  bunches greens, such as
  spinach, chard or dandelion
  greens, leaves only, washed
1 raw garlic clove, cut in half

½ teaspoon vegetable oil
1 raw garlic clove, minced
Freshly ground white pepper
1 tablespoon extra-virgin
  olive oil
2 teaspoons fresh lemon juice

Roast 1 head of garlic (see page 26) omitting rosemary. Set aside 4
roasted cloves for garnish and keep warm; use remaining roasted
garlic as desired. Place greens with whatever water clings to them
(no other water is needed) in a saucepan with a tight-fitting lid.
Cover and cook over high heat, stirring once or twice, about 1
minute or just until leaves are wilted but still bright green. Drain
well, pressing down on greens with paper towels to dry them.

Rub a skillet with cut raw garlic clove, then with vegetable oil.
Discard garlic. Add minced raw garlic and cook over medium heat
until garlic colors. Increase heat to medium-high, add greens and
toss until well heated. Remove from heat; add white pepper and
olive oil and toss again. Sprinkle with lemon juice and serve immediately on a heated platter, topped with warm roasted garlic
cloves. Makes 4 servings.

TIPS

*I like to mix the tender, sweet leaves of early vegetable greens in this dish.
Collards, chard, kale, and mustard, dandelion and beet greens are only
a few possible choices—with or without the spinach. When combining
greens, remember to adjust cooking times to the size and age of the greens
chosen, and to balance their flavors. Mustard greens can be pleasantly
bitter and spicy, for example, and kale mild. More mature greens taste
milder if blanched in water or broth rather than cooked by the steam-
braise method suggested here.*

	kcal	carb(gm)	fat(gm)	chol(mg)	Na(mg)	iron(mg)	Ca(mg)
lavish:	182	10	16	15	538	4.1	121
lean:	73	10	4	0	480	4.1	120

CARROTS WITH TARRAGON & GINGER

Lavish

♦

These lightly caramelized carrots are crunchy outside, soft in the center—
a change from the usual tender-crisp vegetables. If you sauté the carrots
in a copper pan or a heatproof casserole, you can serve them right in the
cooking pan.

4½ tablespoons unsalted
  butter
1 tablespoon grated fresh
  gingerroot
24 medium-size carrots,
  peeled, cut in ½-inch slices

2 tablespoons sugar
½ teaspoon salt or to taste
3 tablespoons chopped fresh
  tarragon leaves or 1½
  teaspoons dried leaf
  tarragon

In a large skillet or sauté pan with a lid, melt 3 tablespoons butter
over medium heat until foamy. Add gingerroot; stir 1 minute or
until aromatic. Add carrots, sugar and salt; toss to mix with ginger.
Reduce heat to medium-low, cover and cook 3 minutes. Uncover,
increase heat to high and cook, stirring occasionally, 5 minutes
longer or until liquid has evaporated and carrot slices are beginning
to brown. Remove from heat; toss with remaining 1½ tablespoons
butter, cut in bits. Stir in tarragon. Serve immediately, in cooking
pan (wipe down sides first) or in a heated serving bowl. Makes 8
servings.

Lean

2 tablespoons *each* frozen
concentrated apple juice
and frozen concentrated
orange juice
1½ tablespoons grated fresh
gingerroot
1 tablespoon grated lemon
zest

24 medium-size carrots,
peeled, cut in ¼-inch slices
2 teaspoons fresh lemon juice
3 tablespoons chopped fresh
tarragon leaves or 1½
teaspoons dried leaf
tarragon

In a large skillet or sauté pan with a lid, combine concentrated apple and orange juices with gingerroot and lemon zest. Cook over medium-high heat 1 minute or until gingerroot foams and liquid has partly evaporated. Stir in carrots; reduce heat to medium-low, cover and cook 5 minutes. Uncover, increase heat to high and stir carrots until liquid has evaporated. Remove from heat; toss with lemon juice and tarragon. Serve immediately, in cooking pan (wipe down sides first) or in a heated serving bowl. Makes 8 servings.

	kcal	carb(gm)	fat(gm)	chol(mg)	Na(mg)	iron(mg)	Ca(mg)
lavish:	162	25	7	17	274	1.1	63
lean:	118	27	.5	0	76	1.2	65

SAUTÉED TOMATOES & SPINACH

Lavish

♦

Robust and colorful, Sautéed Tomatoes & Spinach go well with grilled lamb or poultry.

2 large (about 1-lb. each)
  bunches spinach, leaves
  only, washed well
6 tablespoons butter
4 medium-size firm tomatoes
  (about 1 lb. *total*), peeled,
  seeded, cut in large chunks
Kernels cut from 2 ears fresh
  corn; or 1 cup frozen corn
  kernels, thawed

Salt and freshly ground
  pepper to taste
1 teaspoon fresh marjoram
  leaves or ½ teaspoon dried
  leaf marjoram
Pinch of sugar, if desired

Place spinach leaves with whatever water clings to them (no other water is needed) in a large saucepan with a tight-fitting lid. Cover and cook over high heat, stirring once or twice, about 1 minute or just until wilted but still bright green. Drain very well, chop coarsely and set aside on paper towels.

Melt 2 tablespoons butter in a large skillet over medium-high heat. Add tomatoes and sauté, stirring occasionally, 3 to 4 minutes or until tomatoes have released their juices and liquid has boiled away. Add 2 more tablespoons butter and corn; cook 1 minute, stirring until corn is heated through. Lightly season with salt and pepper. Melt remaining 2 tablespoons butter in skillet, then add drained spinach and marjoram; toss until spinach is warmed and vegetables are mixed. Season with salt and pepper. Add a pinch of sugar, if needed, and toss again. Serve immediately in a heated serving bowl. Makes 4 servings.

Lean

2 large (about 1-lb. each) bunches spinach, leaves only, washed well
½ teaspoon olive oil
2 shallots, minced
1 cup fruity white wine
4 medium-size firm tomatoes (about 1 lb. *total*), peeled, seeded, cut in large chunks
Kernels cut from 2 ears fresh corn; or 1 cup frozen corn kernels, thawed

Pinch of sugar
Freshly ground pepper to taste
1 teaspoon fresh thyme leaves or ⅓ teaspoon dried leaf thyme
1 teaspoon fresh marjoram leaves or ½ teaspoon dried leaf marjoram
2 teaspoons fresh lemon juice

Place spinach leaves with whatever water clings to them (no other water is needed) in a large saucepan with a tight-fitting lid. Cover and cook over high heat, stirring once or twice, about 1 minute or just until wilted but still bright green. Drain very well, chop coarsely and set aside on paper towels.

Rub a large skillet with oil. Add shallots and cook over medium-high heat 3 to 4 minutes or until they begin to brown. Increase heat to high; add wine and reduce to 2 tablespoons. Reduce heat to medium-high, add tomatoes and cook, stirring occasionally, 3 to 4 minutes or until tomatoes have released their juices and liquid has boiled away. Add corn and sugar to skillet; cook, stirring, 1 minute longer or until corn is heated through. Lightly season with pepper. Add drained spinach, thyme and marjoram; toss until spinach is warmed and vegetables are mixed. Then toss vegetables with lemon juice and serve immediately in a heated serving bowl. Makes 4 servings.

	kcal	carb(gm)	fat(gm)	chol(mg)	Na(mg)	iron(mg)	Ca(mg)
lavish:	248	20	18	46	364	6.9	242
lean:	119	22	2	0	194	7	238

MIDGE'S COLD VEGETABLE PLATTER

Lavish

◆

Midge Cowley, artist and fine cook, brings her instinct for beauty and flavor to everything she makes, as evidenced by this handsome dish. It is easily prepared ahead and can double as vegetable dish and salad. When you select the vegetables, imagine their colors in the finished dish; for example, baby beets, baby artichokes, small yellow summer squash and tiny zucchini surrounding a small cauliflower. The choices below are my favorites.

Midge's Dressing
4 Japanese eggplants,
   trimmed, cut in half
   lengthwise
Salt
2 red bell peppers, seeded,
   quartered
1 small (about 1-lb.)
   cauliflower, trimmed
8 small carrots, peeled
16 asparagus spears (about
   1-½ lbs. *total*), trimmed,
   peeled

2 tablespoons extra-virgin
   olive oil
2 tablespoons minced chives
¼ cup fresh cilantro leaves

MIDGE'S DRESSING
⅓ cup minced shallots
1 cup Japanese rice vinegar
2 teaspoons dried leaf basil
1 teaspoon dried dill weed
2 teaspoons *each* sugar and
   salt
⅓ cup olive oil

Prepare Midge's Dressing. Preheat oven to 425F (220C). Sprinkle cut sides of eggplants with salt and let stand 30 minutes; then wipe moisture and salt away with paper towels. Arrange eggplants and bell peppers, cut sides up, in a large, shallow baking dish. Drizzle 3 tablespoons dressing over eggplants and 2 tablespoons dressing over peppers. Bake, uncovered, 35 minutes or until eggplants and peppers are soft. Cool, basting occasionally with additional dressing. Marinate at room temperature up to 3 hours or cover and refrigerate up to 6 hours.

While eggplants and peppers are baking, steam remaining vegetables separately to desired doneness (tender-crisp or soft): whole cauliflower about 15 minutes; carrots about 8 minutes; asparagus 3 to 5 minutes. Set aside in separate dishes. Spoon some dressing over each. Marinate at room temperature up to 3 hours or cover and refrigerate up to 6 hours; toss occasionally.

To serve, arrange all vegetables attractively on a platter. Spoon on dressing to moisten as needed; then drizzle with oil. Sprinkle with chives and cilantro. Makes 8 to 10 servings.

Midge's Dressing: Place shallots and vinegar in a small saucepan. Bring to a boil; then reduce heat and simmer 1 minute. Cool, pour into a glass jar and add basil, dill weed, sugar and salt. Stir until sugar and salt are dissolved. Add oil, cover tightly and shake. Let stand at least 30 minutes before using to allow flavors to blend. Shake before using. Makes about 1¾ cups.

Lean

Follow directions for Midge's Cold Vegetable Platter (lavish), but omit salting step for eggplant and decrease extra-virgin olive oil to 1½ tablespoons (or omit it entirely). Use a lean version of Midge's Dressing. Makes 8 to 10 servings.

Midge's Dressing (lean): Follow directions above, but omit salt, decrease sugar to 1 teaspoon and decrease oil to 2 tablespoons. Makes about 1½ cups.

	kcal	carb(gm)	fat(gm)	chol(mg)	Na(mg)	iron(mg)	Ca(mg)
lavish:	201	21	13	0	570	1.9	75
lean:	143	20	7	0	36	1.9	70

GRILLED BASTED VEGETABLES

Lavish

♦

These are as good at room temperature as they are right off the fire. Grill the vegetables cut side down first to seal in the juices.

Midge's Dressing, page 199
1 garlic clove, minced
1 medium-size eggplant or 4 Japanese eggplants, trimmed
Salt
1 *each* red and yellow bell pepper (or 2 green bell peppers)
4 small sweet red or white onions, peeled, cut in half lengthwise

4 zucchini, trimmed, cut in half lengthwise
8 large mushrooms, cut in half lengthwise
4 Italian (plum) tomatoes, cut in half crosswise
4 small (about 1½-inch diameter) red thin-skinned potatoes, unpeeled, boiled, cut in half
Watercress for garnish

Prepare Midge's Dressing; add garlic to dressing and set aside. Ignite coals and let burn until ash is white and flames have subsided. Set grill 5 to 6 inches above coals.

If using medium-size eggplant, cut in half lengthwise; then cut each half lengthwise in 4 wedges. Or cut Japanese eggplants in half lengthwise. Sprinkle cut sides of eggplant with salt and let stand 30 minutes; then wipe moisture and salt away with paper towels. Cut bell peppers in half lengthwise; remove seeds and white pith. Cut each pepper half in half crosswise.

Just before grilling, moisten cut sides of vegetables with dressing. If vegetables are to be served hot off the grill, add them to grill in order of cooking time—longest cooking time first (see opposite).

To cook, arrange vegetables, cut side down, on grill. Cook until cut sides are browned and vegetables begin to soften; baste uncooked sides with dressing and turn vegetables with tongs. Baste again with dressing; continue to cook until second side is browned and vegetables are as soft as desired. Total cooking times are about 25 minutes for onions, 20 minutes for eggplant, 15 minutes for zucchini, 15 minutes for bell peppers, 15 minutes for mushrooms, 10 minutes for tomatoes and 10 minutes for potatoes.

Serve vegetables immediately; or cover loosely and keep warm in a low oven up to 2 hours; or let stand at room temperature up to 3 hours.

Serve on a heated or room-temperature platter, garnished with watercress. Makes 8 servings.

Lean

Follow directions for Grilled Basted Vegetables (lavish), opposite, using the lean version of Midge's Dressing (see page 199). Use Japanese eggplants and omit salting step. Omit small red thin-skinned potatoes; instead, use 4 small summer squash, such as pattypan squash, cut into 1½-inch chunks. Total grilling time for squash is about 10 minutes. Makes 8 servings.

TIPS

Grilled vegetables soften when they're kept warm after cooking, so if you like them tender-crisp, serve them hot off the grill or at room temperature.

Rinse all unpeeled vegetables well in running water to remove any pesticide or fertilizer residues.

	kcal	carb(gm)	fat(gm)	chol(mg)	Na(mg)	iron(mg)	Ca(mg)
lavish:	163	19	10	0	543	1.6	62
lean:	111	18	4	0	10	1.7	75

ROASTED POTATOES WITH GARLIC

Lavish

♦

Anne Kupper brought this recipe back from Richard Olney after visiting with him in Provence. I find it a particularly good accompaniment for grilled poultry and lamb. Allow about three small potatoes per serving— more for potato lovers. The cooked garlic is mild and creamy; squeeze it right onto the potatoes for a tasty treat.

24 small (about 1½-inch-
   diameter) red thin-skinned
   potatoes, unpeeled
⅓ cup olive oil
1 tablespoon salt
Freshly ground pepper to
   taste

1 tablespoon dried leaf thyme,
   crushed
24 whole garlic cloves,
   unpeeled
5 bay leaves

Preheat oven to 400F (205C). Arrange potatoes close together in a large, shallow baking dish that can come to the table. Coat potatoes well with oil and season on all sides with salt, pepper and thyme. Drop unpeeled garlic cloves between potatoes. Arrange bay leaves decoratively between potatoes. Roast potatoes, uncovered, 1 hour or until tender. Serve immediately. To eat, pinch garlic cloves to squeeze garlic onto potatoes. Makes 8 servings.

Lean

Rub these potatoes with lemon juice and you won't miss the salt.

½ cup fresh lemon juice
24 small (about 1½-inch-
   diameter) red thin-skinned
   potatoes, unpeeled
Freshly ground pepper to
   taste
1 tablespoon dried leaf thyme,
   crushed

24 whole garlic cloves,
   unpeeled
5 bay leaves
1½ tablespoons extra-virgin
   olive oil, if desired

Preheat oven to 400F (205C). Pour lemon juice into a small dish and coat potatoes well with juice; then season potatoes on all sides with pepper and thyme. Let potatoes stand about 15 minutes or until dry, turning as needed to dry evenly. Arrange potatoes close together in a large, shallow baking dish that can come to the table. Drop unpeeled garlic cloves between potatoes. Arrange bay leaves decoratively between potatoes. Roast potatoes, uncovered, 1 hour or until tender. Drizzle potatoes with oil, if desired, and serve immediately. To eat, pinch garlic cloves to squeeze garlic onto potatoes. Makes 8 servings.

	kcal	carb(gm)	fat(gm)	chol(mg)	Na(mg)	iron(mg)	Ca(mg)
lavish:	183	24	9	0	607	1	34
lean:	41	5	3	0	3.2	.7	25

LIA'S RICE, LEEK & ASPARAGUS CUSTARD

Lavish

♦

Lia Benedetti's fine hand in the kitchen comes from her mother, a natural cook, and her father, formerly chef at New York's Waldorf-Astoria Hotel. She's developed her own cooking style, pure and fresh, right out of her Italian past. Lia serves the lean version of this custard with salad for a light but filling supper.

2 tablespoons *each* butter and olive oil
3 leeks, white part only, washed well, chopped
2 garlic cloves, minced
1 pound medium-size fresh asparagus spears, trimmed, cut in ½-inch slices; or 1 (10-oz.) package frozen asparagus spears, cut in ½-inch slices
1½ cups cooked rice
⅓ cup milk

1 scant cup whipping cream
3 large eggs, lightly beaten
¼ cup flat-leaf parsley leaves, chopped
½ cup grated Parmesan cheese (about 1½ oz.)
¾ cup grated mozzarella cheese (3 oz.)
Salt and ground pepper
¾ teaspoon ground nutmeg
2 tablespoons grated Parmesan cheese
Pinch of ground nutmeg

Preheat oven to 325F (165C). Generously butter a medium-size casserole. Melt 2 tablespoons butter in oil in a skillet over medium heat. Add leeks and cook, stirring occasionally, about 10 minutes or until soft. Add garlic and asparagus. Cook, stirring, 3 to 5 minutes or until asparagus softens but is still tender-crisp.

Remove skillet from heat. Add rice, milk, cream and eggs. Add parsley, ½ cup Parmesan cheese and mozzarella cheese; gently toss until well mixed. Season with salt, pepper and ¾ teaspoon nutmeg and toss again. Spoon into buttered casserole. Sprinkle with 2 tablespoons Parmesan cheese and a pinch of nutmeg. Bake, uncovered, 40 minutes or until a thin knife blade inserted in center of custard comes out clean.

Serve custard from casserole onto heated individual plates. Makes 8 servings.

Lean

1 teaspoon olive oil
3 leeks, white part only, washed well, coarsely chopped
2 garlic cloves, minced
1 pound medium-size fresh asparagus spears, trimmed, cut in ½-inch slices; or 1 (10-oz.) package frozen asparagus spears, thawed, patted dry, cut in ½-inch slices
1½ cups cooked rice
1 cup non-fat milk

2 large eggs plus 2 eggs whites, lightly beaten
Freshly ground pepper to taste
1 teaspoon ground nutmeg
¼ cup flat-leaf parsley leaves, chopped
⅓ cup grated Parmesan cheese (about 1 oz.)
½ cup grated skim milk mozzarella cheese (2 oz.)
1 tablespoon grated Parmesan cheese
Pinch of ground nutmeg

Preheat oven to 325F (165C). Rub a medium-size casserole with ½ teaspoon oil; rub remaining ½ teaspoon oil over bottom of a large skillet with a lid. Add leeks and garlic to skillet. Cover and cook over medium heat, stirring occasionally to prevent sticking, 10 minutes or until leeks are soft but not browned. Add asparagus; cover and continue to cook, stirring occasionally, 3 to 5 minutes or just until asparagus is beginning to soften but is still tender-crisp.

Remove skillet from heat. Add rice, milk, eggs and egg whites; season with pepper and 1 teaspoon nutmeg. Add parsley, ⅓ cup Parmesan cheese and mozzarella cheese; gently toss until well mixed. Spoon into oiled casserole. Sprinkle with 1 tablespoon Parmesan cheese and a pinch of nutmeg. Bake, uncovered, 40 minutes or until a thin knife blade inserted in center of custard comes out clean.

Serve custard from casserole onto heated individual plates. Makes 8 servings.

	kcal	carb(gm)	fat(gm)	chol(mg)	Na(mg)	iron(mg)	Ca(mg)
lavish:	328	21	23	158	265	2.3	250
lean:	166	21	5	76	180	2.2	204

POLENTA WITH TOASTED BUCKWHEAT

Lavish

♦

We tasted these flavors in front of a tiny village café in Switzerland's Engadin Valley under the warm, alpine sun. The polenta was made with coarsely cut corn kernels which are hard to find in the United States. Yellow (corn) grits, a kind of coarse cornmeal available in health food stores, make a fine substitute.

2½ cups water, see TIP	1 cup yellow corn grits or
1 cup rich Chicken Stock,	yellow cornmeal, see TIP
page 15, or commercial	2½ ounces imported Gruyère
stock (unsalted)	cheese, grated
1 cup rich Beef Stock, page	½ cup (4-oz.) unsalted butter,
16, or commercial stock	cut in pieces
(unsalted)	2 tablespoons whole
1 teaspoon coarse salt	buckwheat groats (kasha)

Butter a medium-size casserole (for baking and serving). Bring water, stock and salt to a boil in a heavy-bottomed pot. Lower heat until liquid simmers. Slowly sprinkle grits into simmering liquid (to keep lumps from forming), and stir with a wide, flat spoon.

Preheat broiler. Simmer polenta, stirring often to avoid sticking, for 20 minutes. Mixture should look like thick hot cereal. Stir in cheese until melted, then butter until melted. Transfer immediately to casserole. Sprinkle with buckwheat groats and place about 5 inches from broiler until buckwheat is browned, about 4 minutes.

Serve immediately. Makes 4 servings.

TIPS

Corn grits from various parts of the country absorb differing quantities of water. If, when cooking the polenta, the mixture seems too thick, stir in a little boiling water until it is smooth and the water is absorbed.

If cornmeal is used, reduce liquid by 1 cup and reduce cooking time to 5 minutes.

Lean

This polenta gains flavor with the increased quantity of broth, and I like it every bit as well as its butter-enriched cousin. I think it needs salt, but if your stock is double strength, leave it out. The 2½ ounces of Gruyère cheese add a lovely undertone but some fat. You can balance the day's meals and cut fat in other dishes or keep the polenta in line with the American Heart Association's recommended daily fat intake of less than 30 percent of total calories by cutting the quantity of Gruyère in half, to 1¼ ounces. This version is good with ragouts (stews) and pot roasts.

2¼ cups rich Chicken Stock, page 15, or commercial stock (unsalted)
2¼ cups rich Beef Stock, page 16, or commercial stock (unsalted)
1 teaspoon coarse salt
1 cup yellow corn grits or yellow cornmeal, see lavish TIP, opposite

2½ ounces imported Gruyère cheese, grated
2 tablespoons whole buckwheat groats (kasha)

Rub a medium-size casserole with cooking oil. Bring stock and salt to a simmer in a heavy-bottomed pot. Slowly sprinkle grits into simmering stock (to keep lumps from forming), and stir with a wide, flat spoon.

Preheat broiler. Simmer polenta, stirring often to avoid mixture sticking on bottom of pan, for 20 minutes. Mixture should look like thick hot cereal. Stir in cheese until melted. Immediately transfer to casserole. Sprinkle with buckwheat groats and broil 5 inches from heat source until buckwheat is browned, about 4 minutes.

Serve immediately. Makes 4 servings.

	kcal	carb(gm)	fat(gm)	chol(mg)	Na(mg)	iron(mg)	Ca(mg)
lavish:	338	12	29	82	496	1	197
lean:	134	12	6	20	493	.9	191

ROASTED BARLEY & PINE NUTS

Lavish

♦

Barley and I go back to my little girl days when, as a special treat, I shared Scotch Broth at a New York lunch counter with my father. Since then it remains one of my favorite comfort foods, but I've grown to appreciate its inherently nutty flavor and chewy texture when just slightly undercooked. If you like the grain with a softer consistency add about 10 minutes to the cooking time. The dish is a fine complement to roasted and broiled meats.

½ cup (4-oz.) unsalted butter
¾ cup pine nuts
1 cup pearl barley, rinsed and drained
1 medium-size onion, chopped
½ cup chives, chopped
½ cup flat-leafed parsley, chopped

¼ teaspoon freshly ground pepper
1¾ cups Chicken Stock, page 15, or commercial stock
1¾ cups Beef Stock, page 16, or commercial stock
Salt, if desired

Lightly butter a 2½-quart casserole (for baking and serving) with sides that are at least 3½-inches high. Preheat oven to 375F (190C).

Melt 2 tablespoons butter in a heavy skillet, add pine nuts and sauté until nuts are lightly browned. Remove and set aside.

Add remaining 4 tablespoons butter to skillet. Add barley and onion and sauté until barley is brown and toasted and onion is softened. Remove from heat, stir in ¼ cup chives, parsley and pepper and scrape into buttered casserole. Bring stock to a boil and pour over barley mixture, stirring. Bake uncovered for one hour, until all liquid is absorbed and barley is tender. Stir again and taste for seasoning. Season with salt if desired.

To serve, sprinkle with remaining chives. Makes 8 servings.

Lean

To heighten flavors, roast the barley and pine nuts and slowly ''sweat'' the onion.

¼ cup pine nuts
1 cup pearl barley, rinsed
1 medium-size onion, chopped
½ cup wild rice or brown rice
½ cup chopped parsley
½ cup chives, chopped
Freshly ground pepper

2 cups Chicken Stock, page 15, or commercial stock
2½ cups Beef Stock, page 16, or commercial stock
¼ cup lemon juice
1½ tablespoons concentrated apple juice
1 tablespoon unsalted butter, cut in bits
¾ teaspoon salt, if desired

Rub a 3-quart casserole (for baking and serving) and a heavy skillet with a lid with a little cooking oil. Preheat oven to 400F (205C).

Lightly brown pine nuts in oven about 3 minutes or until light brown. Spoon into casserole. Toast barley in oven about 7 minutes or until dark. Spoon into casserole. Watch them carefully so they don't burn!

Lower oven temperature to 375F (190C). Sauté onion in skillet over medium-high heat until it begins to color. Cover tightly, reduce to low heat and sweat the onion 5 minutes, stirring occasionally, until softened and brown. Scrape into casserole. Add rice, parsley, ¼ cup chives and ground pepper to casserole.

Bring stock, lemon juice and apple juice concentrate to a boil. Pour over barley mixture and stir. Bake uncovered for one hour, until liquid is absorbed and barley is tender. Stir again, add butter and taste for seasoning. Season with salt if desired.

To serve, sprinkle with remaining chopped chives. Makes 8 generous servings.

	kcal	carb(gm)	fat(gm)	chol(mg)	Na(mg)	iron(mg)	Ca(mg)
lavish:	282	24	19	32	33	2.7	25
lean:	194	34	5	4	42	2	31

BLACK BEANS CHIAPAS

Lavish

♦

Many years ago I tasted a black bean dish prepared by a fine Indian cook in San Cristobal de las Casas, Mexico. I remembered the flavors and have re-created the dish in my kitchen many times with ingredients from local food stores. Epazote, a dried Mexican herb, is available in Mexican and Latin American markets.

1 pound dried black beans
2 pounds ripe tomatoes
1 large onion, chopped
4 garlic cloves, minced
1 pound bacon, cut in ½-inch
  pieces
Salt and freshly ground
  pepper to taste

Pinch of sugar
2 tablespoons crumbled dried
  epazote or 1½ teaspoons
  dried leaf oregano
½ cup dairy sour cream for
  garnish
Cilantro sprigs for garnish

Place beans in a strainer; wash with cold water. Set aside. Peel and seed tomatoes, reserving juice. Measure juice; add enough water to make 2½ quarts liquid. Coarsely chop tomatoes and set aside.

In a large, heavy pot with ovenproof handles, combine beans and the 2½ quarts juice-water mixture. Stir in onion, garlic and half the bacon. Bring to a boil over high heat. Reduce heat to low, cover pot and simmer 1 hour and 40 minutes, stirring occasionally.

In a medium-size skillet, cook remaining bacon over medium heat until crisp. Drain on paper towels. Discard all but 2 tablespoons of the bacon drippings; cook chopped tomatoes in reserved 2 tablespoons drippings over medium-high heat, stirring frequently, until sauce thickens. Season with salt, pepper and sugar.

Preheat oven to 300F (150C). Stir tomato sauce, cooked bacon and epazote or oregano into cooked beans. Season lightly with salt and pepper. Bake, uncovered, stirring occasionally to prevent sticking, 1½ hours or until most of liquid has been absorbed. If prepared ahead, cool, cover and refrigerate up to 1 week; sauce will thicken and beans become more flavorful. To reheat, bake, uncovered, stirring occasionally, for 1 hour at 300F (150C).

Serve beans on heated individual plates; garnish each serving with 1 tablespoon sour cream and cilantro sprigs. (Or serve beans from pot or in a heated deep earthenware casserole.) Makes 8 generous servings.

Lean

This dish reminds me of a bustling Indian market in Mexico's state of Chiapas, its aisles filled with fresh tomatoes and greens, mounds of beans and onions and rows of herbs and spices. Indians in tribal clothing shop alongside northerners like me and carry their black beans and tomatoes home on their backs in soft, woven bags.

1 pound dried black beans
2 pounds ripe tomatoes
About 9 cups unsalted
    Chicken Stock, page 15, or
    commercial, or water
½ teaspoon olive oil
1 large onion, chopped
4 garlic cloves, minced
4 ounces lean ham, diced
¼ cup fresh lemon juice

2 teaspoons sugar
Freshly ground pepper to
    taste
2 tablespoons crumbled dried
    epazote or 2 teaspoons
    dried leaf oregano
½ cup Creamy Non-fat
    Yogurt, page 22, or
    commercial, for garnish
Cilantro sprigs for garnish

Place beans in a strainer; wash with cold water. Set aside. Peel and seed tomatoes, reserving juice. Measure juice; add enough stock or water to make 2½ quarts liquid. Coarsely chop tomatoes and set aside.

Rub a medium-size skillet with oil. Add onion and cook over medium-low heat, stirring occasionally, until softened. Add garlic and continue to cook until onion begins to brown.

In a large, heavy pot with ovenproof handles, combine beans and the 2½ quarts juice-water mixture. Stir in ham, then cooked onion and garlic (do not rinse out skillet). Bring to a boil over high heat. Reduce heat to low, cover pot and simmer 1 hour and 40 minutes, stirring occasionally.

Place chopped tomatoes and lemon juice in skillet. Cook over medium-high heat, stirring frequently, until sauce thickens. Season with sugar and pepper. Set aside.

Preheat oven to 300F (150C). Stir tomato sauce and epazote or oregano into cooked beans. Bake, uncovered, stirring occasionally to prevent sticking, 1½ hours or until most of liquid has been absorbed. If prepared ahead, cool, cover and refrigerate up to 1 week; sauce will thicken and beans become more flavorful. To reheat, bake, uncovered, stirring occasionally, for 1 hour at 300F (150C).

Serve beans on heated individual plates; garnish each serving with 1 tablespoon yogurt and cilantro sprigs. (Or serve beans from pot or in a heated deep earthenware casserole.) Makes 8 generous servings.

	kcal	carb(gm)	fat(gm)	chol(mg)	Na(mg)	iron(mg)	Ca(mg)
lavish:	468	22	32	54	1460	2.9	61
lean:	145	23	2	8	210	2.1	66

CUCUMBER & YOGURT WITH CARDAMOM

Lavish

♦

Serve this Middle Eastern-style yogurt salad with pita bread and grilled lamb or chicken. You can substitute a teaspoon or so of toasted cumin seeds (see TIP) for the cardamom.

2 cups yogurt
1 large cucumber, peeled,
  seeded, cut in ½-inch dice
1 garlic clove, pressed

1½ to 2 teaspoons ground
  cardamom
Pinch of sugar
Salt to taste

In a medium-size bowl, mix yogurt, cucumber, garlic and cardamom. Season with sugar and salt. If prepared ahead, cover and refrigerate up to 1 day. Remove from refrigerator 15 minutes before serving.

To serve, place in a serving dish; then spoon into individual small bowls. Makes 4 servings.

TIP

To toast cumin seeds, rub a small skillet with ½ teaspoon olive oil. Add cumin seeds and toast over medium-high heat, stirring frequently, about 3 minutes or until seeds begin to darken and pop.

Lean

2 cups Creamy Non-fat
Yogurt, page 22, or
commercial
1 large cucumber, peeled,
seeded, cut in ½-inch dice
3 tablespoons grated red
onion

1 garlic clove, pressed
1½ to 2 teaspoons ground
cardamom
Pinch of sugar

In a medium-size bowl, mix yogurt, cucumber, onion, garlic and cardamom. Season with sugar. If prepared ahead, cover and refrigerate up to 1 day. Remove from refrigerator 15 minutes before serving.

To serve, place in a serving dish; then spoon into individual small bowls. Makes 4 servings.

TIP

To toast cumin seeds, follow directions in TIP opposite, but omit oil. Or toast seeds in the oven as directed on page 30.

	kcal	carb(gm)	fat(gm)	chol(mg)	Na(mg)	iron(mg)	Ca(mg)
lavish:	83	8	4	14	56	.8	156
lean:	57	8	0	2	65	.1	328

ORANGE & TOMATO SALAD WITH CILANTRO

Lavish

♦

Cilantro adds a pungent, assertive flavor to this salad. If it is not available, substitute fresh tarragon or flat-leaf parsley. Seedless Valencia oranges are ideal here, as are ripe, sweet tomatoes.

2 cups diced oranges (½-inch dice), free of all membrane and white pith, seeded, if necessary (about 5 large oranges)
2 cups ½-inch chunks of ripe tomatoes (about 4 medium-size tomatoes)
Dressing
½ cup chopped fresh cilantro leaves

DRESSING
¼ teaspoon salt, or to taste
Freshly ground pepper to taste
1 tablespoon balsamic vinegar; or scant ½ teaspoon sugar dissolved in 1½ tablespoons red wine vinegar
1 tablespoon fresh orange juice
¼ cup extra-virgin olive oil

Drain diced oranges 15 minutes; also drain tomatoes 15 minutes. Set aside 1 tablespoon orange juice for dressing; reserve remaining orange juice and tomato juice for another use. Prepare Dressing. Just before serving, combine Dressing with oranges, tomatoes and cilantro.

Serve salad in a glass bowl to show off its beautiful colors. Makes 8 servings.

Dressing: Whisk salt, pepper, vinegar and orange juice until salt is dissolved. Whisk in oil; taste and adjust seasonings. Whisk again just before using. Makes ⅓ cup.

Lean

2 cups diced oranges (½-inch dice), free of all membrane and white pith, seeded, if necessary (about 5 large oranges)

2 cups ½-inch chunks of ripe tomatoes (about 4 medium-size tomatoes)

Dressing

½ cup chopped fresh cilantro leaves

DRESSING

1 small ripe tomato, seeded, juiced, coarsely chopped

1 tablespoon balsamic vinegar; or scant ½ teaspoon sugar dissolved in 1½ tablespoons red wine vinegar

Freshly ground pepper to taste

2 tablespoons fresh orange juice

1 tablespoon fresh lemon juice

Drain diced oranges 15 minutes; also drain tomatoes 15 minutes. Set aside 2 tablespoons orange juice for dressing; reserve remaining orange juice and tomato juice for another use. Prepare Dressing. Just before serving, combine Dressing with oranges, tomatoes and cilantro.

Serve salad in a glass bowl to show off its beautiful colors. Makes 8 servings.

Dressing: In a blender or a food processor fitted with a metal blade, puree tomato. Strain puree; measure out 2 tablespoons. Whisk tomato puree, vinegar, pepper, orange juice and lemon juice until blended; taste and adjust seasonings. Whisk again just before using. Makes ⅓ cup.

	kcal	carb(gm)	fat(gm)	chol(mg)	Na(mg)	iron(mg)	Ca(mg)
lavish:	95	9	7	0	73	.6	28
lean:	40	10	0	0	8	.7	29

ARUGULA, GREENS & CHEESE SALAD

Lavish

♦

On my counter next to a few stray arugula leaves were some scraps of Appenzeller cheese, grated for a cheese pudding. Tossed together, they made a perfect lunch. You can combine the arugula with other robust greens, such as radicchio, daikon sprouts, and river or watercress.

The greens can be washed and dried, then loosely wrapped in kitchen towels and refrigerated up to 1 day. The cheese can also be grated, loosely covered with plastic wrap and refrigerated up to 1 day ahead.

Dressing
2 quarts arugula leaves or other robustly flavored assorted greens, such as radish greens, radicchio, rivercress, watercress or spinach, washed, dried, torn in pieces
3¼ cups coarsely grated Appenzeller or Gruyère cheese (13 oz.)
¼ cup hazelnut or walnut oil

DRESSING
1 tablespoon balsamic vinegar
2 tablespoons sherry wine vinegar or red wine vinegar
1 garlic clove, unpeeled, halved
½ teaspoon salt, or to taste
Freshly ground pepper
½ teaspoon dry mustard
¼ cup hazelnut or walnut oil
¼ cup light vegetable oil

Prepare Dressing. Place greens in a large salad bowl. Cover greens with grated cheese. Add ¼ cup hazelnut or walnut oil; toss to coat greens and distribute cheese. Whisk Dressing; spoon ½ cup Dressing over cheese and greens. Toss; taste and adjust seasonings. Add remaining dressing as needed. Serve immediately, spooning salad from bowl onto individual plates. Makes 8 servings.

Dressing: In a small glass, ceramic or stainless steel bowl, whisk vinegars, garlic, salt, pepper and mustard until salt is dissolved. Whisk in remaining oils. Let stand at room temperature at least 30 minutes or up to 6 hours. Just before serving, remove garlic and whisk again. Makes ⅔ cup.

Lean

Dressing
2 quarts arugula leaves or other robustly flavored assorted garden greens such as radish greens, radicchio, rivercress, watercress or spinach, washed, dried, torn in bite-size pieces
3¼ cups grated lowfat, low-sodium Swiss cheese such as Swiss Delicat (13 oz.)
3 tablespoons extra-virgin olive oil

DRESSING
2 tablespoons balsamic vinegar
2 tablespoons sherry wine vinegar or red wine vinegar
¼ cup Japanese rice vinegar
1 garlic clove, unpeeled, halved
½ teaspoon dry mustard

Prepare Dressing. Place greens in a large salad bowl. Cover greens with grated cheese. Add oil; toss to coat greens and distribute cheese. Whisk Dressing; spoon over cheese and greens. Toss; taste and adjust seasonings. Serve immediately, spooning from bowl onto individual plates. Makes 8 servings.

Dressing: In a small glass, ceramic or stainless steel bowl, whisk all ingredients until blended. Let stand at room temperature at least 30 minutes or up to 6 hours. Just before serving, remove garlic and whisk again. Makes ½ cup.

	kcal	carb(gm)	fat(gm)	chol(mg)	Na(mg)	iron(mg)	Ca(mg)
lavish:	416	10	39	63	291	1.7	654
lean:	210	10	13	24	97	1.7	232

GREENS WITH WALNUTS & PEARS

Lavish

♦

Assorted fresh greens, some mild, some assertive, mix with tangy-sweet pears in this salad. Try dandelion leaves, baby spinach and tasty local greens for character and flavor.

Dressing
2 firm-ripe pears such as
    Anjou, Bartlett or Bosc; or 3
    firm-ripe Seckel pears
1 pound assorted salad
    greens, washed, dried, torn
    in bite-size pieces
1 cup toasted chopped
    walnuts

DRESSING
3 tablespoons red wine
    vinegar

2 teaspoons balsamic vinegar
    or sherry wine vinegar
1 teaspoon salt
Freshly ground pepper to
    taste
Pinch *each* of dry mustard and
    curry powder
1 garlic clove, unpeeled,
    halved
½ cup *each* walnut oil and
    light vegetable oil, such as
    safflower

Prepare Dressing. Just before serving, peel and core pears; cut into ½-inch chunks. In a large salad bowl, toss greens with Dressing.

To serve, divide dressed greens among 8 salad plates. Arrange pears over and among greens; scatter toasted walnuts on top. Serve immediately. Makes 8 servings.

Dressing: In a small glass, ceramic or stainless steel bowl, whisk vinegars, salt, pepper, mustard, curry powder and garlic until salt is dissolved and seasonings are blended. Whisk in oils. Taste and adjust seasonings. Let stand at room temperature at least 30 minutes or up to 6 hours. Just before serving, remove garlic and whisk again. Makes 1¼ cups.

TIP

Greens can be washed and dried, then loosely wrapped in damp kitchen towels and refrigerated up to 1 day in advance.

Lean

Just ⅓ cup of oil is enough to coat the greens, adding an appetizing smoothness. The dressing is oil-free.

Dressing
2 firm-ripe pears such as
  Anjou, Bartlett or Bosc; or 3
  firm-ripe Seckel pears
1 pound assorted salad
  greens, washed, dried, torn
  in bite-size pieces
⅓ cup walnut oil
⅓ cup toasted chopped
  walnuts

DRESSING
6 tablespoons Japanese rice
  vinegar
1 tablespoon plus 1 teaspoon
  balsamic vinegar or sherry
  wine vinegar
Freshly ground pepper to
  taste
¼ teaspoon *each* dry mustard
  and curry powder
1 garlic clove, unpeeled,
  halved

Prepare Dressing. Just before serving, peel and core pears; cut into ½-inch chunks. In a large salad bowl, toss greens with oil until well coated. Toss again with half the Dressing; add additional Dressing to taste.

To serve, divide dressed greens among 8 salad plates. Arrange pears over and among greens; scatter toasted walnuts on top. Serve immediately. Makes 8 servings.

Dressing: In a small glass, ceramic or stainless steel bowl, whisk all ingredients until blended. Taste and adjust seasonings. Let stand at room temperature at least 30 minutes or up to 6 hours. Just before serving, remove garlic and whisk again. Makes ½ cup.

	kcal	carb(gm)	fat(gm)	chol(mg)	Na(mg)	iron(mg)	Ca(mg)
lavish:	379	13	37	0	303	1.6	78
lean:	155	12	12	0	36	1.3	68

ROASTED JAPANESE EGGPLANTS WITH HOT CHEESE

Lavish
♦

Here's a wonderful eggplant salad that I often serve before a meal with port or sherry.

8 Japanese eggplants,
 trimmed
Salt
3 garlic cloves, minced
½ cup olive oil
1 tablespoon balsamic vinegar
 or 1½ tablespoons red wine
 vinegar or sherry wine
 vinegar
Freshly ground pepper to
 taste

⅓ cup olive oil
8 ounces mild, soft goat
 cheese
½ cup unseasoned fine dry
 bread crumbs
8 butter lettuce leaves or
 leaves of other mild greens
24 tiny yellow pear tomatoes
 or cherry tomatoes
3 tablespoons chopped fresh
 marjoram or chives

Cut eggplants in half lengthwise. Sprinkle cut sides with salt and let stand 30 minutes, then wipe moisture and salt away with paper towels. Preheat oven to 375F (190C). Combine garlic and ½ cup oil. Arrange eggplants, cut sides up, in a large, shallow baking dish. Spoon garlic-oil mixture over eggplants; roast, uncovered, 25 minutes or until soft and beginning to brown. Place eggplants on a large platter; combine any oil from baking dish with vinegar and spoon over eggplants. Season with pepper. If prepared ahead, cover loosely and let stand at room temperature up to 5 hours.

Oil a small, shallow baking dish with some of the ⅓ cup oil. Form goat cheese into 8 small patties; roll in remaining oil, then in bread crumbs. Arrange in baking dish. (At this point, you may cover and refrigerate up to 8 hours.)

Just before serving, bake cheese in 350F (175C) oven 6 minutes or until melting-hot. To serve, place a lettuce leaf on each of 8 salad plates. Arrange 2 eggplant halves over lettuce; spoon oil and vinegar from platter over eggplant halves. Tuck a portion of hot cheese halfway under each lettuce leaf. Garnish each plate with 3 pear or cherry tomatoes and sprinkle with marjoram or chives. Makes 8 servings.

Lean

1 teaspoon olive oil
8 Japanese eggplants
3 garlic cloves, minced
1 tablespoon balsamic vinegar
  or 1½ tablespoons sherry
  wine vinegar
Freshly ground pepper
½ teaspoon olive oil
8 ounces skim milk
  mozzarella cheese

1 egg white
½ cup unseasoned fine dry
  bread crumbs
8 butter lettuce leaves
24 tiny yellow pear tomatoes
  or cherry tomatoes
3 sun-dried tomatoes, cut in
  slivers
3 tablespoons chopped fresh
  marjoram or chives

Preheat oven to 375F (190C). Rub a large, shallow baking dish with 1 teaspoon oil. Cut eggplants in half lengthwise. Sprinkle garlic over cut sides of eggplants; press into flesh. Arrange eggplants, cut sides down, in oiled baking dish. Roast, uncovered, 25 minutes or until soft and beginning to brown. Turn eggplants cut sides up and place on a large platter; scrape cooked garlic bits over eggplants, sprinkle with vinegar and season with pepper. If prepared ahead, cover loosely and let stand at room temperature up to 5 hours.

Oil a small, shallow baking dish with ½ teaspoon oil. Cut cheese into 8 portions. Beat egg white until foamy; roll cheese pieces in egg white, then in bread crumbs. Arrange in baking dish. (At this point, you may cover and refrigerate up to 8 hours.)

Just before serving, bake cheese in 350F (175C) oven 6 minutes or until melting-hot. To serve, place a lettuce leaf on each of 8 salad plates. Arrange 2 eggplant halves over lettuce; spoon any juices and vinegar from platter over eggplant halves. Tuck a portion of hot cheese halfway under each lettuce leaf. Garnish each plate with 3 pear or cherry tomatoes and some slivered sun-dried tomatoes; sprinkle with marjoram or chives. Makes 8 servings.

	kcal	carb(gm)	fat(gm)	chol(mg)	Na(mg)	iron(mg)	Ca(mg)
lavish:	830	13	29	25	442	1.4	176
lean:	148	14	6	16	200	1.4	223

LENTIL SALAD WITH WATERCRESS

Lavish

◆

I like lentils in almost any dish: as soup, hot side dish or salad. This family favorite goes well with grilled meat and poultry; it's especially good with lamb. You can use arugula or young nasturtium leaves for spicy greens in place of the watercress.

1 cup lentils
3 cups cold water
1 medium-size onion,
    quartered
2 garlic cloves, minced
1 bay leaf
1 teaspoon ground cardamom
¾ teaspoon salt
Bouquet Garni
⅔ cup red onion, finely
    chopped

1 cup watercress leaves,
    loosely packed
Zest of 1 lemon, minced
¼ cup extra virgin olive oil
2 tablespoons fresh lemon
    juice
Freshly ground pepper

BOUQUET GARNI
3 whole cloves
3 whole allspice berries

Wash lentils, picking through them to remove any pebbles. Place in a medium-size pot. Add water, onion, garlic, bay leaf, cardamom, salt and Bouquet Garni. Bring to a boil, reduce heat to medium-low and cook uncovered for 20 minutes or until lentils are tender but not mushy; drain and cool. Remove and discard bay leaf, onion and Bouquet Garni and transfer lentils to a bowl. Gently mix red onion, watercress leaves and lemon zest into lentils. Drizzle olive oil over and toss. Add lemon juice and ground pepper. Taste to adjust seasonings. Serve immediately, or cover and refrigerate without watercress up to three days, return to room temperature, and add watercress.

Serve at room temperature. Transfer to serving dish. Makes 4 to 6 servings.

Bouquet Garni: Tie cloves and allspice berries in a piece of washed cheesecloth.

Lean

A generous portion of these lentils combined with rice provides as nutritious a protein as a serving of meat, fish or poultry, see TIP, page 226.

1 cup lentils
2 cups Chicken Stock, page 15, or commercial stock, see TIP, page 266
1 cup Beef Stock, page 16, or commercial stock, see TIP, page 226
1 medium-size onion, quartered
2 garlic cloves, minced
1 bay leaf
1 teaspoon ground cardamom
Salt, if desired
Bouquet Garni
⅔ cup red onion, finely chopped

1 cup watercress leaves, loosely packed
Zest of 1 lemon, minced
1 tablespoon extra virgin olive oil
2 tablespoons fresh lemon juice
1 tablespoon sherry wine vinegar or robust red wine vinegar
Freshly ground pepper

BOUQUET GARNI
3 whole cloves
3 whole allspice berries

Wash lentils, picking through them to remove any pebbles; place in a medium-size pot. Add stock, onion, garlic, bay leaf, cardamom, salt and Bouquet Garni. Bring to a boil, reduce heat to medium-low and cook uncovered for 20 minutes or until lentils are tender but not mushy; drain and cool. Remove and discard bay leaf, onion and Bouquet Garni and transfer lentils to a bowl. Gently mix in red onion and watercress leaves. Drizzle olive oil, lemon juice and vinegar over lentils. Toss gently. Season with ground pepper. Taste to adjust seasonings. Serve immediately, or cover and refrigerate without watercress up to three days, return to room temperature, and add watercress.

Serve at room temperature. Transfer to serving dish. Makes 4 to 6 servings.

Bouquet Garni: Tie cloves and allspice berries in a piece of washed cheesecloth.

TIPS

Use stock that is not too strong (or dilute rich stock) for this dish. The lentils' delicate flavor will be overwhelmed if the stock is too flavorful.

According to U.S.D.A Handbook 8 (Legumes, Cereal Grains and Beef) the protein in 1 cup of lentils eaten with 1 cup of rice is about equal to the protein in 3 ounces of meat.

	kcal	carb(gm)	fat(gm)	chol(mg)	Na(mg)	iron(mg)	Ca(mg)
lavish:	288	33	14	0	449	3.2	74
lean	225	36	4	1	98	3.8	80

WARM POTATO SALAD

Lavish

♦

This family favorite came from Lorenzo Tedesco's kitchen to ours—a memory of Florence, Italy, where he was born.

2½ pounds boiling potatoes, such as red thin-skinned White Rose or Finnish potatoes, unpeeled (choose potatoes of the same size)
Salt and freshly ground pepper to taste

¾ cup extra-virgin olive oil
¼ cup capers
3 tablespoons chopped fresh dill or 1 tablespoon dried dill weed

In a large pot, boil unpeeled potatoes in salted water just until tender. Remove from pot with tongs and place on a medium-size platter. Cut hot potatoes in 1½-inch chunks. Season with salt and pepper and toss gently in oil. Add capers and 2 tablespoons fresh dill or 2 teaspoons dried dill weed; toss gently again. Serve immediately; or cover loosely and let stand at room temperature up to 3 hours. Do not refrigerate before serving.

To serve, wipe off sides of platter. Sprinkle salad with remaining 1 tablespoon fresh dill or 1 teaspoon dried dill weed. Makes 8 servings.

Lean

2½ pounds boiling potatoes, such as red thin-skinned White Rose or Finnish potatoes, unpeeled (choose potatoes of the same size)
Freshly ground pepper to taste
2 tablespoons capers, minced
3 tablespoons chopped fresh dill weed or 2 teaspoons dried dill weed

3 tablespoons chopped chives
¾ cup Creamy Non-fat Yogurt, page 22, or commercial
1 tablespoon fresh lemon juice
2 tablespoons extra-virgin olive oil, if desired

In a large pot, boil unpeeled potatoes in water just until tender. Remove from pot with tongs and place on a medium-size platter. Cut hot potatoes in 1½-inch chunks. Season with pepper, then add capers, dill and 2 tablespoons chives; toss gently. Add yogurt, lemon juice and oil, if desired, and toss gently again. Serve immediately; or cover loosely and let stand at room temperature up to 3 hours. Do not refrigerate before serving.

To serve, wipe off sides of platter. Sprinkle salad with remaining 1 tablespoon chives. Makes 8 servings.

	kcal	carb(gm)	fat(gm)	chol(mg)	Na(mg)	iron(mg)	Ca(mg)
lavish:	304	29	20	0	389	.7	14
lean:	167	31	4	0	23	.6	55

DESSERTS

Today's mix of ethnic foods and cultures has changed our eating habits. We still expect to finish off a meal with a sweet taste, but just how sweet *is* "sweet"?

I like to enhance desserts naturally, using ripe fruit and fruit juices in both lean and lavish recipes. Roasted Winter Fruit (page 230) is one of several dishes in this chapter that takes its delicious taste from the fruits' own fresh flavors. The lean versions of these desserts require little, if any, refined sugar.

Some desserts, though, need sweetening that does not impart another flavor, even that of fruit. For lean recipes of this kind, I prefer not to use concentrated fruit juices or artificial sugar substitutes. Juices contribute a distinct flavor, and sugar substitutes have an aftertaste—less apparent in highly seasoned dishes but (to me) noticeable in delicately flavored desserts. In most lean desserts, I use a little sugar, adding only as much as is needed to develop natural flavor.

A sweet ending is only part of the dessert-lover's pleasure; feeling full and satisfied is a lovely way to finish a meal. In lean desserts, rich whipped cream and egg yolks are replaced whenever possible with airy beaten egg whites —a gastronomic illusion that works.

ROASTED WINTER FRUIT

Lavish

♦

A few years ago, the mellow colors of roasted fruit—blood oranges, grapes, apples and pears—gleamed at me through a glass bowl at Ristorante Buca San Antonio in Lucca, Italy. Arrange the uncooked sliced fruit so plenty of the orange peels face up; they'll brown while roasting and become deliciously chewy.

3 large red-skinned baking
   apples, such as Rome
   Beauty
3 underripe or hard Anjou
   pears or 4 underripe or
   hard Seckel pears

4 blood oranges or 3 thin-
   skinned oranges
2 cups red grapes, seedless or
   with seeds
2 cups sugar

Wash all fruit well; do not peel. Quarter apples and pears lengthwise and cut out cores; then cut each quarter in half lengthwise. Cut oranges lengthwise in quarters; cut each quarter in half lengthwise and remove any seeds.

Set oven rack in upper third of oven. Preheat oven to 400F (205C). Place cut fruit and grapes in a large, shallow baking dish deep enough to hold fruit (fruit will make a layer 2 to 3 inches thick). Sprinkle sugar over fruit and toss to mix. Arrange orange wedges with peels facing up where possible. Roast, uncovered, 1 hour or until top layer of fruit is browned and fruit is softened. Remove from oven and cool to room temperature. Fruit will be juicy and tender. If prepared ahead, cover and refrigerate up to 2 days; return to room temperature before serving.

Serve in a glass bowl to show off the fruits' color; spoon into individual dishes. Makes 8 servings.

Lean

3 large red-skinned baking apples, such as Rome Beauty
3 underripe or hard Anjou pears or 4 underripe or hard Seckel pears
4 blood oranges or 3 thin-skinned oranges
2 cups red grapes, seedless or with seeds
2 tablespoons grated fresh gingerroot
¾ cup *each* apple juice and fresh orange juice
½ cup crème de cassis, port wine or cream sherry

Wash all fruit well; do not peel. Quarter apples and pears lengthwise and cut out cores; then cut each quarter in half lengthwise. Cut oranges lengthwise in quarters; cut each quarter in half lengthwise and remove any seeds.

Set oven rack in upper third of oven. Preheat oven to 400F (205C). Toss cut fruit with grapes and ginger and place in a large, shallow baking dish deep enough to hold fruit (fruit will make a layer 2 to 3 inches thick). Pour apple juice, orange juice and crème de cassis, port or sherry over fruit. Arrange orange wedges with peels facing up where possible. Roast, uncovered, 1 hour or until top layer of fruit is browned and fruit is softened. Remove from oven and cool to room temperature. Fruit will be juicy and tender. If prepared ahead, cover and refrigerate up to 2 days; return to room temperature before serving.

Serve in a glass bowl to show off the fruits' color; spoon into individual dishes. Makes 8 servings.

TIP

The alcohol in the crème de cassis, port or sherry will evaporate after 15 minutes of cooking, leaving the liquor's flavor but fewer calories.

	kcal	carb(gm)	fat(gm)	chol(mg)	Na(mg)	iron(mg)	Ca(mg)
lavish:	314	82	1	0	2	.4	42
lean:	159	40	1	0	3	.6	47

BAKED APPLES CALIFORNIA

Lavish

♦

*A fine California port (such as Ficklin) or any good imported Muscatel,
Marsala or cream sherry can be used as the fortified wine in this recipe.*

8 large red-skinned baking
  apples, such as Rome
  Beauty
Sugar
2 cups *each* fortified sweet red
  wine and fresh orange juice
⅔ cup fresh lemon juice

Zest of 3 oranges (about
  twenty ¼″ × 3″ strips)
Zest of 1 lemon (about
  fourteen ¼″ × 3″ strips)
2 cups whipping cream,
  unwhipped

Preheat oven to 350F (175C). Core apples. Starting from stem end, peel apples a third of the way down. Arrange in a medium-size baking dish. Fill each apple cavity with about 2 tablespoons sugar. Pour wine, orange juice and lemon juice over and around apples. Push orange and lemon zests into liquid around apples. Sprinkle 1½ cups sugar over and around apples. Bake, uncovered, basting twice, 45 minutes or until apples are tender when pierced with a wooden pick. Remove apples from baking dish and arrange in a ceramic or glass dish.

Strain liquid from baking dish into a 3-quart saucepan, reserving zests for garnish. Add 1 cup sugar and reduce liquid by half over high heat. Watch pan carefully; liquid will foam up as it boils away. Spoon reduced liquid frequently over apples as they cool; liquid will have a slightly jellied consistency when cooled or chilled. Strew orange and lemon zests over cooled apples. If prepared ahead, cover and refrigerate up to 1 day.

Serve apples at room temperature; if refrigerated, remove from refrigerator 1 hour before serving. To serve, place each apple in an individual bowl. Spoon jellied juices into cavity and over and around apple. Pass a pitcher of cream. Makes 8 servings.

Lean

8 large red-skinned baking
   apples, such as Rome
   Beauty
⅓ cup frozen concentrated
   apple juice, thawed
2 cups *each* fortified sweet red
   wine and fresh orange juice
⅔ cup fresh lemon juice
¼ teaspoon *each* ground
   cinnamon, ground cloves
   and ground allspice

Zest of 3 oranges (about
   twenty ¼″ × 3″ strips)
Zest of 1 lemon (about
   fourteen ¼″ × 2″ strips)
⅓ cup sugar, if desired
2 cups Creamy Dessert
   Topping, page 279

Preheat oven to 350F (175C). Core apples. Starting from stem end, peel apples a third of the way down. Arrange in a medium-size baking dish. Spoon concentrated apple juice into apple cavities. Pour wine, orange juice and lemon juice over and around apples. Sprinkle cinnamon, cloves and allspice into liquid. Push orange and lemon zests into liquid around apples. Bake, uncovered, basting twice, 45 minutes or until apples are tender when pierced with a wooden pick. Remove apples from baking dish and arrange in a ceramic or glass dish.

Strain liquid from baking dish into a 3-quart saucepan, reserving zests for garnish. Add sugar, if desired. Reduce liquid by half over high heat. Spoon reduced liquid frequently over apples as they cool; strew orange and lemon zests over cooled apples. If prepared ahead, cover and refrigerate up to 1 day.

Serve apples at room temperature; if refrigerated, remove from refrigerator 1 hour before serving. To serve, place each apple in an individual bowl. Spoon juices into cavity and over and around apple. Pass a bowl of Creamy Dessert Topping. Makes 8 servings.

	kcal	carb(gm)	fat(gm)	chol(mg)	Na(mg)	iron(mg)	Ca(mg)
lavish:	531	87	23	81	25	.5	65
lean:	222	48	2	4	192	.7	67

PEARS POACHED IN TWO WINES

Lavish

♦

As they simmer, these golden pears absorb the flavors of wine and spices. Cool, tart cheese provides a lovely contrast to the fruity syrup.

8 barely ripe Anjou or Bartlett pears
1 cup dry white wine, such as Chardonnay
1 cup Marsala or port wine
1 cup sugar
¼ cup *each* fresh lemon juice and fresh orange juice

8 (¼" × 2") strips orange zest
8 (¼" × 2") strips lemon zest
4 whole allspice berries
2 whole cloves
2 cinnamon sticks
8 ounces fresh goat cheese

Peel and core pears from blossom end, leaving stems intact. Arrange in a large, heavy pot. Add wines, sugar, juices, zests and spices; bring to a boil over high heat. Reduce heat, cover and simmer, turning pears every 20 minutes, about 1 hour or until pears are tender. Drain pears and arrange on a platter.

Over high heat, reduce cooking liquid to 1½ cups syrup; strain syrup, then cool and pour over pears. If prepared ahead, cover and refrigerate up to 1 day.

Serve pears at room temperature; if refrigerated, remove from refrigerator 1 hour before serving. To serve, divide cheese in 8 portions. Place pears on individual plates; spoon a little syrup over each pear, then arrange cheese next to pear over syrup. Makes 8 servings.

Lean

8 barely ripe Anjou or Bartlett pears
½ cup dry white wine, such as Chardonnay
½ cup Marsala or port wine
1 cup pear nectar plus ¼ cup fresh orange juice; or 1¼ cups fresh orange juice
¼ cup fresh lemon juice
8 (¼" × 2") strips orange zest
8 (¼" × 2") strips lemon zest
4 whole allspice berries
2 whole cloves
2 cinnamon sticks
1 cup Creamy Dessert Topping, page 279

Peel and core pears from blossom end, leaving stems intact. Arrange in a large, heavy pot. Add wines, pear nectar or orange juice, lemon juice, zests and spices; bring to a boil over high heat. Reduce heat, cover and simmer, turning pears every 20 minutes, about 1 hour or until pears are tender. Drain pears and arrange in a pretty serving dish or on a platter.

Over high heat, reduce cooking liquid by half. Strain liquid; discard zests and reserve spices. Cool liquid and pour over pears. If prepared ahead, cover and refrigerate up to 1 day.

Serve pears at room temperature; if refrigerated, remove pears from refrigerator 1 hour before serving. Spoon sauce over pears and strew spices decoratively over and in sauce. Pass a small bowl of Creamy Dessert Topping. Makes 8 servings.

	kcal	carb(gm)	fat(gm)	chol(mg)	Na(mg)	iron(mg)	Ca(mg)
lavish:	359	69	9	0	179	.7	149
lean:	185	40	1	2	162	.8	63

BERRIES!

Lavish

♦

Sun-warmed, unembellished berries say summer. Try this colorful mix at breakfast or brunch, or as dessert at dinner. You can substitute your favorite fresh berries for any of those suggested below.

2 cups blueberries	1 large banana
1 cup raspberries	1 tablespoon fresh thyme
1 cup blackberries or	leaves
boysenberries	⅓ to ½ cup fresh lemon juice
3 cups strawberries	1 to 1½ cups powdered sugar

Pick over berries to remove stems and leaves. Wash berries and immediately pat dry. Slice strawberries and banana. Place all fruit in a pretty glass bowl. Sprinkle with thyme, lemon juice and powdered sugar, toss gently, then taste and adjust amounts of sugar and lemon juice.

Let stand 10 minutes; then gently toss again, wipe down sides of bowl and serve. (Fruit is best served at room temperature, about 10 minutes after it is combined.) Makes 8 servings.

VARIATION

Substitute 2 tablespoons finely sliced fresh mint or basil leaves for minced thyme leaves.

Lean

2 cups ripe pineapple chunks or 1 small cantaloupe	2 cups strawberries
2 cups blueberries	1 tablespoon fresh thyme leaves
1 cup raspberries	3 tablespoons fresh lemon juice, or to taste
1 cup blackberries or boysenberries	½ cup powdered sugar

Drain pineapple and reserve juice. If using cantaloupe, cut in half and discard seeds. Scoop melon into bite-size balls, then set in a strainer to drain; reserve juice. If desired, pour pineapple or cantaloupe juice into a small saucepan and reduce over high heat by two-thirds or until syrupy.

Pick over berries to remove stems and leaves. Wash berries and immediately pat dry. Slice strawberries. Place pineapple or cantaloupe and berries in a pretty glass bowl. Sprinkle with thyme, lemon juice and powdered sugar; toss gently, then taste and adjust amount of lemon juice. Add pineapple or cantaloupe juice or syrup for sweetening, if desired.

Let stand 10 minutes; then gently toss again, wipe down sides of bowl and serve. (Fruit is best served at room temperature, about 10 minutes after it is combined.) Makes 8 servings.

VARIATION

Substitute 2 tablespoons finely sliced fresh mint or basil leaves for minced thyme leaves.

	kcal	carb(gm)	fat(gm)	chol(mg)	Na(mg)	iron(mg)	Ca(mg)
lavish:	131	33	1	0	3	.5	21
lean:	95	24	1	0	3	.5	21

APPLE PUDDING WITH RASPBERRY VINEGAR

Lavish

♦

Chuck Williams of Williams-Sonoma cooks this tempting creation in his quality ovenware. Raspberry vinegar is a perfect complement to the tart apples.

4 cooking apples, such as
    pippin or Granny Smith
    (about 2 lbs. *total*), peeled,
    cored, sliced
½ cup *each* water and
    granulated sugar
1½ cups soft bread crumbs
2 to 3 tablespoons raspberry
    vinegar

1 cup demerara sugar or
    packed light brown sugar
3 tablespoons butter, cut in
    small pieces
1½ cups Crème Fraîche, page
    278, or whipped cream

Generously butter a medium-size ovenproof casserole. Place apples, water and granulated sugar in a medium-size, heavy pot. Bring water to a boil over high heat; reduce heat and simmer, uncovered, about 20 minutes or until apples are soft. Press through a sieve or food mill into a bowl; cool.

Preheat oven to 350F (175C). Gently mix apples with bread crumbs and vinegar; spoon into buttered casserole. (At this point, you may cover and refrigerate up to 1 day; return to room temperature before baking.) Sprinkle apple mixture with demerara or brown sugar. Top with bits of butter. Bake 20 to 25 minutes or until bubbly and browned on top.

Serve pudding warm or at room temperature; spoon from baking dish into individual bowls. Pass Crème Fraîche or whipped cream. Makes 4 generous servings.

Lean

4 cooking apples, such as
  pippin or Granny Smith
  (about 2 lbs. *total*), peeled,
  cored, sliced
½ cup fresh orange juice
2 tablespoons crème de cassis
  or Framboise (raspberry
  liqueur)

1½ cups soft bread crumbs
2 to 3 tablespoons raspberry
  vinegar
¼ cup demerara sugar or
  packed light brown sugar
1½ cups Creamy Dessert
  Topping, page 279

Rub a medium-size ovenproof casserole with a little vegetable oil on a paper towel. Place apples, orange juice and liqueur in a medium-size, heavy pot. Bring to a boil over high heat; reduce heat and simmer, uncovered, about 20 minutes or until apples are soft. Press through a sieve or food mill into a bowl; cool.

Preheat oven to 350F (175C). Gently mix apples with bread crumbs and vinegar; spoon into oiled casserole. (At this point, you may cover and refrigerate up to 1 day; return to room temperature before baking.) Sprinkle apple mixture with demerara or brown sugar. Bake 20 to 25 minutes or until sugar is melted and pudding is bubbly around edges.

Serve pudding warm or at room temperature; spoon from baking dish into individual bowls. Pass Creamy Dessert Topping. Makes 4 generous servings.

	kcal	carb(gm)	fat(gm)	chol(mg)	Na(mg)	iron(mg)	Ca(mg)
lavish:	751	108	37	122	218	2.2	133
lean:	260	51	2	3.5	401	.9	96

CHILLED PRUNE MOUSSE

Lavish

♦

French mousse meets American prune whip and turns into this rich, faintly spicy dessert. Be sure the cardamom is aromatic and fresh.

10 ounces (1½ cups packed)
   dried pitted prunes
Zest of 1 small lemon, cut in
   strips
About 2 cups water
½ cup sugar
Prune juice, if needed
1 cup cottage cheese

½ teaspoon ground
   cardamom, or to taste
1 tablespoon Cointreau or
   Grand Marnier
1 cup whipping cream,
   whipped
1 cup Crème Fraîche, page
   278, or dairy sour cream for
   garnish

In a saucepan, combine prunes, lemon zest and enough water to cover prunes (about 2 cups). Simmer 20 minutes or until prunes are soft. Stir in sugar, cover and simmer 10 minutes longer. Drain prunes and discard lemon zest. Reserve cooking liquid. If needed, add prune juice to make 1 cup. Pour liquid into a saucepan and reduce by half. Pour into a dish, cover and refrigerate.

In a food processor fitted with a mctal blade, process cottage cheese 2 minutes or until *completely* smooth. Scrape pureed cheese into a bowl. Process drained prunes in food processor until smooth, scraping down sides of work bowl often. Fold pureed prunes into cottage cheese. Fold in cardamom, then liqueur, then whipped cream until blended. Spoon into 8 individual ramekins or small bowls. Cover and refrigerate until chilled or up to 1 day.

Remove mousse from refrigerator 10 minutes before serving; mousse should be served slightly chilled. Spoon a dollop of Crème Fraîche or sour cream over each serving; drizzle a spoonful of reduced prune syrup over Crème Fraîche or sour cream. Makes about 8 servings.

Lean

10 ounces (1½ cups packed)
dried pitted prunes
3 cups fresh orange juice
Zest of 1 small lemon
1 vanilla bean or 1 teaspoon
vanilla extract
1 cup lowfat cottage cheese

¾ teaspoon ground cardamom
or to taste
1 envelope unflavored gelatin
4 egg whites, room
temperature
¼ teaspoon cream of tartar
1 cup Creamy Dessert
Topping, page 279, for
garnish

In a saucepan, combine prunes, orange juice, lemon zest and vanilla bean, if used. Simmer 30 minutes or until prunes are soft. Drain prunes. Reserve cooking liquid; you should have about 2 cups. Discard lemon zest; remove vanilla bean, rinse and save to reuse.

In a food processor fitted with a metal blade, process cottage cheese 2 minutes or until *completely* smooth. Scrape pureed cheese into a bowl. Process drained prunes in food processor with ½ cup of the reserved cooking liquid, cardamom and vanilla extract (if used) until smooth; scrape down sides of work bowl often. Fold pureed prunes into cottage cheese. Cover and refrigerate.

In a saucepan, sprinkle gelatin over remaining 1½ cups cooking liquid; let stand 10 minutes to soften. Bring to a simmer over medium heat, stirring to dissolve gelatin. Cool and refrigerate about 45 minutes or until gelatin begins to thicken, stirring frequently. Remove from refrigerator and whisk 2 to 3 minutes or until foamy. Fold into prune mixture, half at a time. Beat egg whites with cream of tartar until stiff but not dry. Gently fold into prune mixture. Spoon into 8 individual ramekins. Cover and refrigerate until chilled or up to 1 day.

Remove mousse from refrigerator 10 minutes before serving; mousse should be served slightly chilled. Spoon a dollop of Creamy Dessert Topping over each serving. Makes 8 servings.

	kcal	carb(gm)	fat(gm)	chol(mg)	Na(mg)	iron(mg)	Ca(mg)
lavish:	371	37	22	86	136	.9	76
lean:	182	35	1	2	232	1.2	66

LEMON MERINGUE MOUSSE

Lavish

♦

Smooth lemon custard combines deliciously with chewy meringue. Cornstarch thickens the custard and makes it easier to serve, but if you don't mind a softer filling, you can leave out the cornstarch and increase the butter to 9 tablespoons. In that case, take care to remove the custard from the heat just as soon as it thickens.

Meringue Crust
4 large eggs, room
    temperature
4 egg yolks, room temperature
    (reserve whites for crust)
1½ cups sugar
1 tablespoon cornstarch
1 cup fresh lemon juice
2 tablespoons finely grated
    lemon zest
5 tablespoons unsalted butter,
    room temperature, cut in
    pieces

1 cup whipping cream,
    whipped
1 teaspoon grated lemon zest
    for garnish

MERINGUE CRUST
4 egg whites, room
    temperature
¼ teaspoon cream of tartar
1 cup sugar

Prepare Meringue Crust. Beat eggs and egg yolks in top of a double boiler or in a medium-size bowl until thick and lemon-colored. Add sugar; whisk until mixture forms a ribbon when whisk is lifted. Whisk in cornstarch, lemon juice and 2 tablespoons lemon zest. Whisk in butter, a piece at a time, until all ingredients are well blended. Place over simmering water and cook, stirring, until mixture is smooth and thick; it should have the consistency of sour cream. Remove from heat. Cool, stirring occasionally. Fold whipped cream into cooled lemon mixture. Spoon into Meringue Crust. Cover loosely and refrigerate 24 hours.

Remove mousse from refrigerator 15 minutes before serving; garnish with 1 teaspoon lemon zest. Cut in wedges. Makes 8 to 10 servings.

Meringue Crust: Set oven rack in center of oven. Preheat oven to 300F (150C). Generously butter a 10-inch glass pie plate or a 10-inch ceramic dish 2 inches deep. Beat egg whites until they hold soft peaks; add cream of tartar. Gradually add sugar, beating until whites hold stiff, glossy peaks. Spoon meringue into buttered pie plate, pushing meringue up sides with spoon. Bake 20 minutes. Reduce oven temperature to 225F (105C) and continue to bake 40 minutes longer or until golden. Cool before filling.

VARIATION

Chilled Lemon Mousse: Prepare recipe above, but omit Meringue Crust. Fill 6 individual ramekins with lemon mousse. Cover and refrigerate at least 4 hours or up to 1 day. Garnish with Crème Fraîche, page 278, and grated lemon zest. Makes 6 servings.

Lean

Intensely lemony and fresh.

Meringue Crust
1¼ teaspoons unflavored
  gelatin
¼ cup non-fat milk
1 cup lowfat cottage cheese
2 tablespoons cornstarch
2 tablespoons finely grated
  lemon zest
1 cup fresh lemon juice
¾ cup sugar
4 egg whites, room
  temperature

¼ teaspoon cream of tartar
1 teaspoon grated lemon zest
  for garnish

MERINGUE CRUST
4 egg whites, room
  temperature
¼ teaspoon cream of tartar
⅓ cup sugar

Prepare Meringue Crust. Sprinkle gelatin over 2 tablespoons milk and let stand 10 minutes to soften.

Meanwhile, in a food processor fitted with a metal blade, process cottage cheese 2 minutes or until completely smooth, scraping down sides of work bowl as needed. Dissolve cornstarch in remaining 2 tablespoons milk, add to blended cottage cheese and process 1 minute longer. Scrape into a medium-size, heavy saucepan. Whisk in 2 tablespoons lemon zest, lemon juice and ¼ cup sugar. Mixture may appear to curdle and thicken; continue to whisk until curdled look disappears. Cook over medium heat, whisking constantly, until mixture is thickened and beginning to bubble. Remove from heat; add softened gelatin, return to heat and whisk 1 minute longer or until gelatin is completely dissolved. Scrape mixture into a large bowl and cool, gently folding occasionally.

With an electric mixer, beat egg whites with cream of tartar at high speed 2 to 3 minutes or until they hold soft peaks. Slowly add remaining ½ cup sugar, continuing to beat until mixture is very glossy and stiff but not dry.

If you used a copper bowl for beating egg whites, scrape them into a large glass, ceramic or stainless steel bowl. Then slowly pour cooled lemon mixture over egg whites and gently fold until blended. Scrape into Meringue Crust; smooth and slightly mound filling. Cover loosely and refrigerate 24 hours.

Remove mousse from refrigerator 15 minutes before serving. Sprinkle with 1 teaspoon lemon zest. Cut in wedges. Makes 8 to 10 servings.

Meringue Crust: Set oven rack in center of oven. Preheat oven to 300F (150C). Spray a 10-inch glass pie plate or a 10-inch ceramic dish 2 inches deep with non-stick spray; or lightly grease with margarine or vegetable oil. Beat egg whites until they hold soft peaks; add cream of tartar. Gradually add sugar, beating until sugar is dissolved and whites are stiff and glossy. Spoon into prepared pie plate, pushing meringue up sides with a spoon. Bake 20 minutes. Reduce oven temperature to 225F (105C) and continue to bake 40 minutes longer or until golden. Cool before filling.

	kcal	carb(gm)	fat(gm)	chol(mg)	Na(mg)	iron(mg)	Ca(mg)
lavish:	465	65	22	325	147	1	56
lean:	172	36	1	2.5	169	.1	37

RICE PUDDING WITH APRICOT SAUCE

Lavish

♦

This creamy pudding is adapted from one in Huntley Dent's fine book The Feast of Santa Fe. *It's a sensuous dessert, custardy and comforting. My Apricot Sauce provides a tart, fresh contrast to the rich pudding and a chance to use up any white wine leftovers.*

Apricot Sauce
2 cups *each* whipping cream
   and half and half
¼ cup butter
½ cup long-grain white rice
⅔ cup sugar
Pinch of salt
2 cinnamon sticks or ½
   teaspoon ground cinnamon
1 teaspoon vanilla extract

2 large eggs, room
   temperature, separated
Pinch of cream of tartar

APRICOT SAUCE
8 ounces dried apricots
3 cups dry white wine (use
   up remainders of bottles)
2 cups sugar
Fresh lemon juice, if desired

Prepare Apricot Sauce. Set oven rack in center of oven. Preheat oven to 300F (150C). In a medium-size saucepan, scald cream and half and half over medium-high heat. Pour into a 2-quart ovenproof casserole. Stir in butter, rice, sugar, salt and cinnamon until sugar is dissolved. Bake, uncovered, without stirring, 1½ hours. Continue to bake, stirring every 20 minutes, 20 to 40 minutes longer or until thick and creamy.

Remove pudding from oven and cool 5 minutes. Remove cinnamon sticks, if used, from pudding with tongs. Beat in vanilla and egg yolks. Beat egg whites with cream of tartar until stiff but not dry; fold into pudding. Pudding is best served warm and freshly made; but you may bake it up to 2 days ahead, cool, cover and refrigerate. Return to room temperature or reheat in oven before serving.

To serve, spoon pudding into individual bowls. Pass Apricot Sauce. Makes 4 servings.

Apricot Sauce: In a medium-size saucepan, combine apricots, wine and sugar. Bring to a rolling boil over high heat; reduce heat, cover and simmer 15 minutes or until soft. Cool. Remove about a third of the apricots with a slotted spoon, coarsely chop and set aside. In a blender or a food processor fitted with a metal blade, process remaining apricots with cooking liquid in 2 batches until pureed. Pour into a bowl. Stir in chopped apricots and a few drops of lemon juice if a tarter taste is desired. If prepared ahead, cool, cover and refrigerate up to 2 days. Return to room temperature or reheat before serving. Makes about 4½ cups.

TIP

Use leftover Apricot Sauce on ice cream, puddings and dessert omelets.

Lean

The starchy rice breaks down and combines with the milk to give this pudding a lovely, creamy consistency. Don't use Enriched Non-fat Milk, page 22, here; it will change the pudding's texture.

Apricot Sauce
1 quart non-fat milk
½ cup long-grain white rice
2 cinnamon sticks or 2
   teaspoons ground cinnamon
¼ cup sugar
1 teaspoon vanilla extract
1 large egg, room
   temperature, separated
2 egg whites, room
   temperature

Generous pinch of cream of
   tartar

APRICOT SAUCE
8 ounces dried apricots
3 cups apricot nectar (two
   12-oz. cans)
1 tablespoon fresh lemon
   juice

Prepare Apricot Sauce. Set oven rack in center of oven. Preheat oven to 300F (150C). In a medium-size saucepan, scald milk over medium-high heat. Pour into a 2-quart ovenproof casserole. Stir in rice, cinnamon and sugar until sugar is dissolved. Bake, uncovered, without stirring, 1 hour. Continue to bake, stirring every 10 minutes, 30 to 45 minutes longer or until thick and creamy.

Remove pudding from oven and cool 5 minutes. Remove cinnamon sticks, if used, from pudding with tongs. Beat in vanilla and egg yolk. Beat all 3 egg whites with cream of tartar until stiff but not dry; fold into pudding. Pudding is best served warm and freshly made, but you may bake it up to 2 days ahead, cool, cover and refrigerate. Return to room temperature or reheat in oven before serving.

To serve, spoon pudding into individual bowls. Pass Apricot Sauce. Makes 4 servings.

Apricot Sauce: In a medium-size saucepan, combine apricots, apricot nectar and lemon juice. Bring to a rolling boil over high heat; reduce heat, cover and simmer 15 minutes or until apricots are soft. Cool.

Remove about a third of the apricots with a slotted spoon, coarsely chop and set aside. In a blender or a food processor fitted with a metal blade, process remaining apricots with cooking liquid in 2 batches until pureed. Pour into a bowl. Stir in chopped apricots. If prepared ahead, cool, cover and refrigerate up to 2 days. Return to room temperature or reheat before serving. Makes about 3½ cups.

TIPS

Use leftover Apricot Sauce on sliced fresh pears or apples and on lowfat cottage cheese.

Egg whites increase their volume and stability when beaten or whisked in a deep, clean copper bowl at room temperature; the chemical interaction between copper and the alkaline whites stabilizes the whites as they're whipped. Cream of tartar—¹⁄₁₆ teaspoon for each white—is another stabilizer. To bring chilled eggs in their shells to room temperature quickly, put them in a bowl filled with hot (not boiling) water for 5 minutes.

	kcal	carb(gm)	fat(gm)	chol(mg)	Na(mg)	iron(mg)	Ca(mg)
lavish:	1044	93	72	375	253	2.5	238
lean:	306	59	2	72	173	2.7	340

CREAMY YOGURT, BERRIES AND GRAINS
Birchermuesli

Lavish

◆

Birchermuesli for dessert? Well, the Swiss have such a love affair with this dish that when I saw it all dressed up in a Basle pastry shop window it didn't seem strange at all. A small portion topped with sweetened Crème Fraîche and berries really is a great way to end a meal; a large portion makes a whole breakfast or lunch. Use frozen berries (thawed and drained) when fresh ones aren't available.

½ to ⅔ cup Unsweetened
　Muesli, see opposite, or
　commercial unsweetened
　muesli
1 pint mild yogurt
⅔ cup fresh blueberries
⅔ cup fresh raspberries
⅔ cup fresh blackberries
1 cup fresh strawberries, cut
　into ½-inch pieces
(Or about 3 cups diced fresh
　fruit)

⅔ cup sugar
2 tablespoons Framboise
　(raspberry liqueur)
3 tablespoons powdered sugar
1 cup Crème Fraîche, page
　278, or sour cream
24 berries for garnish
8 fresh mint leaves

Soak muesli in 1½ cups cold water for 30 minutes. Drain. Mix yogurt and muesli in a medium-size bowl. Add berries, sugar and Framboise. Stir gently until mixture becomes pink. Serve immediately or cover and refrigerate up to 12 hours. Stir powdered sugar into Crème Fraîche.

To serve, spoon muesli into glass goblets. Top each serving with a dollop of Crème Fraîche, 3 berries and a mint leaf. Makes 8 servings.

UNSWEETENED MUESLI
(Lavish)

¾ cup rolled oats
¾ cup barley flakes
¾ cup wheat flakes
¾ cup rye flakes
(Or any combination of the
  grains above to make 3
  cups)

⅓ cup oat or wheat bran
1 teaspoon salt
⅓ cup canola oil or light
  cooking oil
¾ cup diced pecans, toasted

Preheat oven to 350F (175C). Toss grains, bran and salt in a medium-size bowl. Add oil and stir until grain flakes and oil are well mixed. Spread evenly on a large, shallow baking pan and toast in oven 15 minutes or until lightly browned, stirring every 5 minutes to prevent burning. Cool and add nuts. Cover and store at room temperature for 3 weeks or freeze. Makes about 3 cups.

Lean

Muesli, yogurt, nuts and fruit gets its name—Birchermuesli—from Dr. Bircher-Brenner, a Swiss nutritionist, who used it with great success in the early part of this century. Even if it's nutritionally virtuous, it is an absolutely delicious dish.

½ to ⅔ cup Unsweetened Muesli, see opposite, or commercial unsweetened muesli
1 pint mild non-fat yogurt
⅔ cup fresh blueberries
⅔ cup fresh raspberries
⅔ cup fresh blackberries
1 cup fresh strawberries, cut into ½-inch pieces

(Or about 3 cups diced fresh fruit)
⅓ cup sugar
1 cup Creamy Dessert Topping, page 279
24 berries for garnish
8 fresh mint leaves

Soak muesli in 1½ cups cold water for 30 minutes. Drain. Mix yogurt and muesli in a medium-size bowl. Add berries and sugar. Stir gently until mixture becomes pink. Serve immediately or cover and refrigerate up to 12 hours.

To serve, spoon muesli into glass goblets. Top each serving with a dollop of Creamy Dessert Topping, 3 berries and a mint leaf. Makes 8 servings.

UNSWEETENED MUESLI
(Lean)

Follow the lavish recipe for Unsweetened Muesli, omitting oil and salt. Substitute toasted soy beans (lower in fat and calories than pecans) for the lavish nuts.

TIP

The Swiss use small pieces of fresh apple and pear as well as dried fruits in the muesli, with or without the fresh fruit or berries.

Creamy Yogurt, Berries and Grains (includes 1 tablespoon muesli)

	kcal	carb(gm)	fat(gm)	chol(mg)	Na(mg)	iron(mg)	Ca(mg)
lavish:	291	34	16	48	83	.6	104
lean:	119	18	2	3	138	.7	151

Muesli (only) (8 tablespoons or ½ cup)

	kcal	carb(gm)	fat(gm)	chol(mg)	Na(mg)	iron(mg)	Ca(mg)
lavish:	371	32	25	0	358	2.3	31
lean:	256	36	7	0	3	2.9	50

CUSTARDS IN BERRY SAUCE

Lavish

♦

When carefully cooked, this classic custard has a delicate, creamy texture and flavor, a silky contrast to the Berry Sauce.

Berry Sauce
1 cup milk
1½ cups whipping cream
1 vanilla bean, split
  lengthwise, or 1 teaspoon
  vanilla extract
3 large eggs
3 egg yolks
¾ cup sugar
24 fresh berries for garnish, if
  desired
8 fresh mint leaves for
  garnish, if desired

BERRY SAUCE
3 cups frozen sweetened
  raspberries, boysenberries,
  blackberries or blueberries
  (or a mixture), thawed,
  undrained
1 to 2 tablespoons fresh
  lemon juice
Sifted powdered sugar to
  taste

Prepare Berry Sauce. Set oven rack in center of oven. Preheat oven to 300F (150C). Cut 8 rounds of parchment to fit 8 (4-oz. or 6-oz.) custard cups or ramekins. Butter custard cups and both sides of parchment rounds; fit rounds into cups. Choose a baking pan large and deep enough to hold custard cups and enough water to come halfway up sides of cups; set baking pan in center of oven. Boil water in a kettle; keep at a simmer.

In a saucepan, scald milk and cream with vanilla bean, if used, over medium heat. In a bowl, beat eggs and egg yolks until well blended; add sugar and vanilla extract, if used, and beat until lemon-colored. Slowly pour hot liquid into egg mixture, continuing to stir until sugar is dissolved. Strain into a pitcher, then pour into custard cups. Arrange cups in baking pan in oven. Pour enough boiling water into pan to come halfway up sides of cups. Lay a sheet of foil over cups. Water should be steaming hot as custards bake, but should not boil in baking pan; add ice cubes to water as necessary. Bake

20 to 30 minutes or until blade of a thin knife inserted in center of custard comes out clean.

Remove custards from hot water, uncover and cool. Cover; refrigerate until well chilled, at least 5 to 6 hours (or up to 2 days). Do not remove from custard cups until well chilled.

Remove custards from refrigerator 10 minutes before serving. Run a sharp knife around cups to loosen sides of custards; loosen bottoms gently with a spatula. Invert each cup over center of a dessert plate, shaking gently to dislodge custard. Peel off parchment. Carefully spoon Berry Sauce around inverted custards. Garnish each custard with 3 berries and a mint leaf, if desired. Makes 8 servings.

Berry Sauce: In a blender or a food processor fitted with a metal blade, process berries with their juice until smooth. Strain to remove seeds. Add lemon juice and powdered sugar to taste. If prepared ahead, cover and refrigerate up to 2 days; return to room temperature before serving. Makes 2½ cups.

Lean

Berry Sauce
2½ cups Enriched Non-fat
   Milk, page 22, or non-fat
   milk
2 vanilla beans, split
   lengthwise, or 2 teaspoons
   vanilla extract
¾ cup liquid egg substitute
⅓ cup sugar
24 fresh berries for garnish, if
   desired
8 fresh mint leaves for
   garnish, if desired

BERRY SAUCE
3 cups fresh or frozen
   unsweetened raspberries,
   boysenberries, blackberries
   or blueberries (or a
   mixture), thawed and
   undrained, if frozen
¼ to ⅓ cup fresh orange juice
Fresh lemon juice to taste
Sifted powdered sugar, if
   desired

Prepare Berry Sauce. Set oven rack in center of oven. Preheat oven to 300F (150C). Cut 8 rounds of parchment to fit 8 (4-oz. or 6-oz.) custard cups or ramekins. Lightly oil custard cups and both sides of parchment rounds; fit rounds into cups. Choose a baking pan large and deep enough to hold custard cups and enough boiling water to come halfway up sides of cups; set baking pan in center of oven. Boil water in a kettle and keep at a simmer.

In a saucepan, scald milk with vanilla bean, if used, over medium heat. Beat egg substitute with sugar and and vanilla extract, if used, until well blended. Slowly stir hot milk into sugar mixture until ingredients are completely blended and sugar is dissolved. Strain into a pitcher, then pour into custard cups. Arrange cups in baking pan in oven. Pour enough boiling water into pan to come halfway up sides of cups. Lay a sheet of foil over cups. Water should be steaming hot as custards bake, but should not boil in baking pan; add ice cubes to water as necessary. Bake 20 to 30 minutes or until blade of a thin knife inserted in center of custard comes out clean.

Remove custards from hot water, uncover and cool. Cover and refrigerate until thoroughly chilled, at least 5 to 6 hours (or up to 2 days). Do not remove from custard cups until well chilled.

Remove custards from refrigerator 10 minutes before serving. Run a sharp knife around cups to loosen sides of custards; loosen bottoms gently with a spatula. Invert each cup over center of a dessert plate, shaking gently to dislodge custard. Peel off parchment. Carefully spoon Berry Sauce around inverted custards. Garnish each custard with 3 berries and a mint leaf, if desired. Makes 8 servings.

Berry Sauce: In a blender or a food processor fitted with a metal blade, process berries and their juice until smooth. Strain to remove seeds. Add orange juice to give sauce desired consistency. Add lemon juice and powdered sugar to taste. If prepared ahead, cover and refrigerate up to 2 days. Return to room temperature before serving. Makes about 2½ cups.

	kcal	carb(gm)	fat(gm)	chol(mg)	Na(mg)	iron(mg)	Ca(mg)
lavish:	408	53	19	259	60	1.5	105
lean:	129	25	1	1.5	82	.9	125

CHOCOLATE RAMEKINS

Lavish

♦

A smooth, rich mousse for special occasions. Use bittersweet Belgian, Swiss or French chocolate if possible.

1 cup whipping cream
8 ounces imported bittersweet
   chocolate, chopped
2 ounces unsweetened
   chocolate, chopped
Pinch of salt
4 large eggs, room
   temperature, separated

1 cup whipping cream,
   chilled
¼ teaspoon cream of tartar
⅓ cup sugar
Shaved bittersweet chocolate
   for garnish

In a medium-size saucepan, scald 1 cup cream over medium-low heat. Add chopped bittersweet and unsweetened chocolates and salt; reduce heat to low and stir until chocolate and cream are blended. Flecks will appear in cream, but will disappear as chocolate is cooked and stirred. Remove from heat and scrape into a large bowl; cool until tepid.

Beat egg yolks, 1 at a time, into chocolate. Beat ½ cup chilled cream until stiff; set aside. Beat egg whites until foamy; add cream of tartar and continue to beat until whites hold soft peaks. Gradually add sugar and continue to beat until sugar is dissolved and whites hold stiff, glossy peaks. Fold whipped cream into chocolate mixture, then lightly fold in egg whites just until blended. Spoon into individual ramekins, cover and refrigerate at least 4 hours or up to 2 days.

Remove ramekins from refrigerator 20 minutes before serving. Beat remaining ½ cup cream until stiff; spoon a dollop of whipped cream over each ramekin and sprinkle with shaved chocolate. Makes 12 servings.

VARIATION

Chocolate-Espresso Ramekins: Stir 1 teaspoon instant espresso or coffee powder (regular or decaffeinated) into cream as it scalds. Proceed as directed above.

Lean

Whipping cream and solid chocolate aren't missed when extra egg whites and cocoa replace them.

2 tablespoons cornstarch
2 cups Enriched Non-fat
 Milk, page 22, or non-fat
 milk
½ cup unsweetened cocoa,
 sifted
Pinch of salt, if desired
4 egg whites, room
 temperature

¼ teaspoon cream of tartar
⅔ cup packed brown sugar
1 cup Creamy Dessert
 Topping, page 279, for
 garnish
Additional sifted
 unsweetened cocoa for
 garnish

Place cornstarch in a heavy saucepan. Stirring constantly, add enough milk, a few drops at a time, to make a smooth paste. Stir in remaining milk. Whisk in ½ cup cocoa until blended; add salt, if desired. Cook over medium heat, stirring constantly, until mixture thickens and begins to bubble. Reduce heat and cook 2 minutes longer, stirring to prevent sticking. Scrape mixture into a large bowl. Cool, stirring frequently to prevent a skin from forming.

In a medium-size, deep bowl, beat egg whites and cream of tartar until whites hold soft peaks that bend over at the tips. Gradually beat in brown sugar; continue to beat at high speed 2 to 3 minutes longer or until beaten whites are thick and shiny. Fold a third of the beaten egg whites into cocoa mixture. Fold in remaining whites, a third at a time, just until streaks disappear. Spoon into individual ramekins, cover and refrigerate at least 1 hour or up to 4 hours.

Remove ramekins from refrigerator 10 minutes before serving. Spoon a dollop of Creamy Dessert Topping over each ramekin; sprinkle with a pinch of cocoa. Makes 12 servings.

	kcal	carb(gm)	fat(gm)	chol(mg)	Na(mg)	iron(mg)	Ca(mg)
lavish:	283	19	23	135	37	1.2	46
lean:	94	18	1	1	136	.8	8

BLUEBERRY ICE CREAM

Lavish

♦

You won't need an ice cream maker for this recipe, though you can use one if you have it. The lemon juice, blueberries and sugar thicken the cream; when frozen, the mixture forms very small crystals. Reprocessing before serving is optional, but for the best flavor, serve the ice cream slightly softened. Top each serving with fresh blueberries when they're in season; bring summer back any time of year with ice cream made from frozen blueberries.

2 cups fresh or frozen
   unsweetened blueberries,
   partially thawed and
   drained if frozen
1 cup sugar
3 tablespoons fresh lemon
   juice

2 cups whipping cream
Fresh blueberries for garnish,
   if in season
Bittersweet Chocolate Sauce,
   page 276, if desired

In a food processor fitted with a metal blade, process 2 cups blueberries with sugar until blueberries are broken down but not smooth. Scrape into a small bowl, add lemon juice and cream and stir until sugar is dissolved. Spoon into a freezer container with a tight-fitting lid; gently press plastic wrap directly on surface of unfrozen ice cream. Cover with lid and freeze 6 hours or until soft-frozen. (Or pour mixture into an ice-cream maker and freeze according to manufacturer's directions.) Ice cream can be prepared and frozen up to 1 week ahead.

Let hard-frozen ice cream stand at room temperature 15 minutes before serving. If desired, reprocess ice cream before serving to soften berry chunks. Serve soft-frozen.

Use a scoop to remove ice cream from container and place in a serving dish or individual dishes. Garnish with fresh blueberries, if available; pass Bittersweet Chocolate Sauce, if desired. Makes 10 servings.

Lean

My friend Alison Stein and her mother, Midge Cowley, prepare countless variations on this theme; they use strawberries, melons, peaches or mangoes (sometimes in combination, sometimes alone) in place of the blueberries. My version of this frozen yogurt is based on delicious results from their kitchens.

2 cups fresh or frozen
   unsweetened blueberries,
   partially thawed and
   drained if frozen
2 tablespoons powdered sugar
2 tablespoons fresh lemon
   juice
1 medium-size ripe banana,
   cut in chunks

½ cup Creamy Non-fat
   Yogurt, page 22, or mild
   commercial
Fresh blueberries for garnish,
   if in season
Lean Bittersweet Chocolate
   Sauce, page 277, if desired

In a food processor fitted with a metal blade, process 2 cups blueberries with powdered sugar until blueberries are broken down but not smooth. Add lemon juice and banana and process until banana chunks disappear and mixture is smooth. Add yogurt and process until blended. *If using fresh berries*, pour mixture into a freezer container with a tight-fitting lid. Gently press plastic wrap directly on surface of unfrozen dessert, cover with lid and freeze 6 hours or until soft-frozen. *If using frozen berries*, you may serve dessert without freezing it, or freeze as directed.

Dessert can be prepared and frozen up to 1 week ahead. Let hard-frozen dessert stand at room temperature 15 minutes before serving; reprocess until smooth. Serve soft-frozen. Use a scoop to remove dessert from container and place in individual dishes. Garnish with fresh blueberries, if available; pass Bittersweet Chocolate Sauce, if desired. Makes 6 servings.

	kcal	carb(gm)	fat(gm)	chol(mg)	Na(mg)	iron(mg)	Ca(mg)
lavish:	228	25	15	53	17	.1	36
lean:	63	15	.5	0	15	.2	43

CHOCOLATE CAKE WITH FRESH ORANGE GLAZE

Lavish

♦

Chocolate and orange are made for each other. I've been making this cake without the orange since my college days, but when I wanted to boost flavor in the lean cake, the two seemed a natural combination. It's a happy marriage in both versions.

2 cups flour
1 teaspoon baking powder
1 teaspoon baking soda
Pinch salt
4 squares (4-oz.) unsweetened chocolate
1 cup hot water
½ cup (¼-lb.) unsalted butter, room temperature
2 cups sugar
2 large eggs, room temperature
1 cup sour cream

Grated zest from one medium-size orange, minced
2 teaspoons vanilla extract
Fresh Orange Glaze

FRESH ORANGE GLAZE
1 cup powdered sugar, sifted
⅓ cup fresh orange juice
2 tablespoons fresh lemon juice
Grated zest from 1 orange

Preheat oven to 325F (165C). Butter a 9-inch springform or a 9" x 13" × 2" baking pan. Cut some waxed paper to fit bottom. Butter paper on both sides; fit into bottom. Dust pan lightly with flour; rap out excess flour.

Sift dry ingredients together. Melt chocolate in hot water, stirring until smooth. Cream butter and sugar together until light. Beat in eggs, one at a time, and continue to beat until light and fluffy. Blend in sour cream, minced orange zest and vanilla. Add dry ingredients to butter-egg mixture in three parts, stirring each time just until blended. Blend in chocolate-water mixture. Pour into baking pan and bake in top third of oven for 1 hour and 10 minutes or until a toothpick in center of cake comes out clean.

As cake bakes, prepare Fresh Orange Glaze. Cool cake in open oven for 5 minutes; remove to rack. When cool enough to handle run a knife around sides of cake and invert onto rack. Remove waxed paper. Place a fresh piece of waxed paper under rack with cake. Spoon Orange Glaze gradually over cake (the bottom is now the top) as it cools. Use two broad spatulas to slip cake onto cake plate. Spoon glaze drips from waxed paper onto cake. Serve immediately, or cover cake and let stand at room temperature for up to four days. Cake may be tightly wrapped and frozen. Makes 12 servings.

Fresh Orange Glaze: Stir juices into powdered sugar until blended. Mix in orange zest. Makes about 1 cup glaze.

Lean

Cocoa, non-fat yogurt and reduced sugar and oil replace the Lavish recipe's richer ingredients—and make this cake considerably less caloric. The prune juice, orange and increased vanilla lend depth and richness to its flavor.

⅔ cup cocoa
1 cup prune juice
⅓ cup light cooking oil
¾ cup mild non-fat yogurt
Grated zest from one
  medium-size orange,
  minced
1 tablespoon vanilla extract
2 cups flour
1 teaspoon baking powder
1 teaspoon baking soda
Pinch salt, if desired
4 egg whites, room
  temperature

Pinch cream of tartar
¾ to 1 cup dark brown sugar,
  packed, then loosened with
  a fork
Fresh Orange Glaze

FRESH ORANGE GLAZE
½ cup powdered sugar, sifted
⅓ cup fresh orange juice
2 tablespoons fresh lemon
  juice
Grated zest from 1 orange

Preheat oven to 350F (175C). Rub a 9-inch springform pan or a 9" × 13" × 2" baking pan with oil. Cut some waxed paper to fit bottom. Lightly oil paper on both sides; fit into bottom. Dust pan lightly with flour; rap out excess flour.

In a large mixing bowl, blend cocoa into prune juice until powder is dissolved and smooth, about 1 minute. Add oil, yogurt, minced orange zest and vanilla and mix until ingredients are blended.

Sift dry ingredients together into a mixing bowl. Beat egg whites with cream of tartar until soft peaks form. Sprinkle in brown sugar a tablespoon at a time, continuing to beat until peaks hold their shape and sugar is dissolved.

Add dry ingredients in two parts to cocoa-yogurt mixture stirring just until blended. Fold in beaten egg whites in two parts just until blended. Pour into prepared cake pan and bake in upper third of oven for 45 to 50 minutes or until a toothpick in center of cake comes out clean. As cake bakes, prepare Fresh Orange Glaze.

Turn off heat and cool cake in open oven for 10 minutes; remove to rack. When cool enough to handle run a knife along sides of cake and invert onto rack. Remove waxed paper; place a fresh piece of waxed paper under rack with cake. Spoon Orange Glaze gradually over cake (the bottom is now the top) as it cools.

When cool, use two broad spatulas to transfer cake to serving plate. Spoon glaze drips from waxed paper onto cake. Serve immediately, or cover cake and let stand 2 days at room temperature. Cake may be tightly wrapped and frozen. Makes 12 servings.

Fresh Orange Glaze: Stir juices into powdered sugar until blended. Stir in orange zest. Makes about ¾ cup glaze.

	kcal	carb(gm)	fat(gm)	chol(mg)	Na(mg)	iron(mg)	Ca(mg)
lavish:	405	62	18	65	142	1.4	49
lean:	245	43	7	.2	132	2	64

WALNUT CAKE

Lavish

♦

This nutty Greek-style karidopeta *is moistened with syrup (or drenched with it, if you like) and keeps beautifully for a week at room temperature. I serve it with fresh fruit and cheese or with Roasted Winter Fruit, page 230*

3 tablespoons all-purpose
  flour
2½ teaspoons baking powder
Pinch of salt
1 tablespoon ground
  cinnamon
½ teaspoon ground nutmeg
1 teaspoon ground cardamom
2 cups butter, room
  temperature
1 cup sugar
8 large eggs, room
  temperature
1 cup semolina or regular
  farina
1 cup unseasoned fine dry
  bread crumbs
2 cups ground or finely
  chopped walnuts

1½ tablespoons finely grated
  orange zest
Spiced Syrup

SPICED SYRUP
2 cups sugar
½ cup honey
3 cups water
2 cinnamon sticks or 1
  teaspoon ground cinnamon
½ teaspoon *each* ground
  nutmeg and ground
  cardamom
1 *each* lemon and orange
  wedge
¼ cup Cointreau or Triple Sec

Set oven rack in center of oven. Preheat oven to 350F (175C). Generously butter, then flour a 9″ × 13″ baking pan. Sift 3 table-spoons flour, baking powder, salt and spices into a small bowl; set aside.

In a large bowl, cream butter with sugar until fluffy. Beat in eggs, 1 at a time. Stir in semolina or farina, bread crumbs, walnuts and orange zest until well mixed. Blend in flour mixture (batter will be thick). Pour into prepared pan; spread evenly. Bake 30 to 35 minutes or until a wooden pick inserted in center of cake comes out clean.

Cool cake in baking pan on rack. Meanwhile, prepare Spiced Syrup. When cake is cooled, spoon half the syrup over it, a little at a time, until syrup is absorbed. Cake is best served 4 or more hours after baking; it can be covered and left at room temperature up to 1 week.

To serve, trim ½ inch off each 9-inch side of cake. Cut cake into 3-inch squares and place on individual plates. Spoon remaining syrup over each piece. Makes 12 servings.

Spiced Syrup: In a deep 3-quart saucepan, combine sugar, honey, water and spices. Add juice and rinds from lemon and orange wedges. Bring to a boil, stirring until sugar is dissolved; boil 15 minutes. Remove cinnamon sticks, if used, and lemon and orange rinds. Remove from heat; add liqueur. If prepared ahead, cool, pour into a glass container and refrigerate up to 2 weeks before using. Use at room temperature. Makes 3½ cups.

Lean

Food writer Selma Morrow created this delicious spiced cake; it's as good at breakfast as at lunch or dinner. Vegetable oil, non-fat yogurt and a little brown sugar replace the butter, eggs, sugar and honey used in the lavish version. The cake can be frosted, but I prefer to dust it lightly with powdered sugar.

1 cup all-purpose flour
1½ teaspoons baking powder
½ teaspoon baking soda
Pinch of salt, if desired
1 tablespoon ground
  cinnamon
1 teaspoon ground cardamom
½ teaspoon *each* ground
  nutmeg and ground ginger
½ cup safflower oil
2 cups Creamy Non-fat
  Yogurt, page 22, or
  commercial
1 tablespoon *each* finely grated
  lemon zest and orange zest

1 tablespoon vanilla extract
¾ cup unsalted fine dry bread
  crumbs
1 cup semolina or regular
  farina
8 egg whites (from large
  eggs), room temperature
½ teaspoon cream of tartar
¾ cup packed dark brown
  sugar
1 cup walnut pieces, lightly
  toasted, cooled
¼ cup powdered sugar

Set oven rack in center of oven. Preheat oven to 350F (175C). Coat a 9" × 13" baking pan with non-stick spray. Sift flour, baking powder, baking soda, salt, if desired, and spices into a small bowl. Set aside. In a large bowl, whisk oil, yogurt, zests and vanilla until well blended. Stir in bread crumbs and semolina or farina. Batter will be stiff.

With an electric mixer, beat egg whites with cream of tartar at high speed until whites hold soft peaks. Gradually beat in brown sugar; continue to beat at least 5 minutes or until whites are thick and hold peaks that bend over at the tips. Fold a fourth of the egg whites into yogurt mixture. Fold in half the dry ingredients. Fold in a third of the remaining egg whites, then fold in remaining dry ingredients. Gently fold in remaining egg whites, then walnuts. Spread batter evenly in prepared pan.

Bake 30 minutes or until a wooden pick inserted in center of cake comes out clean and cake pulls away from sides of pan. Cool cake in baking pan on a rack. If prepared ahead, cover cooled cake and let stand at room temperature up to 3 days; or double-wrap and freeze up to 2 weeks.

To serve, trim ½ inch off each 9-inch side of cake. Sift powdered sugar over cake. Cut cake into 3-inch squares and place on individual plates. Makes 12 servings.

	kcal	carb(gm)	fat(gm)	chol(mg)	Na(mg)	iron(mg)	Ca(mg)
lavish:	617	80	32	224	330	1.7	171
lean:	338	42	16	1	194	1.3	210

OATMEAL COOKIES

Lavish

♦

Contrary to oatmeal cookies' hearty image, these are crisp and delicate, elegant with poached pears or any fruit dessert. If you bake them on a damp day put the cookies in an airtight container as soon as they cool to keep them crunchy. Or re-crisp them by heating for a few minutes in a low oven.

1 scant cup unsalted butter	3 cups rolled oats
1 cup flour	1 cup brown sugar, packed
1 teaspoon baking soda	¼ cup strong coffee, or
Pinch salt	decaffeinated coffee

Preheat oven to 375F (190C). Melt butter over low heat; set aside and keep warm. Sift flour, baking soda and salt into a large mixing bowl. Add oats and brown sugar and mix well. Pour melted butter and coffee over mixture and stir until well blended. Use a spoon to form walnut-sized pieces of dough, and drop onto a large cookie sheet about 2 inches apart. (Cookies will spread). Bake in upper third of oven 8 to 10 minutes or until cookies are a deep, golden brown. Remove with a spatula onto a rack and cool. Cookies will harden as they cool. Store in an airtight container. Makes about 64 cookies.

Lean

These are hearty cookies, great with fresh fruit or ice cream. If you don't have to watch your sugar intake and you like sweet cookies, use the two-thirds cup of brown sugar.

1 cup flour or whole wheat
   flour
¾ teaspoon baking soda
1 teaspoon ground cinnamon
Pinch salt, if desired
3 cups rolled oats
½ to ⅔ cup brown sugar,
   packed

⅓ cup light cooking oil
½ cup liquid egg substitute
¼ cup strong coffee, or
   decaffeinated coffee

Lightly oil a cookie sheet or use a non-stick cookie sheet. Preheat oven to 350F (175C). Sift flour with baking soda, cinnamon and salt if used. Mix oats and brown sugar in a large mixing bowl. Stir in canola oil. Add egg substitute and coffee; mix well. Fold in dry ingredients until blended. Use a spoon to form walnut-sized pieces of dough, and drop onto cookie sheet. Flatten cookies to ¼ inch with fork tines. Bake in upper third of oven about 15 minutes or until cookies are lightly browned on bottoms and sides. Remove with a spatula onto a rack and cool. Store in an airtight container. Makes about 64 cookies.

For three cookies:

	kcal	carb(gm)	fat(gm)	chol(mg)	Na(mg)	iron(mg)	Ca(mg)
lavish:	183	22	10	24	60	1	18
lean:	121	17	4	.07	42	1	16

JANE ULLMAN'S DARK CHOCOLATE DIAMONDS

Lavish

♦

These thin, delicate morsels are so easy to fix that Jane Ullman bakes them in between planning her sculptures. I like the little diamonds slightly moist, so I trim off the cake's crisp edges before slicing it.

1 cup unsalted butter	4 large eggs, room
4 ounces unsweetened	temperature, beaten
chocolate, chopped	1 tablespoon vanilla extract
2 ounces semisweet chocolate,	1 cup all-purpose flour
chopped	Pinch of salt
2 cups granulated sugar	1 cup powdered sugar

Set oven rack in center of oven. Preheat oven to 400F (205C). Generously butter and flour a 12″ × 18″ × 1″ baking pan.

In a medium-size, heavy-bottomed saucepan, melt butter with unsweetened and semisweet chocolates over low heat, stirring occasionally. Add granulated sugar, increase heat to medium and cook 5 minutes or until mixture boils, stirring constantly. Remove from heat.

Mix in eggs, vanilla, flour and salt just until blended. With a rubber spatula, spread batter evenly in prepared pan (it will be about ½ inch thick). Bake 14 to 15 minutes or just until a wooden pick inserted in center comes out clean.

Meanwhile, sift ⅔ cup powdered sugar over a large piece of waxed paper. When cake is baked, immediately trim ½ inch off each side; freeze trimmed strips and corner pieces for another use. Then cut cake lengthwise into 1-inch strips. On the diagonal, cut into 1½-inch diamonds. Remove from baking pan with a metal spatula and place on sugared waxed paper. Trim triangular pieces to match size of diamonds. When cakes are cool, sift remaining ⅓ cup powdered sugar over them. If prepared ahead, cover and let stand at room temperature up to 2 days or freeze up to 3 weeks (diamonds may require an additional dusting of powdered sugar before serving).

Serve on a pretty platter. Makes about 120 (1″ × 1½″) pieces.

Lean

These little cakes are moist and bittersweet, with fewer calories than the lavish recipe and only half the fat.

2 tablespoons unsweetened mashed Stewed Prunes	1 cup all-purpose flour
¾ cup unsweetened cocoa	Pinch of salt, if desired
¾ cup granulated sugar	3 tablespoons powdered sugar
¾ cup liquid egg substitute	STEWED PRUNES
6 tablespoons light cooking oil	⅓ cup water
1 tablespoon vanilla extract	7 medium-size pitted prunes

Prepare Stewed Prunes and mash as directed.

Set oven rack in center of oven. Preheat oven to 350F (175C). Coat a 9" × 13" baking pan with non-stick spray; or use a non-stick pan.

Sift cocoa into a medium-size bowl. Add granulated sugar and mix. Blend in egg substitute, oil, mashed prunes, and vanilla. Stir in flour and salt, if desired. Batter will be thick. Spread batter evenly in prepared pan. Bake 14 minutes or just until a wooden pick inserted in center comes out clean. Remove from oven and immediately trim ½ inch off each 9-inch side of cake; freeze trimmed-off strips for another use. Cut cake crosswise into 8 (1½-inch) strips. Then, on the diagonal, cut into 1-inch diamonds. Remove from baking pan with a metal spatula and place on waxed paper. Trim triangular pieces to match size of diamonds. If prepared ahead, cover and let stand at room temperature 3 to 4 days (diamonds will become more moist) or freeze up to 3 weeks.

Just before serving, sift powdered sugar over diamonds. Serve diamonds arranged on a pretty platter over white paper doilies. Makes about 60 (1" × 1½") pieces.

Stewed Prunes: Combine water and prunes in a small saucepan. Bring to a boil; reduce heat, cover and simmer 20 minutes or until prunes are soft. Drain and mash with a fork. Makes about ¼ cup (recipe calls for 2 tablespoons).

TIP

The taste of chocolate, whether solid chocolate or cocoa, deepens with the addition of flavor extracts, a little salt, or fruit (I like prunes and rasp-berries). Of course, for those on a low-sodium diet, salt is optional.

For 2 1″ × 1½″ diamonds:

	kcal	carb(gm)	fat(gm)	chol(mg)	Na(mg)	iron(mg)	Ca(mg)
lavish:	111	14	6	190	5.5	.1	4.2
lean:	72	10	3	0	29	.4	8

BITTERSWEET CHOCOLATE SAUCE

Lavish

♦

The finer the chocolate, the better the sauce. I recommend using quality Belgian, Swiss or French chocolate, sold in bars at many markets.

8 ounces imported bittersweet   Pinch of salt
   chocolate, broken in pieces   2 teaspoons vanilla extract
1 cup whipping cream

Place chocolate in top of a double boiler and set over very hot, but not boiling, water. Stir until chocolate is melted. In a small saucepan, scald cream over medium heat; blend into chocolate along with salt, whisking until smooth and shiny. Beat in a little hot water or additional cream for a thinner consistency, if desired. Remove sauce from heat and stir in vanilla. Serve warm or at room temperature. If prepared ahead, cool, cover and refrigerate up to several weeks; sauce will harden when chilled.

To serve, return to room temperature and reheat over hot water until liquefied; or place container in a saucepan filled with very hot, but not boiling, water. To further thin sauce, beat in hot cream or hot water, 1 tablespoon at a time. Makes 2 cups.

TIP

This sauce and the lean version opposite are ideal for fruit fondue, a lovely summer desert. Arrange a platter of fresh strawberries, bananas, peaches and pears (or a selection of your favorite fruits) around a bowl of heated Bittersweet Chocolate Sauce; provide fondue forks for dipping.

Lean

Cocoa, cornstarch and milk replace solid chocolate and cream, making this rich-tasting sauce considerably lower in fat than its lavish counterpart. If Dutch-processed cocoa is available, use it; it has a rich, mellow flavor. You can adjust the sauce's consistency by using more or less cornstarch.

1 cup powdered sugar	2 cups Enriched Non-fat
1 cup unsweetened cocoa	Milk, page 22, or non-fat
1 tablespoon plus 1 teaspoon	milk
cornstarch	2 teaspoons vanilla extract
¼ teaspoon salt, if desired	

Sift powdered sugar, cocoa, cornstarch and salt, if desired, into a small saucepan. Slowly whisk in 1 cup milk until mixture is well blended. Stir in remaining 1 cup milk and cook over medium heat, stirring constantly, until sauce bubbles. Reduce heat and simmer 2 minutes, stirring constantly. Remove from heat and blend in vanilla.

Serve warm or at room temperature; if serving tepid or cool, stir frequently to prevent a skin from forming. If prepared ahead, cool, cover and refrigerate up to 2 days; to cover, gently press plastic wrap directly onto surface of cooled sauce. Return to room temperature or reheat over hot water, stirring, before serving. Makes about 2½ cups.

TIP

Cornstarch helps to emulsify or suspend the cocoa particles in liquid; without such a thickener, the cocoa would settle to the bottom. Lecithin is often used as an emulsifier in commercial sauces.

For ¼ cup sauce:

	kcal	carb(gm)	fat(gm)	chol(mg)	Na(mg)	iron(mg)	Ca(mg)
lavish:	246	17	21	41	12	.7	28
lean:	78	18	2	1	87	.9	73

CRÈME FRAÎCHE
Creamy Dessert Topping

Lavish

♦

*Crème fraîche, common in France and now available in this country, is
cultured cream that thickens and becomes slightly tart when left to stand
at room temperature. It adds something special when spooned over berries
or warm chocolate pudding, and a tablespoon or two stirred into soups
or sauces gives them a velvety texture and silky sheen. There are several
ways to make crème fraîche; you can use an imported starter, sour cream
as a starter, or this simple recipe.*

2 cups whipping cream   **2 tablespoons buttermilk**

Pour cream into a 3-cup glass jar or plastic container with a tight-
fitting lid. Add buttermilk. Cover and shake 1 minute. Let stand
covered and undisturbed at room temperature 6 to 12 hours or until
thickened. If a soft consistency is desired, serve at once; for a thicker
consistency, refrigerate 12 hours. To store, refrigerate up to 10 days;
flavor will become slightly stronger as Crème Fraîche matures.
Makes 2 cups.

VARIATIONS

Sweetened Crème Fraîche: Gently fold ½ cup powdered sugar and
1 tablespoon vanilla extract into 2 cups thickened Crème Fraîche
until blended. Cover and refrigerate.

Crème Fraîche with Liqueur: Gently fold 1 tablespoon liqueur, such
as Grand Marnier, Cointreau, or cognac, into 2 cups thickened
Crème Fraîche until blended. Sweeten to taste with powdered sugar.
Cover and refrigerate.

TIP

*When making Crème Fraîche with Liqueur, match the liqueur to the
flavor of your dessert. For example, citrus-flavored liqueurs enhance citrus
desserts; a coffee-flavored liqueur goes well with a coffee-flavored dessert.*

Lean

Tomi Haas, an expert in cutting calories, makes a lowfat meal taste like a banquet. This cool, creamy topping is her creation.

2 cups lowfat cottage cheese
¼ cup Enriched Non-fat Milk, page 22, or non-fat milk

3 tablespoons powdered sugar
2 teaspoons vanilla extract

In a food processor fitted with a metal blade, process cottage cheese 2 minutes or until completely smooth. Add milk, powdered sugar and vanilla and process 1 minute longer. Cover and refrigerate until topping thickens, about 2 hours (or refrigerate up to 3 days). Makes about 2½ cups.

VARIATIONS

Lemon Dessert Topping: Blend minced zest of 1 lemon into topping.

Orange Liqueur Topping: Omit milk. Blend 3 tablespoons Grand Marnier or Cointreau and minced zest of 1 orange into topping.

For ¼ cup sauce:

	kcal	carb(gm)	fat(gm)	chol(mg)	Na(mg)	iron(mg)	Ca(mg)
lavish:	207	9	18	66	25	0	45
lean:	50	4	1	4	187	.1	38

GLOSSARY

In this book, I have used American English terms to describe cooking techniques and foods, except when words from another language are in common use.

Blanch: To immerse food briefly in boiling water. Cooks blanch and quickly cool food to control its texture and flavor. Blanching green vegetables intensifies their color and slightly tenderizes them; plunging them into cold water stops the cooking action. Bacon and vegetables such as cabbage are blanched to reduce their strong flavors. Blanching tomatoes for 20 seconds makes it easy to remove their skins.

Braise: To brown (usually in oil or fat) over medium-high heat in a heavy pot, then cover and cook slowly in a low oven or over low heat on top of the range. Liquid and/or vegetables are often added for this slow, moist cooking process. Braising tenderizes both meat and vegetables and develops their flavor. After browning meat, drain the fat before adding any liquid.

Bruise: To release the oil and essence of fresh herbs by crushing them with the back of a heavy knife or by rubbing them together between your hands. Bruised herb leaves infuse stews or roasts with flavor and add a garden-fresh taste to vegetables.

Deglaze: To pour liquid into a hot pan and loosen browned, crusty bits of food that cling to the pan after sautéing, pan-frying or roasting. These flavorful caramelized bits and juices enrich the flavor of gravies, sauces and soups.

Poach: See *Simmer*.

Puree: To liquefy or break down solid foods into a mixture with a smooth, uniform texture. To puree foods, you can process them in a blender or food processor, put them through a food mill, or press them through a sieve. Raw or cooked fruits and vegetables contain so much liquid that they usually need no more for pureeing. Serve seasoned pureed vegetables as an accompaniment to a main course, or use them in soups and gravies in place of more caloric thickeners. Fruit purees make natural sauces for desserts.

Reduce: To boil away liquid. Reducing concentrates flavor and thickens stocks, sauces and gravies.

Sauté: To fry, usually with a little fat or oil, in an uncovered pan over medium-high or high heat on top of the range. *Sauté* comes from the French verb *sauter*, "to leap or jump"; the term describes the way the food jumps and sizzles in the hot pan. When you sauté food, be sure not to crowd the pan; if you do, the food will stew or steam instead of browning nicely. See *Sweat* for a lowfat, low-calorie alternative to sautéing.

Simmer: To heat liquid to a bare bubble, just at the boiling point. Meats and vegetables are simmered in broth to tenderize them and/ or extract their flavors. The French say liquid shivers during *poaching* or slow simmering when bubbles barely break the surface. Poaching preserves the texture and flavor of delicate foods.

Sweat: To cook meat or vegetables over low to medium heat in a covered heavy skillet, with little or no added fat, oil or liquid. Sweating softens vegetables and tenderizes meats as they cook in their own juices; it's ideal for lowfat, low-calorie cooking. Food is sometimes lightly browned over medium-high heat to develop flavor before sweating. Non-stick pans work best; to prevent sticking and burning, stir food occasionally as it sweats.

Waterbath: A hot waterbath stabilizes cooking temperatures in a dish. Set a baking pan or saucepan in a larger pan on top of the range or in the oven. Pour boiling water into the larger pan and maintain it at a simmer. Sauces and custards cooked in a waterbath won't overcook, and they will have an even, delicate texture.

Zest: The colored outer peel of citrus fruit. Zest is oily, flavorful and rich in vitamin C. The pithy white layer just beneath the zest (also vitamin C-rich) is bitter, so cooks are careful to grate or peel only the zest. Used sparingly, citrus zests enhance salads, stews, braised meats, vegetables and desserts.

SOURCES

United States Department of Agriculture (U.S.D.A.), Human Nutrition Information Service, Agriculture Handbook 8–13, *Composition of Foods: Raw, Processed and Prepared*, Nutrition Monitoring Service, Series 8-1 to 8-16.

United States Department of Agriculture, *Nutritive Value of American Foods in Common Units*, Agriculture Handbook No. 456, 1975.

Pennington and Church, *Bowes and Church's Food Values of Portions Commonly Used*, 14th Edition, J.B. Lippincott, Philadelphia, 1985.

Food and Agriculture Organization of the United Nations (U.N.F.A.O.), *Food Composition Table For Use in East Asia*, 1972.

Dietary Guideline for Healthy American Adults, American Heart Association, 1988.

Recommended Dietary Allowances (RDA), National Research Council, National Academy of Sciences, 1989.

Nutritionist III, N-Square Computing, Silverton, Oregon, 1985–1990.

INDEX